Prayers for the People

Prayers for the People

Homicide and Humanity in the Crescent City

REBECCA LOUISE CARTER

The University of Chicago Press   Chicago and London

The University of Chicago Press, Chicago 60637
The University of Chicago Press, Ltd., London
© 2019 by The University of Chicago
All rights reserved. No part of this book may be used or reproduced
in any manner whatsoever without written permission, except in
the case of brief quotations in critical articles and reviews. For more
information, contact the University of Chicago Press, 1427 E. 60th St.,
Chicago, IL 60637.
Published 2019
Printed in the United States of America

28 27 26 25 24 23 22 21 20 19   1 2 3 4 5

ISBN-13: 978-0-226-63552-1 (cloth)
ISBN-13: 978-0-226-63566-8 (paper)
ISBN-13: 978-0-226-63583-5 (e-book)
DOI: https://doi.org/10.7208/chicago/9780226635835.001.0001

Library of Congress Cataloging-in-Publication Data

Names: Carter, Rebecca Louise, author.
Title: Prayers for the people : homicide and humanity in the Crescent
    City / Rebecca Louise Carter.
Description: Chicago ; London : The University of Chicago Press, 2019. |
    Includes bibliographical references and index.
Identifiers: LCCN 2018058214 | ISBN 9780226635521 (cloth : alk. paper) |
    ISBN 9780226635668 (pbk. : alk. paper) | ISBN 9780226635835 (e-book)
Subjects: LCSH: Homicide—Louisiana—New Orleans—Religious aspects. |
    Violence—Louisiana—New Orleans—Religious aspects. | African
    Americans—Louisiana—New Orleans—Religion. | African Americans—
    Louisiana—New Orleans—Social conditions. | Church work with the
    bereaved—Louisiana—New Orleans. | African American mothers—
    Louisiana—New Orleans. | African American neighborhoods—Louisiana—
    New Orleans. | Religion and sociology—Louisiana—New Orleans.
Classification: LCC HV6197.U52 .N43 2019 | DDC 362.88/130976335—dc23
LC record available at https://lccn.loc.gov/2018058214

♾ This paper meets the requirements of ANSI/NISO Z39.48-1992
(Permanence of Paper).

*In Memory of James Puckette Carter Sr., MD, DrPH (1933–2014)
and James Puckette Carter Jr. (1964–2019)*

Contents

The Crescent City

Site of My Father's House (photo by author)

So the beginning of this was a woman and she had come back from burying the dead. Not the dead of sick and ailing with friends at the pillow and the feet. She had come back from the sodden and the bloated; the sudden dead, their eyes flung wide open in judgment. The people all saw her come because it was sundown. The sun was gone, but he had left his footprints in the sky. It was the time for sitting on porches beside the road. It was the time to hear things and talk.

ZORA NEALE HURSTON (1937, 1)

"Grieve well and you grow stronger. That's the way it is," Sister Anne said finally.[1] The room fell silent with the women around the table processing this particular bit of wisdom. Danielle was the first to respond. "Well you know" she said, "May the twelfth made four years for Rock's death." She paused, remembering that day and how she had mourned. "I was in the Winn Dixie making groceries. And you know how the Winn Dixie plays all the old songs, and it just be relaxing as you shop? So, this song came on, and it was, 'It's So Hard to Say Goodbye to Yesterday.'"

The other women gathered at the church that evening nodded their heads in recognition. Written by Motown industry duo Freddie Perren and Christine Yarian for the 1975 film *Cooley High*, "It's So Hard to Say Goodbye to Yesterday" plays during the burial scene of Cochise, a young Black man who is brutally murdered on the streets of Chicago. An a cappella version was more famously released in the early 1990s by Boyz II Men, the contemporary R & B group. The accompanying video is also set at a funeral, the lyrics carrying significant weight given the intensified violence in Black communities at the time and ever since. Danielle's experience of the song nearly two decades later was no less affecting, given Rock's death in unfortunately familiar circumstances.

How do I say goodbye to what we had?
. . . .
I thought we'd get to see forever,
But forever's gone away.

2

. . . .
And I'll take with me the memories
To be my sunshine after the rain.
It's so hard to say goodbye to yesterday.

The lyrics triggered an acute experience of grief within an otherwise steady undercurrent of death and mourning in Black New Orleans.

"As I reached through the freezer that's when I noticed that song was playing," Danielle continued. "I was getting the ice cream and when that song came on, *it hit my ear*, and I reached, and I stopped, and I listened. You know when you walk into Winn Dixie out there on Chef . . . Where is it?" She looked around for confirmation of the location, thinking of the grocery store located on Chef Menteur Highway. "Yes, it's on Chef," Sister Anne confirmed, and Danielle went on. "Yeah, and in the front my friend was sitting out there waiting on me. And when that song went playing, I left the basket, I left the ice cream, and I ran by him. And my heart was just *overwhelmed* with that song. And he said, 'What's the matter?' And I couldn't say a word, I just pointed up. I said, 'You see what they playing?' And I thought about my baby."

Her words settled on the hot summer air—a Thursday evening in New Orleans in the early part of June 2009. The sun was still high, and the air conditioning inside the building offered little relief, the whirring sound mixing with the rush of traffic at the tail end of the daily commute. We were gathered in the community development center across the street from Liberty Street Baptist Church, a large, predominantly African American community of faith located in the heart of the Central City neighborhood.[2] While Central City was on the other side of town from the Winn Dixie on Chef, Black residents across the city dealt with disproportionate levels of violence. Sister Anne, Danielle, and the others had all lost family members, and they now met weekly in a support group Danielle had founded shortly after the death of her son Hiroki. Known to family and friends as "Rock," he was murdered in 2005, just a few months before Hurricane Katrina. For Danielle to situate her memories as "sunshine after the rain" in a world where it was "so hard to say goodbye to yesterday" was thus both personal and political. It situated the mourned death of a young Black man as both inextricable from the devastation and central to the recovery of the postdisaster city.

This particular meeting marked the one-year death anniversary of Brian, whose mother Monica sat quietly, dabbing her eyes dry from time to time. The other women shared their experiences of grief in part to reassure Monica that it was okay to cry and that this was a necessary part of the mourning process, the "good grief" and accompanying strength of which Sister Anne spoke. Danielle, still in the Winn Dixie, continued her story. "I stood there . . . , [took] a deep breath, and pulled myself together," she recalled.

So what Sister Anne is saying is very true. Because no matter where you are . . . people are going to ask you "How do you feel today?" You know? And we don't have to cover up and say, "Oh, I'm alright" when we know that we are hurting. The pain is there of missing our child . . . because that is our grief. And like she just said, you can express it anywhere you need to.

To grieve well, however, went beyond expression. It translated into a certain depth of knowledge that Danielle felt she now possessed because of her son's death. "I just give God the glory today" she continued. "Because I have gained so much *knowledge* on death . . . I never knew this before so, you know, the Bible has a way . . . God's words have a way, of letting us know."

What does it mean to grieve well? To look, in the space of violence, death, and mourning, for sunshine after the rain? What is the source of this warmth and light and the resulting "knowledge on death" it produces? How is that knowledge then shared, and what does it do? Does it make one grow stronger, as Sister Anne believed? Whom do we find at the center of these processes? Black women like Sister Anne, Danielle, Monica, and the others who were gathered at the church that evening. And what does it mean to find them there with the dead—the young Black men who are the primary victims of violence in the contemporary American city? How might this relatedness, which Danielle affirmed in glory and gratitude, strengthen a city and its people?

I explore these questions in New Orleans, at the intersection of Black death, religious work, and the process of social change. I follow the pathways set by several diverse communities of faith; however, I focus in particular on the history, mission, and forward motion of religious work at Liberty Street Baptist Church in Central City. Directed by clergy holding firm to a vision of a beloved community and guided by mothers and grandmothers celebrating birth and death anniversaries to "raise" the dead, I trace the emergence of an old and new African American religious ideal. I examine how the faithful, building on a legacy of Black social Christianity attuned to the conditions of the present day, worked against the violent ruptures of life in Black families and communities. They asserted Black humanity, in this world and the next, challenging assumptions about the nature of violence or the limits of death and demonstrating the possibilities of Black urban life far beyond the ways in which it has been determined. To grieve well was to chart a generative path through death into new and more expansive ways of being, relating, and dwelling. It was a path toward peace that others could also follow in an increasingly precarious world.

The Flood and the Fire

I had come to New Orleans for fieldwork in 2007, but I already knew the city—a second home for many years. I spent most of my childhood in Tennessee, but in the early 1970s my parents divorced and my father moved to New Orleans, where he eventually met and married my stepmother. They lived Uptown, in a townhouse on Napoleon Avenue, comfortably set back along the far edge of a small park but uneasily situated between the struggling Freret Street neighborhood and the grandeur of the St. Charles Avenue corridor. My siblings and I visited them frequently, for holidays and for longer periods over the summer. As a middle-class African American family connected, through my father's work, to the wealth of Uptown university life, we found ourselves part of a vibrant intellectual community. Yet although I was greatly enriched by the diverse educational, cultural, and social experiences this provided, my overall experience of New Orleans was somewhat sheltered. There were parts of the city to which we rarely ventured.

Decades later, I watched with horror as the city I thought I knew disappeared. It was late August of 2005, and Hurricane Katrina had devastated the Gulf Coast. I was many miles away, and my family in New Orleans thankfully had evacuated. But the images on the television were no less heartbreaking. Floodwaters submerged whole neighborhoods and thousands of people were missing and presumed dead. Many more waited, endlessly it seemed, for help. My father and stepmother considered themselves extremely fortunate even though they had already received word that their house was under a foot of water. Still, they were fairly confident that they would be able to return home soon, to salvage what they could. I hoped that this was true.

A week later, in early September, I was lying in bed half asleep when the telephone rang. It was my mother, calling from Tennessee. "Are you awake?" she asked. Then, "I have some terrible news. Your father's house

5

burned." Dazed but upright, I listened as she shared what she knew. The cause of the fire was unknown, but it had started in the house next door and grew with such force that it consumed eight homes. Miraculously no one was hurt, but the loss was devastating. The lessons we were learning about the structural conditions of violence, the process of disaster, and the legacies of loss in Black communities were fast and furious. My father, a physician and professor, was well regarded in his field. However, after the storm he lamented that although he had lived on the edge of a well-to-do (and still dry) neighborhood, he was clearly "not Uptown enough" to escape disaster. We were all alive and accounted for, but with the house reduced to rubble, we, too, looked to the heavens for sunshine after the rain.

Foundations of Love

In academic and public inquiry alike, Black lives have long been under scrutiny. In the United States the focus tends to be on the extraordinarily high rates of poverty and violence found in poor Black communities, with growing though still inadequate attention to police brutality and its intensification within an increasingly militarized urban state. While some analyses continue to confine these conditions, historically and statistically, to the "ghetto," for the participants of a still-rising progressive movement, they are traced, regardless of their predominant location, to the same root: "a world where Black lives are systematically and intentionally targeted for demise" (Garza 2014). From this fraught terrain, the #BlackLivesMatter project and the larger Black Lives Matter movement have emerged.

We now understand that Black lives are challenged by multiple factors, from the brutal legacy of slavery to a status of free but not yet equal American citizenship, from disfranchisement to the continued unevenness with which essential goods and services are distributed, from the persistence of poverty to the ubiquity of violent crime, and from the systematic incarceration of poor Blacks to the fractured communities in which many people are left. We further understand that such processes fundamentally rest on the devaluing of Black lives and that they intensify as the quest for wealth and power ramps up in an increasingly polarized world.

We know far less, however, about the systems and structures of Black humanity, especially beyond the assertions that ring out forcefully from resistance and social justice movements. Despite the tendency to characterize the Black Lives Matter movement as a radical or even violent response, it is important to remember that the movement began as a "love letter" to Black people penned and posted by Alicia Garza and disseminated by cofounders Garza, Patrice Cullors, and Opal Tometi (Bailey and Leonard 2015, 69–71). Yet love—referring here to the expressions and practices that affirm, value, strengthen, and celebrate Black people—has not received the attention it deserves, not just in studies of Black urban life but in studies of contemporary life more broadly.

In New Orleans I explore these themes in two directions, looking back at the histories and ideologies that inform present frameworks and thinking forward about what they provide for the crafting of a sustainable, Black, and urban future. To take up this inquiry is not to deny that conditions of suffering still exist. Rather, it is to bring forward the knowledge that comes from the Black experience as new frameworks and methods of change are developed. The conclusions to which this study leads, therefore, are not confined to the Black community. As George Lipsitz (2011, 6) argues, "Black negotiations with the constraints and confinements of racialized space often produce ways of envisioning and enacting more decent, dignified, humane, and egalitarian social relations for everyone."

The call to examine such processes is already made by scholars and activists who emphasize the need for concurrent religious, moral, and spiritual progress. Angela Davis (Davis and Davis 2016), for example, in an interview for *Yes!* magazine, states, "I think our notions of what counts as radical have changed over time. Self-care and healing and attention to the body and the spiritual dimension—all of this is now a part of radical social justice struggles." Later that same year, Michelle Alexander, author of the celebrated book *The New Jim Crow: Mass Incarceration in the Age of Colorblindness* (2010), resigned her position as a professor of law at Ohio State University and joined the faculty at Union Theological Seminary. Posting on social media, she gave a similar statement, writing,

I no longer believe we can "win" justice simply by filing lawsuits, flexing our political muscles or boosting voter turnout. Yes, we absolutely must do that work, but none of it—not even working for some form of political revolution—will ever be enough on its own. Without a moral or spiritual awakening, we will remain forever trapped in political games fueled by fear, greed and the hunger for power. . . . At its core, America's journey from slavery to Jim Crow to mass incarceration raises profound moral and spiritual questions about who we are, individually and collectively, who we aim to become, and what we are willing to do now.[3]

Before considering such awakenings in New Orleans, through the work of clergy and parishioners, including the women who gathered in support at Liberty Street, I take three main steps through several connected bodies of literature. In the first, I call for a more expansive conceptualization of Black urban life, one that moves beyond the confines of the "ghetto" and the assumptions still held about life and death therein. Rather than an uncritical acceptance of violence as customary in Black communities, I cast New Orleans as a simultaneously precarious and productive place and situate the people I encountered there as vital agents who find life in the "space of death" (Taussig 1987, 5; Holland 2000, 4). Second, I consider how African American religion has been understood, what new frameworks are emerging, and how they might direct us, as M. Shawn Copeland (2013, 626) suggests, toward "a future with authentic and luminous possibility." Third, finding Black women of faith at the center of these processes in New Orleans, I bring their experiences and insights to the forefront, merging studies of religion, death, and kinship to understand the reconfiguration of Black social and spiritual value in the space of death through everyday acts of relatedness in multiple realms.

Conditions of Loss

The windows of the community development center looked out on a fragile landscape. It had been nearly four years since Hurricane Katrina, but Central City had not recovered; indeed, this was fragile ground long before the storm ever materialized. To understand Katrina's causes and effects, therefore, one must do away with notions of a "natural" disaster and look instead at the determinations of difference that made this neighborhood and population vulnerable to begin with—the risky moves of urban expansion, the racism and forced settlement of Blacks in areas below sea level, the poor design and upkeep of levee systems. The tragic loss of life that resulted from the hurricane was directly related, with rates of mortality for African Americans four times higher than those for whites.[4]

Katrina's devastation also stemmed from neoliberal approaches to disaster management and recovery in which many Black residents were further abandoned—deemed "disposable, an unnecessary burden on state coffers, and consigned to fend for themselves" (Giroux 2006, 10). Disaster capitalism continued after the storm, with public and private entities taking advantage of the "opportunity" to strategically remake and repopulate the city (Klein 2007; Gunewardena and Schuller 2008; Johnson 2011). New Orleans remained a majority African American city. It had been so since at least 1980 (Arena 2004, 378), but the African American population had dramatically decreased.[5] Life in Central City nonetheless went on, and Danielle and the other women made their way to church and home, past shuttered businesses and blighted properties, past corner markets with little sustenance, past recovering schools and neighborhood centers, past crime sites and memorials for those whose deaths were sudden but still situated, as all of them were, in a condition of vulnerability and violence that had long been accumulating.

Like most major cities in the United States, New Orleans experienced an abrupt rise in violent crime over a twenty-five-year period, from around 1970 to 1995. Most accounts attribute this to the drug trade, particularly following the introduction of crack cocaine into urban markets beginning in the 1980s (Grogger and Willis 2000, 528).[6] New Orleans was at the top of this trend; local homicide rates rose during this period by a staggering 329 percent (Currie 1998, 23). Even though rates started to decline in many cities after 1991, the worst year on record for New Orleans is 1994 when there were 414 murders. While this number has been higher in other cities, New Orleans is consistently set apart by its per capita murder rate. In 2009, at the time of my research, this rate was approximately 52.0, based on 174 homicides and a population estimate of 336,425. It was the highest rate in the nation for that year, compared to a national rate of 5.0.[7]

In the wake of Katrina, the problem of homicide was magnified, becoming a pivot point around which the discourse on recovery turned. It featured prominently in conversations about the future of the city, standing in the way of the peaceful and prosperous comeback that city officials and developers envisioned. What was striking, however, was the fact that many of the proposed solutions seemed to hinge on the exclusion of "violent" people, namely, the poor Black people on whom the characterization was routinely projected (Woods 2005, 1014–1015; Arena 2012, 146). The associated redevelopment projects, which overlapped with the demolition of low-income housing, gained traction through narrow statistical analyses that confirmed violence's location, such as a study of crime in New Orleans over a two-year period (2009–2010) that found that the majority of homicides occurred in poor Black communities and involved young Black men as both perpetrators and victims (Wellford, Bond, and Goodison 2011).

Efforts to end the violence were more generally supported, especially by residents who perceived a shift in the nature of violence after the storm, as it spilled out of its usual Black boundaries. Several killings took the lives of "innocent" people—those who were clearly unconnected, at least by race or status, to the kind of criminal activity that would explain, or even warrant, their demise. As I discuss in a later chapter, this expanded and less predictable location of violence was finally unacceptable and it spurred public outcry, most visibly in a March for Survival in January 2007 that was attended by several thousand people. This mobilization fueled another—as some residents decried the suggestion, explicit or not—that certain deaths (white, wealthy, and presumed innocent) were worthy of collective outrage and mourning while other deaths (Black, poor, and declared criminal) were not. This set the stage for a renewed assertion of Black social value regardless of one's status, location, or criminal history.

From the "Ghetto" to the Crescent City

Neighborhoods like Central City have historically been characterized as the "ghetto," their residents cast simultaneously as the perpetrators and victims of violence. This remains the case even when violence's multiple causes are understood. Such characterizations make it difficult to learn from local experience, as people are more frequently imagined as responsible for, or at least confined by, their circumstances. To bring forward the responses they nonetheless develop, therefore, requires that we first interrogate what we think we know about Black urban life. In doing so we might better identify the institutions, structures, and agents of change and follow their lead past assumptions into the new ways of being they suggest.

The history of the ghetto can be traced from the sixteenth century when the term designated the confinement of Jewish people on a Venetian island where a foundry or *geto* had once been located (Duneier 2016, ix). This classification of urban space according to forced settlement and restricted movement and its association with a population identified by a particular feature such as race or religion would remain a key feature of how ghettos were subsequently defined in Europe and around the world (Haynes and Hutchinson 2008, 347–52). The term was first applied to African American settlement in the United States at the turn of the twentieth century, denoting the Black enclaves of northern cities such as Philadelphia and Chicago.[8] By the mid-twentieth century it had entered the mainstream of the growing field of urban studies.

In the latter part of the twentieth century a lively debate emerged about the characteristics that were most important in defining the ghetto, such as geography, race, income level, employment, segregation, social isolation, or subjugation (Wilson 1987; Jargowsky and Bane 1991; Pattillo 2003). For example, while some scholars identify ghettos by their high rates of poverty, others, such as Loïc Wacquant (1997, 341), maintain that this "obfuscates the racial basis and character of this poverty and divests the term [*ghetto*] of both historical meaning and sociological content." Wacquant's (1997, 343) own definition, by contrast, understands the ghetto as "an ethnoracial formation that combines and inscribes in the objectivity of space and group-specific institutions all four 'elementary forms' of racial domination, namely, categorization, discrimination, segregation and exclusionary violence."

More recent inquiries focus on the process of ghettoization, examining the ways that ghettos are produced and maintained, rather than reinforcing the "ghetto" "as an unambiguously discrete category" (Chaddha and Wilson 2008, 284). This fits with a call, again by Wacquant (2014, 1696), to see the "ghetto" as part of a larger system of "peculiar institutions" that have worked to define and confine African Americans over the last four centuries—from slavery to Jim Crow to the ghettos of northern cities in the first half of the twentieth century to the ghettos and hyperghettos of the present time.[9] These analytical shifts unfortunately have little impact on the everyday lives of poor people, which continue and end under the influence of both old and new forms of domination. Thus, the *ghetto* (or the "inner city" or the "urban margin") remains inhabited by poor people of color, ethnic and religious minorities, immigrants, outcasts, and others—and persists as a necessary, though not predetermined, backdrop for the study of urban life.

Anthropological contributions to this inquiry began to coalesce in the 1940s and 1950s, with urban anthropology emerging as a distinct subfield in the 1960s. By the political economic turn of the early 1980s, scholars were situating their work both *in* and *of* the city (Low 1996, 384), examining larger systems of inequality while simultaneously tracing the ways that people navigate, sustain, and transform their lives and communities (Liebow 1967; Hannerz 1969; Stack 1974; Merry 1981; Susser 1982). The study of violence has been a persistent concern, especially in an approach to urban ethnography that is increasingly interdisciplinary across anthropology, sociology, geography, and attendant fields. While I follow Nancy Scheper-Hughes and Philippe Bourgois in situating violence as a "continuum" to reflect its structural, physical, social, symbolic, and other dimensions (2004, 1), it is true that the ethnographic study of violence in the United States was founded in the "ghetto," with a particular focus on gangs and drug trafficking (Bourgois 1995; Vigil 1988; Anderson 1999; Venkatesh 2008). Scholars are increasingly outspoken about the implications; Kilanski and Auyero (2015, 2) argue that "the tendency of ethnography to focus on the types of violence that shape daily life in poor Black and brown communities—when read collectively—can help to (re) produce negative stereotypes of racial/ethnic minorities circulating in the wider culture." They call instead for scholarship that brings those who are most directly affected by violence to the center of the discourse in order to better understand how "violence is 'lived' and 'acted upon'" (3).

This call has been met by those who make clear the connection between local and structural forms of violence such as the devastating impact of the United States' War on Drugs and the rise of the neoliberal, carceral, and militarized state. Their findings reveal the continued oppression and erasure of poor people of color—from displacement and death wrought by poverty, joblessness, poor education, disease, and the inadequacies of social services to the growth of illicit economies, drug trafficking, and associated violence to the ongoing impact of criminalization and increasingly punitive forms of urban governance and social control (Bergmann 2009; Bourgois and Schonberg 2009; Rios 2011; Contreras 2012; Ralph 2014). Findings also reveal how residents move, as much as they are able, beyond the limits of violence to forge sustainable urban futures. Laurence Ralph's (2014) exploration of the "underside of injury" in gangland Chicago, with injury cast as "a potential, an engine, a generative force that propelled new trajectories" (17), is such a study.

With this inspiration, I do not situate my research in New Orleans as being in or of the "ghetto." I do not see the people I encountered—parishioners, members of the clergy, residents, and others—as responsible for, confined within, or incapacitated by the conditions of poverty and violence they nonetheless experience. Instead, I follow the lead of scholars such as Katherine McKittrick and Clyde Woods (2007), who frame a Black geography that frees those who occupy the margins from the places to which they have been relegated, tracing the ways that people refashion their lives in and through the "geographies of exclusion" that have been historically established for them (4). I thus propose a study of urban life and death in the "crescent city."

The Crescent City, of course, refers first to New Orleans—it is an existing moniker referencing the city's location along a crescent-shaped curve of the Mississippi River. I also use this term, however, to signify the cusp of change, viewing the city as a generative space in "a world that is crescent rather than created; that is 'always in the making'" (Hallam and Ingold 2007, 3). *Crescent* comes from the Latin word *crēscere*, whose present participle *crēscent* means "to come into existence, increase in size or numbers." The word commonly refers to the phases of the moon, specifically the period of increasing illumination (the waxing crescent moon) that follows the new moon. This emphasis on illumination inspires my suggestion of the crescent city, with the city and the "ghetto" in particular reconfigured as emergent spaces where new revelations and ways of being come to light. However, a "crescent moon" has come to designate either a period of waxing or waning, of increasing or decreasing illumination, and this ambiguity seems also relevant to the crescent city, where the direction of change is not always clear and where the shifts, be they toward lightness or darkness, are cyclical and continuous.[10] The inhabitants of the crescent city, the socially devalued in particular, thus become the vital agents, mediators, and guides who develop and share their visions—now and in the city and world to come. My intent here is not to shift attention away from the continued impact of violence; rather, the idea is to reframe negative characterizations of the "ghetto" so that we can better attend to and follow the transformative responses found therein.

The Space of Death and Transformation

There are many ways to mourn the dead. Following Brian's death, for example, Monica requested a funeral at the Baptist church she attended in Marerro, on the Westbank and outskirts of New Orleans. After the service, the family processed to the cemetery for the burial. In the year that followed, Monica mourned with such intensity that it was alarming. Her close family members and friends, increasingly worried about her health, did everything they could to support and care for her. Someone told her about the support group at Liberty Street, and finally she came. She prayed with the others, listened to their testimonies, and when she was ready shared her own. When Danielle asked whether she would like to honor Brian on the one-year anniversary of his death, she said yes. Not only would it give her the chance to acknowledge her own journey, the fact that she had "made it" thus far, it would affirm Brian's continued relatedness— absent in the body but now present with the Lord. The significance of such practices is indeed revealed in the crescent city, where life or death is not a fixed calculus, as traditional notions of violence in Black communities would have us believe. To "grieve well" was a less-defined and more encompassing experience of death-in-life and life-in-death, one that reflected more accurately people's beliefs and capacities, including their ability to move beyond the limits of the world so firmly laid before them.[11]

In New Orleans, the boundaries between life and death have long been blurred. The poet Brenda Marie Osbey describes a "peculiar fascination with the dead" exhibited by many residents through everyday practices of relatedness and care. As Osbey (2015, 25) encourages, "Honor the dead as they ought to be honored. Live among your dead, whom you have every right to love." Helen Regis (2001, 764) identifies a range of related traditions, including jazz funerals and second lines, which make up a broad and "complex cultural repertoire of memorial discourse." For Regis, to honor the dead is also to transform the present by "summoning death to the stage of the living human body" (Taussig 1977, 77, cited in Regis 2001, 766)—claiming space for the articulation of Black subjectivity, especially given conditions of continued oppression and suffering. This fascination with the dead thus has social and political import; it facilitates a critique of the current order (see also Osbey 1996; Breunlin and Regis 2006; Sakakeeny 2013).

Regis (2001, 766) draws on Michael Taussig's work to situate such practices as "death-work"; however, I find Taussig's conceptualization of "the space of death" more apt for a consideration of life, death, and *transformation* in the crescent city. This is a physiological and social condition of terror that emerges out of a painful world history of conquest and colonization seen, for example, in "the space of death where the Indian, African, and white gave birth to a New World" (1987, 5). With the culture of the conqueror inextricably bound to that of the conquered (5), it is only by coming close to death that there might be "a more vivid sense of life" (7). Taussig understands this way of living and thinking through terror as transformative; thus, the space of death becomes "important in the creation of meaning and consciousness" (4).

Sharon Patricia Holland takes up these ideas to think through the relationship between death and subjectivity in twentieth-century African American literature and culture. The existence of a space of death in the United States cannot be denied, Holland argues, as "our boundary is filled with the blood from five hundred years of slavery, removal, and conquest and . . . our border is a constant space of death and terror" (2000, 4). In considering this space, however, the objective is not solely to discover who resides there past and present; it is also to determine why they are kept there and how to free those confined (4). Holland examines in particular the contributions of writers, artists, critics, and others who are "raising the dead, allowing them to speak, and providing them with the agency of physical bodies in order to tell the story" (4). This connection between the living and the dead is also transformative; as Holland asserts, "Perhaps the most revolutionary intervention into conversations at the margins of race, gender, and sexuality is to let the dead—those already denied a sustainable subjectivity—speak from the place that is familiar to them" (4).

The space of death and transformation, when applied to New Orleans, does not simply reveal the terror and violence that plagues poor Black communities. It directs us to the shifts that are simultaneously possible as people live their lives within and through the conditions they inhabit. As Taussig argues, the space of death allows for "illumination" as much as it brings about "extinction" (1987, 4). Holland agrees, arguing that "speaking from the site of familiarity, from the place reserved for the dead, disturbs the static categories of black/white, oppressor/oppressed, creating a plethora of tensions *within* and *without* existing cultures" (2000, 4–5, emphasis in original).

As provocative as this framing is, for the women at Liberty Street it is not enough, despite the illumination, the disturbance, or even the shift in consciousness that the space of death might provide. Theirs were the three-times dead, the ones who were essentially dead to the world when they were alive, dead again when life left their physical bodies, and dead once more from the mourning the world forgot. The transformation that is attached to the space of death, therefore, must also be social and political in nature. Monica's son Brian had been shot multiple times, targeted by three assailants who fled and had not been apprehended. His death was reported by the police department, but there was no collective outrage; it was instead another case of "black-on-black crime," an "incident" for which the investigators did not believe robbery was a motive. The mourning was left to his mother.

Such realities require us to open up the space of death as a productive arena in which the connection between death and the determination of human value can be examined and reconfigured. The inquiry into social death, for example, typically begins with Orlando Patterson's comparative study *Slavery and Social Death* (1982), where the slave is situated as a "socially dead person" (38) with no existence outside of the master's violent domination.[12] Vincent Brown (2009) offers a useful critique, however, of an inquiry that has been overly focused on Patterson's notion "as the basic condition of slavery," an inquiry that has resulted in a lack of sufficient knowledge about the *experiences* of those who are rendered as "socially dead" (1233).[13] To illustrate, Brown takes an example from the atrocities of the Middle Passage, describing the death in 1786 of an African woman on the slave ship *Hudibras* and the rite of mourning that ensued—performed by the other enslaved women on that vessel who protested, as much as they were able, to make sure that she was properly buried (1231). While many accounts of slavery gloss over such events, Brown argues that they "typif[y] the way that people who have been pronounced socially dead, that is, utterly alienated and with no social ties recognized as legitimate or binding, have often made a social world out of death itself" (1232–33). The women on the *Hudibras* are thus recast: "[They] were not in fact the living dead; they were the mothers of gasping new societies. . . . This was first and foremost a battle over their presence in time, to define their place among ancestors, kin, friends, and future progeny" (1241).

In contemporary contexts such as New Orleans, social death continues in an urbanized world engendered by corporate capital and the neoliberal and carceral state (Cacho 2012, 4, 7). As Lisa Marie Cacho argues, human value is now made intelligible through "racialized, sexualized, spatialized, and state-sanctioned violences" whereby certain populations (namely Black, Latinx, and other communities of color—as well as those individuals who are also identified as "illegal aliens," "gang members," "terrorist suspects," and the like) are *permanently* criminalized and therefore "ineligible for personhood . . . subjected to laws but refused the legal means to contest those laws as well as denied both the political legitimacy and moral credibility necessary to question them" (2012, 6).

It is extraordinarily difficult to counter these effects. Outright demands for the recuperation of social value are understandable but can ultimately be disempowering—not only do they reinforce the idea that human value is achieved or bestowed rather than inherent (Cacho 2012, 7), they necessitate the disavowal of certain relationships, particularly disassociation from other devalued groups and status categories (17–18). This frequently pits criminalized groups against each other "in a way that essentially hides, disguises, and displaces American racism, stabilizing rather than subverting practices and processes of criminalization" (13). While stressing that it is important to continue to fight for basic rights and essential resources (33), Cacho proposes an "unthinkable politics," which brings forward other kinds of value practices or the refusal of value altogether (31). This requires letting go of the outcome of struggle, thinking counterintuitively, and exploring the contexts that demonstrate why life is valuable in the first place. With this, an exploration of religious work at Liberty Street might proceed in the space of death and transformation—from violence to the determinations of human value that underpin its location and impact to the relational reconfiguration of value in the continuous raising of the dead.[14]

Follow the People to Church

Upon arriving in New Orleans in the late spring of 2007, I initially stayed with my father and stepmother, who were getting by in a small apartment outside of the city on the Northshore of Lake Pontchartrain. My father in particular took refuge in his work, bracketed by the incessant drone of cable TV news. I wanted to assist with their recovery, but the fire had taken everything, there was nothing tangible *to* recover. It seemed that all we could do was to sit and wait, and for what I wasn't sure—settlement, direction, some kind of resolution? The related research with which I had charged myself provided little guidance. The project had been quickly formed, more of a reaction than an arrangement, and thus I had only a broad notion of what I would study as well as many reservations given the very fragile state in which I found the place and the people.

As my interactions broadened to include extended family, friends, and neighbors, a number of key concerns emerged that seemed relevant for understanding the production of vulnerability, the scope of disaster, and the ways in which people were responding. Chief among them was the concern about violent crime. While homicide had long been a problem, residents were reeling from a recent rash of murders, and the March for Survival had occurred just a few months earlier. This compounded the traumatic impact of the storm and colored the discourse on recovery. How had such conditions come to be, and how might they, finally, be addressed? Rebuilding the city would mean nothing, it seemed, without the concurrent remaking of its people.

I followed residents as they made their way through this uncertain terrain, and the paths they took frequently led to church. This was perhaps not surprising given the high degree of religiosity in New Orleans (over 50 percent report a religious affiliation) and the historically close relationship between religious expression, public life, and the process of social and political change.[15] Most interesting, however, were the diverse ways in which religious groups addressed the issue—from providing support for those experiencing violence first hand to crafting visions for the moral recovery that many believed was necessary for the redevelopment of a nonviolent urban society.

My research thus took shape through an unscripted journey across a diverse religious landscape. I spent time with a group of white Catholics in Uptown New Orleans who were praying at a Marian shrine for peace and the conversion of sinners; I followed members of a multiracial Episcopal congregation in the Tremé who publicly named all victims of violence, regardless of who they were or what they had been doing at the time of their deaths; and I observed the work of a Vodou *sosyete* in the Bywater whose initiates, the majority of them young, white, and relatively new to the city, performed anticrime ceremonies at specific neighborhood crossroads. By the time this survey was complete, I had left the Northshore and was living in New Orleans, with my research based primarily at Liberty

Street. The religious work I observed there seemed especially significant; it suggested a slow reframing of the moral architecture of the city—one that was guided by Black residents with a contemporary vision of faith, equality, community, and peace. It was unclear what change, if any, their work would bring about. The message was certainly clear, but its reception by a broader public accustomed to listening elsewhere was undetermined.

Religious Encounters

The pastor at Liberty Street, Pastor Samuel, was a generous man and a powerful driving force. Since the late 1980s he had focused much of the church's work on the problem of violence, pervasive as it was in the community to which he ministered. He gave his full support to the group that Danielle had founded while also leading the congregation in worship, through funerals, on crime walks, to vigils, and in related outreach and advocacy work. All of these activities, however, were driven more deeply by faith in God and a commitment to the church covenant, which focused on salvation and baptism, the responsibilities of Christian living, the duties one had to the church and fellow members, and the obligation to remain engaged with the covenant and with God's word in all other places. It was to God that Sister Anne, Danielle, Monica, and the other women looked for support, and it was to God that they gave glory for the "knowledge on death" they had gained. As Danielle had made clear, "God's words have a way, of letting us know."

In studies of vulnerability, violence, and death in Black communities, the role of religion is inadequately explored. This is especially striking given the evidence we have of religion—"the encounter of human beings with the 'sacred' or 'divine'" (Lincoln and Mamiya [1990] 2003, 2)—as a central phenomenon in the realization of Black social being. The "black sacred cosmos," as Lincoln and Mamiya describe the religious worldview of African Americans (2), should thus come forward in analyses of urban conditions and processes of change, particularly in the crescent city.

Such inquiry would impel us to move, as many scholars have already done, past outdated characterizations of the Black Church as functioning either as a space of accommodation or of resistance. As Fredrick Harris (1999, 5) historically traces, the idea that African American religion operates as an "opiate" or other means of social control has Marxist roots; it suggests that religion "offer[s] African Americans a way to cope with personal and societal difficulties and thus undermin[es] their willingness to actively challenge racial inequalities." These ideas have been gradually replaced with a more balanced perspective, described by Marla Frederick (2003, 5) as a "shift in focus from viewing black faith as one embedded in escapist theology . . . to viewing it as a faith which acknowledges the power of practitioners to not only endure, but also resist structures of oppression." This comes closest to Lincoln and Mamiya's ([1990] 2003, 15) dialectical model of the Black Church as a "mediating institution" in which the tension that exists between resistance and accommodation is just one set of polarities along a continuum that shifts in response to changing conditions (16).

Religious work at Liberty Street certainly had this dynamic quality, as the church attended to the shifting needs of the congregation and the community. However, religious work also had forward motion, as clergy and parishioners imagined more expansive ways of human being, relating, and dwelling. This suggests that analyses of the Black Church might also expand beyond a concern for how the church functions to a consideration of where the church might lead. The idea fits with recent scholarship that considers African American religious ideals as central frameworks for the refashioning of the world, for example, through alternative routes to "black religious consciousness" (Copeland 2013, 636), or a *theological thinking of love*" that leads to new and freer possibilities "for living and being otherwise" (C. D. B. Walker 2013, 653, emphasis in original).[16]

Black Women, Religion, and Restorative Kinship

Black women, in New Orleans and elsewhere, are frequently at the center of these expansions. Their presence and powerful work, however, are not well recognized; the pathways they set are not broadly followed. As Patricia Hill Collins (2000a, 3) argues, the systemic suppression of Black women "makes it easier for dominant groups to rule . . . [and] has been critical in maintaining social inequalities" in the United States and across the African diaspora. Such suppression takes multiple forms (economic, political, and ideological), and while Black women counter in a wide variety of ways, their concerns remain subordinate to the agendas of white male elites, white feminists, and a Black intellectualism with a "prominent masculinist bias" (7). I thus follow Collins in a corrective centering, to bring Black women's experience and knowledge to the forefront, at the very least in scholarly inquiry (2000b, 44).[17]

Especially relevant for my project is the centering of African American religious women. As Cheryl Townsend Gilkes (2001, 10) asserts, religion is central to the African American experience, "and black women's activities and commitments form the backbone or indispensable central framework on which every expression of black religion survives." Judith Casselberry thus summarizes the contributions of historical studies on Black women's religious (primarily Christian) work and organization (Casselberry 2017, 3–4; see also Collier-Thomas 1997, 2010; Higginbotham 1993; Weisenfeld 1997). Such inquiries focus more on the politics of religious work and less on religion itself. However, more recent ethnographic studies shed valuable light on religious experience without detaching it from persistent conditions of oppression or limiting it to standard time frames and settings (Gilkes 2001; Frederick 2003; Abrums 2010; Day 2012; Manigault-Bryant 2014; Casselberry 2017).[18]

Casselberry's (2017) own ethnographic study examines Black women's religious labor at a Pentecostal church in present-day Harlem. Focusing on the contemporary nature of women's social and religious lives within the still gendered hierarchies of the church, Casselberry finds "an unmediated relationship with Jesus" at the center of women's negotiations of religious and institutional authority (171). The networks and "women-driven patriarchies" these women create are thus emboldened by the knowledge that like Jesus, women "have the power to submit" (171). Casselberry's broader intent, however, is to explore "the circumstances of producing a *holy Black female personhood* within faith communities" (5, emphasis added). In this way, women's religious work is fundamentally about their development as "authentic religious subject[s]" while growing the church as institution and Kingdom of God (172).

In New Orleans, the production of a holy Black female personhood was connected more directly to women's ability to mediate the space of death, and they did so in ways that reconfigured standard boundaries of time, place, and existence. For example, the women at Liberty Street worked steadily to address what Danielle described as "kin pain," referring to the pain that women experienced following the violent severing of relatedness, which for these women occurred most directly in the deaths of their children. The labor they performed, therefore, was about repairing family, social, and spiritual bonds—a *restorative kinship* that affirmed value among the living, between the living and the dead, on earth, and in God's eternal kingdom.

I develop this framing within an expanded field of kinship studies that now includes forms of relatedness far beyond kinship's traditionally biological conceptualization. This reinvigorated inquiry brings diverse forms of recognition, connection, and care to the forefront while also revealing the persistent processes of invisibility, disconnection, and neglect alongside and against which they work. Sarah Franklin and Susan

McKinnon (2001, 7), for example, examine how kinship "can be put to use in ways that destabilize the 'obviousness' of its conventional referents, while expanding the scope of its purchase." The notion of "relatedness" emerges out of this endeavor. Janet Carsten (2000, 4) develops the term "in opposition to, or alongside, 'kinship' in order to signal an openness to indigenous idioms of being related rather than a reliance on pre-given definitions."

Regarding the women at Liberty Street, a consideration of relatedness creates space for an examination of family and social rupture as well as the connections that women forge through outreach and fellowship, in mourning, and in their overall raising of the dead. Relatedness also reveals an important extension of these processes beyond traditional realms, for example, in earthly as well as heavenly dimensions where connectivity, value, and eternal life are assured. Two processes are especially relevant here. The first, as Carsten (2007, 1) again argues, is the intersection that exists between loss, the forms of relatedness that emerge in such situations, political processes, and the imagining and crafting of the future.[19] The second process is the development, frequently at this juncture, of new strands of connectivity. The restorative kinship I frame is thus "co-poietic" in the sense that Robert Desjarlais (2016, 15) describes, constituting a "collaborative fashioning and unfashioning of self and other, as well as . . . a poiesis-on-behalf-of-another." As Desjarlais asserts, "the call for the living to labor on behalf of the deceased makes such efforts a matter of care, responsibility, and honor, implying an ethics of mourning" (15). In Central City and in other places where disconnection and rupture are intensified, these forms of relatedness are also deeply political, with poiesis connected to processes of healing and justice. As the women at Liberty Street raised the dead, they also situated them (and each other) in valued relation—as some mother's son, some father's daughter, and all God's children. As Gilkes (2001, 140) argues, identifications such as these form "an intergenerational and inter-gender basis for unity" signified by an assertion of personhood within a Black sacred cosmos attuned to freedom in response to death and in the (continued) context of racial and other forms of oppression (Lincoln and Mamiya [1990] 2003, 4).[20]

Failure as Fieldwork

These ideas, while compelling, did not fully address the reservations I still had about living and working in New Orleans. Even after the scope of my project was clear, the research, especially my role and presumed authority in carrying it out, raised a long-standing disciplinary and personal concern about the ethics of fieldwork in precarious urban settings. While extensive scholarship over the past several decades has refined methods of knowledge production and dissemination, a troubling characterization of the fieldworker, set out for unfamiliar and even "exotic" settings, still persists. Laurence Ralph brings this concern forward, citing Victor Rios (2011) to describe the care urban ethnographers must take so as not to rehearse what Rios describes as "'the jungle-book trope,' the notion that the researcher got 'lost in the wild,' the people of 'the wild' subsequently adopted her, put her on a pedestal, and she has 'lived to tell civilization about it'" (Ralph 2015, 442). One cannot assume that today's ethnographers know better and are able to successfully navigate these pitfalls, and the fallout is high if they do not, as detailed in both Rios's and Ralph's critique of Alice Goffman's (2014) work (Ralph 2015; Rios 2015).

Such situations highlight more broadly the dilemmas of speaking "for" or "with" others (Alcoff 1991), a dilemma with extra weight in already vulnerable communities and especially in violent, postdisaster, or war-torn settings (Howell 1990; Daniel 1996; Gill 2004). While expectations for an immersed experience of fieldwork still exist, I, or any other researcher, cannot expect to be welcomed into such communities without question or concern. Nor can we imagine that our research will have only a positive impact for the already overburdened people we encounter or for the long-standing social issues and problems they face. My own instinct, therefore, was to tread lightly—I did my best to make sure I had permission and whenever possible I took a back seat in proceedings in order to minimize my intrusion.

This was a fine line to walk given the disciplinary associations that continue to be made between the depth of one's immersion and the quality and application of resulting data. To what extent can and should researchers immerse in such settings? How do we learn from the encounters we are permitted to have? When reciprocal relationships form, to what degree do they reflect the validity of research findings? How, in turn, do we assess findings when these kinds of relationships do *not* develop?

I raise these questions as I think back on an experience of fieldwork that was very difficult. While I was supported by the close relationships I already had, I nonetheless landed in New Orleans as something of an outsider. This, plus the state of the post-Katrina city, made my research challenging to organize and carry out. Appointments were made then suddenly canceled, locations were hard to pin down, and in some cases my own follow-through was poor, overcautious as I was about the added stress my queries might cause and stressed myself from trying so hard, in such precarious circumstances, to do no additional harm.

Nonetheless, over a period of two years, from 2007 to 2009, I came to know the members of a diverse community of faith, developing most of my connections at Liberty Street, especially with the women in the support group. I relied on participant observation and interviews as primary methods of data collection. This work, however, was fundamentally about listening, and I tried to do so with as little presumption as possible (Angel-Ajani 2004, 142). The narratives and testimonies that resulted were extended and full; their details of disaster, violence, death, and mourning frequently elicited strong emotions in both the sharer and the recipient. I did my best to structure these encounters safely by informing participants about the potential risks of my inquiry, by arranging for support during and following interview sessions, and by making sure participants understood their right to disengage. I also followed up to make sure that people were comfortable with what they had revealed, although the need to tell one's story, to testify, seemed to override most concerns about its translation or broadcast.

My work primarily took place within religious settings, but it also extended to the surrounding community, as participants brought me into their homes, workplaces, and to the public sites they claimed around town. I structured my time in accordance with their scheduled services, prayer groups, vigils, demonstrations, community meetings, and other related activities. The conversations I had in these settings were informal but equally rich, and they broadened the scope of my inquiry beyond the members of a particular congregation to the community leaders, teachers, law enforcement personnel, and city officials with whom they were also involved. Finally, some of my research took place in the archives, where I studied the history and mission of specific religious organizations and traced the development, decline, and recovery of surrounding neighborhoods.

In the long period of analysis and writing that ensued, my data nonetheless seemed diffuse and thin. As George Marcus observes in an article on the sharing of fieldwork stories, anthropologists do not talk about their fieldwork experiences as much as they used to, particularly when research is carried out within complex and increasingly interdisciplinary domains (Marcus 2006, 114). In fact, contemporary fieldwork "may no longer be very ethnographic in the traditional way that it is imagined" (115). While valuable findings still emerge, they often do so through an extensive period of *post*fieldwork reflection. In this way, "it is the fieldwork that provides stimulation and ideas, but is relatively 'thin' in materials, while it is the diffuse efforts to come to terms with the lacks and failures of fieldwork afterward that provide the richest and 'thickest' materials" (115).

While I am somewhat relieved by this view, I wonder about the implications, particularly given the emphasis on postfieldwork analysis and the relationship that sets up between the fieldwork and what must be salvaged from it. To what extent might a salvage ethnography be the new norm for the study of the increasingly precarious urban world? What can we expect such an inquiry to generate? That is, what does fieldwork in the crescent city look like, how does it fail, and what might that failure reveal? In coming to terms with the failures of my own fieldwork, I listened to and transcribed interviews, read and reread my field notes, and delved more deeply into related geography and history. It was in this process that Liberty Street was confirmed as a primary site of analysis, the diffuse nature of my data reflecting the scattered state of the recovering city and the practices of Black women emerging to direct an otherwise drifting project and world.

I have organized the book to bring these revelations forward in the clearest way possible. Following the introduction, the book is divided into three parts—an arc that extends from the histories of vulnerability and violence in the Black urban delta to the legacies and current frameworks of Black love at Liberty Street to the processes of restorative kinship at work in the raising of the dead. Each begins with a short "message" in the spirit of a pastoral or lay message one would receive in Baptist worship service. These have two purposes. The first is to position the experiences of Black women as the central framing of the book, the gateway through which one enters into broader context and explanation. The second is to facilitate a sense of connection, or at least recognition, an essential perspective as the reader comes to know and follow these women through the text. The book is also anchored by a series of photographs that provide a visual point of entry for the messages and the material that follows. Rather than use images to illustrate specific locations or events, my intention is to *let in light* at key moments. This is a rough play on the idea of an illuminated manuscript, and I hope it will enhance and not prescribe the reader's own discovery, with greater access to sacred meaning across the histories, stories, and ideas the book contains.

One final yet central failing, of heart and body, explains the process of my work and the final substance of the book. My fieldwork took place alongside my family's recovery from disaster, and five years later, as I struggled to make sense of my findings, my father passed away. While his death resulted from a specific illness, it was not disconnected from the impact of flood and fire—a physical, social, and emotional loss from which he never fully recovered. My writing was thus unexpectedly furthered through my own experience of death and mourning.

Renato Rosaldo, in the introduction to *Culture and Truth: The Remaking of Social Analysis* ([1989] 2001), describes the insight such experience provides, referring specifically to the sudden and very tragic death of his wife, which took place during a period of fieldwork in the Philippines while researching the relationship between bereavement and rage among Ilongot headhunters. Writing about this fieldwork some fifteen months after his wife's passing, Rosaldo understands his personal experience as "a vehicle" for making the qualities of Ilongot grief more accessible to his readers. The writing itself became simultaneously "an act of mourning, a personal report, *and* a critical analysis of anthropological method" (Rosaldo [1989] 2001, 11, emphasis in original).

My own work is similarly attuned—a way to reflect on my father's life and death while considering how the experience brought me closer to the conditions and responses I observed in New Orleans.[21] Such comparisons are tricky, as personal experience does not necessarily give greater access to the lives of others. Nonetheless, this particular failing has been insightful not just in terms of feeling and thus better seeing the contours of sorrow but through a greater awareness of the aspects of humanity revealed in the process of loss and recovery. This insight is developed by tracing the connections between what we have experienced and what we believe, who we are and what we value, and what this affirms about the kinds of awakenings we inherit and inspire. Certainly, this seems a central part of the "good grief" that Sister Anne described.

In many ways, therefore, the book remains a work in progress, reminiscent of Scheper-Hughes's (1993, 28) notion of "good enough ethnography," where in perilous times anthropologists "struggle to do the best we can with the limited resources we have at hand—our ability to listen and observe carefully, emphatically, and compassionately." Bourgois and Schonberg (2009, 298) call for a "good-enough *applied* anthropology" (emphasis added), grounded in critical theory and working to alleviate suffering, particularly for the socially vulnerable. I am not yet sure whether this book is either, which does not make it not worth sharing but perhaps loosens the grip on its determination just slightly so that its methods and findings can flounder and fail in unexpected and perhaps informative ways, as life and death in the crescent city would suggest.

PART ONE

On Fragile Ground

Grand Bayou (photo by author)

Clouds

It finally rained yesterday, the clouds opening up with a promise of relief they could not keep. The air in Central City felt fresh afterward, but it was only for a moment, as the steam rose from the pavement and the world was again what it was. Uselessly fanning herself as she sat at the table in the community development center across the street from the church, Danielle began her testimony by describing a conversation she had recently enjoyed with her five-year-old grandson. The two of them had been sitting on the front porch of her house looking out at a similar sky. This boy was the child of Danielle's firstborn son "Rock," and "Little Rock," as he was called, was as inquisitive as his father had been. It had been three years since Rock's death, and his son had many questions. What had happened to him? He asked his grandmother. Where was he now? Danielle told him that his dad was in heaven, pointing him out in the clouds above. As she recounted,

I told him, "That's your dad up there." He said, "How Grandma?" I said, "Just look at his head, round and everything." I said, "Just look at how the cloud is shaped." He said "Oooh, how did he get up there?" You know I had to tell him that his spirit went up there . . . I told him, I said, "The Bible said your daddy is absent from the body and present with the Lord and we would see him again." He said, "When will we see him again?" I said to him, "The Bible said when Jesus comes back." You know what he asked me then? He said, "When's Jesus coming back?" [*laughter*] So you know I told him, I said, "We have to wait on him." I said, "He's coming back sooner than we think."

The other women, gathered with Danielle for the support group that evening, smiled, their spirits collectively lifted by Little Rock's reaction to an impromptu but powerful teaching.

Danielle had long been fascinated with clouds, but they took on new meaning after Rock's death. Their sighting reminded her of Rock's heavenly ascension, which provided some comfort as she continued to mourn his passing. This religious significance was further confirmed when Danielle came across a short religious text, published by her pastor's wife, in which there was a section titled "Clouds." Drawing on Scripture and subtitled "His strength is in the clouds (Psalm 68:34)," the text moved from the common perception of clouds as dark and foreboding to their affirmation as an important resource that brought solace in times of need. "It was amazing when I found this topic in this book," Danielle told the group. "Because when Rock got killed I used to always look up in the cloud, and I did find strength."

"Clouds" became the central reading at special meetings of the support group, when the women gathered to mark the birth and death anniversaries of lost loved ones. Danielle would distribute copies, and each woman would read a passage. Just after the psalm referencing God's strength, the text continued in a more somber tone: "What is your perception of clouds?" it read. "In this life, we have a great tendency to think of clouds as something deep, dark, and dismal. We have heard or perhaps said expressions like: 'There is a dark cloud hanging over.' 'I cannot see for the dark clouds.' Or 'How I long for an unclouded day.'" It was a sense of foreboding doom that the women well understood, given the conditions of violence that surrounded them.

Danielle had founded the support group in 2005, shortly after Rock's passing. His death was devastating but not unexpected, caught up as he was in violence associated with drug trafficking and murdered on the street, just a few blocks from the church. In fact, violence, in all its forms, went back for decades in this poor African American community, its impact accumulating across many generations. Danielle was raised primarily by her grandmother and brought up in the church, but her life took a turn at age eleven, when her father was released from prison. Spending time with his extended family in the housing projects of Central City, the dark clouds of poverty, poor education, teenage pregnancy, joblessness, and substance abuse settled around her. She dropped out of school and became involved with drugs, as a dealer and then a user, addicted by the age of twenty-six. She nonetheless managed to provide for her son and the children that followed, making sure that they were baptized and that they finished high school. It had not been possible, however, to fully clear the skies for Rock, and this kept Danielle, and many other mothers, in a constant state of anxiety as they waited for the phone call that eventually came to announce, in her words, "jail or death."

In a later return to the church, and with sobriety, Danielle made her way to another perspective. Her trust in God was restored, and she believed that He would "keep" her through whatever the clouds might unleash. The emphasis thus shifted to strength over sorrow, to clarity over a clouded mind and heart. She read carefully the next passage from the text: "When we examine the biblical history of clouds, we see our Lord is indeed in the clouds of our lives. The Bible declares His strength is in the clouds. The children of Israel were led by a pillar of clouds by day. (Exodus 13:21) This should be good news for the children of God, that there is help in the clouds. The prophet Elijah was encouraged by a cloud that it would rain. We are grateful for the clouds that bring rain because it is essential for life."

The passage triggered Danielle's memory of the rain yesterday that had brought some relief, albeit short lived, to the heat of a summer day in the urban delta. "And guess what?" she said, looking around the table, "It was so *hot* yesterday that when I seen that rain came down, I just stood up and said, '*Thank you Jesus*, for cooling off the earth!'" The other women agreed, emphatically, "Oooh child, *yes!*" Needing no encouragement, Danielle began to preach: "It was so hot yesterday, the heat was actually . . . I felt the *weight* of the heat. But his Word is just awesome." She returned to the text. "And like it says here: 'And Psalms 36:5 reminds us, 'Your mercy, O Lord, is in the heavens, Your faithfulness reaches to the clouds.' And we can all testify for that."

One's connection to the clouds, therefore, was not solely based on the conditions of violence that were close to the ground, nor was it singularly transformed through the recognition of God's strength and mercy; it was *atmospheric* in nature, inseparable from the pervasive context and climate. Showers and thunderstorms were frequent from an unpredictable tropical air, and weather systems could quickly intensify, as everyone certainly understood. While this added to an existing state of anxiety, it was also conceptualized as a blessing. Another woman read the next passage: "It will do us good to remember the lower our clouds hang the more blessed we are. How, you may ask, can this be? When in the clouds, we cannot see our way clearly. That's when our Lord draws closer, nearer because we need Him most. Thank God that His mercy is always in proportion to our troubles. Our generous, gracious God would not give us a cup of grace when our situation calls for a gallon."

Danielle was always moved by this passage and she stopped the meeting that evening to comment, "I just want to share with you all, we go through so much, you know? But God knows just what we need. I mean sometimes we have big troubles, we have little troubles. But God, He will supply our every need. And if we need a gallon of it, He got it. If we need just one cup of it, He got it. . . . There's nothing too big and nothing too small that He can't handle." It was an important reassurance, especially for those whose suffering was acute. She asked a longtime member to conclude:

The next time you find yourself overtaken by dark clouds you must remember, there is peace, hope, and help in the clouds because God's strength is within them. Let us also not forget that the glory of the Lord is in the clouds (Exodus 16:10). Wherever, whenever and whatever His children are in need of, He is there, even in dark clouds. When our dark clouds are hanging low, all we need is to draw closer to Him, whose strength is in the clouds. If we just keep our eyes on Him, we will be able to consider our ways and see our way clear. Recognize the voice of our Lord, and walk in His will, and know that by faith we will receive the strength that is ours for the asking.

Luke 21:27 reminds us that we shall see the "Son of man coming in a cloud with power and great glory" . . . 1 Thessalonians 4:17 tells us the day will come when "we who are alive and remain shall be caught up together with them in the clouds to meet the Lord in the air, and we shall always be with the Lord." Heaven . . . I am going there . . . (2 Corinthians 5:1).

"Amen," the women said when the reading was finished. "Praise the Lord."

ONE

The Black Urban Delta

The wealth of a world is here,—unworked gold in the ore, one might say; the paradise of the South is here, deserted and half in ruins. I never beheld anything so beautiful and so sad. When I saw it first—sunrise over Louisiana—the tears sprang to my eyes. It was like young death,—a dead bride crowned with orange flowers,—a dead face that asked for a kiss. I cannot say how fair and rich and beautiful this dead South is. It has fascinated me. I have resolved to live in it. LAFCADIO HEARN ([1907] 2007, 42–43)

I first met Danielle at a public vigil against urban violence held in New Orleans over the New Year's Day holiday in 2009. Organized by the clergy at Liberty Street Baptist Church, the three-day event took place in the heart of the Central City neighborhood—at the foot of a memorial to the Reverend Dr. Martin Luther King Jr., which stands in the middle of the "neutral ground" (median) on South Claiborne Avenue between Martin Luther King Jr. Boulevard and Felicity Street.[1] The location was not far from the church and also not far from the Uptown neighborhood that I called home. Driving to the vigil in the early afternoon, I followed Napoleon Avenue toward the lake, turning right on South Claiborne. Nearing the intersection of Felicity Street, I could make out a small group of about ten people standing on the neutral ground. Positioned at the base of the King monument, they were also under the protection of a few trees, which gave some shelter from the drizzling rain. It was a dreary afternoon, but they had built a small sanctuary of sorts, huddled together with three lanes of traffic rushing by on either side. I parked and crossed the street to reach them.

Pastor Samuel, the pastor at Liberty Street and the vigil's main organizer, was easy to spot. I recognized him from a televised interview I had seen the afternoon before announcing the vigil and describing its purpose—to bring attention to the problem of violence that continued to plague the Black community. Participants were there to pray for those who were suffering, but they also wanted to reach people outside of the community—to raise awareness about violence as a problem of collective concern, not one confined to poor Black neighborhoods. A tall man with a formidable but gentle presence, Pastor Samuel was already making a statement, wearing a black T-shirt and matching cap with the word "ENOUGH" printed across the front in bold white letters. I introduced myself and he welcomed me without hesitation, inviting me to join in the prayer and fellowship that was planned for the day.

I walked around and met the participants who were already gathered. They had set up camp in the center of the neutral ground on a small paved area. There were a few benches there, interspersed with lawn chairs, blankets, and sleeping bags from the night before. Someone had carried in a small metal fire pit, which sat smoldering with coals. The participants were mostly men of various ages, although a few women, including Danielle, were present. Most were positioned along the perimeter of the neutral ground in close proximity to cars when the traffic light turned red. They held printed and hand-lettered signs that read "I will NOT take a life," "I will not take the life of my brother," "Homicides in 2008: 178, Homicides in 2009: 0," and "Yes We Can," in reference to Barack Obama's campaign slogan and recent election as the first Black president of the United States.

Danielle was at the center of the neutral ground, close to the monument. She was lettering her own sign, which read, "I am a mother hurting because of violence." As we introduced ourselves she told me a bit about her affiliation with the church. A member of Liberty Street since childhood, she expressed loyalty and gratitude for Pastor Samuel because of the support he had given her and for the leadership he provided for the community. She finished lettering her sign and then pulled a flyer from her purse, handing it to me before joining the others along the edge. It advertised a support group she had founded for grieving mothers like herself. "You are welcome to stop by" she said, "if you are interested in seeing what we do."

I remained by the monument, taking in the scene. This was a busy intersection along a major commercial corridor. Thousands of people rushed through on any given day and many rushed through with purpose, it seemed, to minimize their time in what was known as a poor, African American, and violent neighborhood. They kept to South Claiborne, on either side of the long median, rarely frequenting the mix of gas stations, fast food restaurants, and discount stores that served a mostly local clientele. From where I stood, facing the monument, my eyes followed the traffic as it proceeded Uptown to eventually skirt behind prestigious universities before extending into Jefferson Parish. Turning the opposite way, I watched the cars travel up and over the I-10 overpass, veering off to get on the highway or continuing past the Superdome and into the Central Business District (CBD). Central City spanned primarily to the left and right, toward the "river side" or the "lake side" of Claiborne where it encompassed the B. W. Cooper Apartments (Calliope Projects).[2]

It occurred to me, standing there, that Pastor Samuel had chosen a strategic site for this work. When he had a moment to chat, I shared my observations: "We're standing at the busiest of intersections, located in the heart of Central City but also between Uptown and the CBD," I said. "I mean thousands of people pass through here every day, and *fast*. Does it mean anything to you spiritually or otherwise to be at such a place, at *this* particular crossroads?" He answered quickly and emphatically, "*Yes*. First of all because it's familiar. But the monument also reminds me of what we as a people are able to do. It reminds me of a debt I feel I owe. I mean how can we just sit by idly when this kind of battle is going on in our community?" He gestured to the surrounding area as he continued to speak.

You know, we have given out maybe five thousand bibles at this intersection since Katrina. Because you know people were reestablishing their lives and everything, but everybody was replacing everything that they had lost except for their bible. So, we started giving them away. And it's so funny because whenever you stand on the corner, people assume you are trying to raise money. So, they ask me, "Are you giving those away?" And you say, "Yes, would you like one?" And they say "Yeah . . ." and then, "*Who are you?*" They just can't believe that somebody is giving away something for free, and when you tell them you are from a church, they are shocked. And I'm thinking, you're not supposed to be shocked if the church gives you a bible. I mean that's how far away we are from the Word and from where we want to be. So, we've given away literally millions of tracts, even way before Katrina, and we've had times when we've just flooded this area at *every* intersection; all the way down Martin Luther King [*pointing to the left and right*] and Claiborne [*pointing behind him and to the front*]. It's always been impactful when we've sustained it.

The Life and Death of a Son

I contacted Danielle a few weeks later, and she agreed to an interview so that we could get to know each other before I attended the support group that she had founded. We sat in her office, tucked away in the community development building across the street from the church. I thanked her for taking the time, and then I asked about the history of the group, when and why it had formed, and the nature of their work. Danielle took a long minute before responding and then revealed that her primary source of inspiration had been the sudden, but not altogether unexpected, death of her own son. "In 2005 Rock was murdered, which was very hard for me," she began.

And Pastor Samuel called me up and asked about me coming to share with the news media . . . and his reason for asking was because he said that he saw that I was one of the stronger mothers that have dealt with this tragedy, how God gave me the strength to deal with it. And at my son's funeral he was there, and it was just amazing how God kept me and helped me to stand in the midst of it all.

I immediately expressed my condolences, feeling foolish for not anticipating the painful memories such a question would likely trigger. Yet I was also struck by how quickly Danielle had moved from grief to an affirmation of religious strength. God had "kept" her and helped her to stand. Stepping lightly, I asked her to elaborate on the source of this strength and what it provided. Her response came in the form of a long narrative, which she later described as her "testimony." As I would come to understand, sharing this testimony was an essential part of how she communicated, survived, and flourished in the troubled city she nonetheless called home.

Well what it was, to be honest about it, was that God guided my heart. Because my son was in the drug life. He was a drug dealer for ten years, and when he got murdered he was thirty-two years old. And I always tried to help him to come out of drug life, as far as not selling drugs . . . And I knew it wasn't nothing good in the drugs . . . that if he didn't stop, it was going to be jail or death. So even before he got killed, I prayed and asked God to give me the strength when that phone rang.

As she continued to speak, it became apparent that the source of Danielle's strength was also tied to the knowledge she possessed, gained from an experience and awareness of how the world worked, at least in this regard. This was not separate from the strength and knowledge she attributed to God; rather, it stemmed from a belief that God supported her through death and mourning, and this gave her the capacity to stand and to support and strengthen others. She continued,

Just weeks before he got killed, he was coming home by me, he didn't live with me, and he was crying out to me saying, "Mama, I'm tired." I would just look at him in the chair, and I would rub his head, and we would pray. I knew what my son wanted. He wanted money, he wanted things in life, and he got caught up in drug life in the community, and he made a wrong choice in life, and it was hard for him to get out because once you get in . . . it's not easy to walk away.

One night, he was just like, "Whew," went to sleep in the chair, and I said, "Something wrong?" And he said, "No Mama. I'm just tired of this, tired of this." And I said, "I know you are, but you just gotta continue to pray and ask God to deliver you from these drugs." And he never was a user, he always was a dealer and he wound up losing his life around it, he got set up . . . someone hire someone to kill him. I knew that this was going to take place because I saw it coming. So, I guess that's what give me the strength today to go on. Because I was not in denial of what the circumstances were.

Beautiful Dead South

As I describe in the introduction to this book, my conceptualization of New Orleans as a crescent city goes beyond the city's well-known moniker to signal an important process of urban being and becoming, one that requires a less bounded view of the city itself, particularly the urban margins. It claims the space of death, characteristic of many poor Black neighborhoods, as a simultaneously generative space for the envisioning and crafting of a sustainable Black urban future. It also identifies the people therein—the socially devalued in particular—as vital agents, makers, and guides in the transformation of self and society. In this chapter, I introduce a key group of individuals who were engaged in this work in New Orleans—including Pastor Samuel, Danielle, and the others at the vigil that New Year's Day.

To better situate this community, I take a historical and social-geographic approach that brings the "Black urban delta" into view, revealing the evolution of vulnerability for people of African descent in New Orleans from the eighteenth century forward. My intent is to make clear the connection that exists between the development of the urban delta and the contemporary social problems that disproportionately affect Black people in socially, economically, and environmentally precarious places. This approach also sheds light on the various forms of adaptation, resistance, resilience, and recovery that have simultaneously emerged, as Black people have fought to survive and thrive in a society in which they have never been fully valued or welcomed.[3]

To give structure to this task, I anchor this chapter in my own navigation of the city at the start of my research through key sites, events, and encounters. For example, as I describe the location of my own New Orleans–based family as well as the state of the city upon my arrival, I provide an overview of the development of Uptown but "back-of-town" neighborhoods. As I return to my first encounter with the clergy and parishioners from Liberty Street at the King memorial, I recount the history of oppression and the fight for Black citizenship correlated with the racialization then reclaiming of urban space. As I introduce participants' life histories and experiences of violence, I give necessary context for understanding related processes, such as the development and decline of public housing and the disfranchisement and increased marginalization of poor Black communities. Such detail forms an essential backdrop for understanding the conditions that many of my research participants confronted. Neighborhoods like Central City are not removed, for example, from local histories of slavery and racial oppression, and the conditions of violence found there must be understood in terms of their overlapped structural and social causes. The responses to violence are equally complex, inspired by Black political, social, and religious thought and forged over centuries in the home, in the church, and on the connecting streets of the Crescent City.

Lafcadio Hearn, a nineteenth-century writer based in New Orleans from 1877 to 1888, presents a similarly integrated view of life and death in southeast Louisiana—where "paradise" is a world that is simultaneously "deserted" and "half in ruins" (Hearn [1907] 2007, 42–43). Yet it is within this space of beauty and sadness that Hearn is resolved to live. Thus, "sunrise over Louisiana" is "like young death,—a dead bride crowned with orange flowers,—a dead face that asked for a kiss." This resolve to contend with the complexities of a "beautiful . . . dead South," is one that I keep in sight as I examine the diverse histories, encounters, and ways of being in the Black urban delta. While this chapter focuses on the evolution of precarity in poor Black neighborhoods, it does so to anticipate the frameworks and practices that guide life as it is determined to proceed in a still-rising city and world.

Arrival and Departure

I left Ann Arbor in the spring of 2007, flying first to my mother's home in Tennessee and purchasing a car to drive from there to New Orleans. I had made this drive before, but I was particularly anxious this time— just a year and a half after Hurricane Katrina—to traverse what I knew would be a radically changed landscape. My father and stepmother, who had evacuated just before the storm, had since returned to Louisiana. They were settled in an apartment in Mandeville, on the Northshore of Lake Pontchartrain, some forty-five minutes from New Orleans. I gratefully accepted the single mattress on the floor of their second bedroom and rested among stacks of insurance papers and other documents piled up on every available surface.

A few days later we headed across the Causeway and into New Orleans, to see the site where my parents' house had stood before the flood and fire. They had already been by there, but only once, as it was difficult to take in. There were other parts of the city that they had not seen since the storm, so we drove through those areas first. Our conversation was sparse, and in hard-hit communities such as Lakeview and the Lower Ninth Ward, we slowed and fell silent, stunned by the destruction. Here were whole neighborhoods upturned, the leaning structures of damaged houses, razed lots of dirt and concrete, debris piled up in the street. The primary signs of life were other uncomfortable observers like ourselves along with some birds and stray animals. We did visit some people that we knew who were living in still-standing homes among FEMA trailers dotting the landscape.

Approximately 80 percent of New Orleans flooded in the wake of Hurricane Katrina after levees and floodwalls failed. Many people had evacuated, but a sizeable number did not or could not, and with floodwaters reaching over ten feet in some neighborhoods, there were thousands who lost their lives. Those who stayed and survived and those who had managed to return faced enormous challenges as they worked to meet basic needs—food, shelter, employment, healthcare, education—in a city long known for its simultaneous richness and scarcity and in which some people had already felt abandoned.

This overall sense of loss was complicated by a strong assertion of recovery. For example, New Orleans's population decreased by more than half after Hurricane Katrina, from 484,674 in 2000 to an estimated 230,172 in 2006. However, by July 2015, the population had recovered by 80 percent, to 386,617.[4] City officials touted additional statistics suggesting economic stability despite a national recession, claiming that rebuilding efforts and a postdisaster reinvestment in cultural economy had helped shield New Orleans from job loss (Quillen 2009). Local poverty rates had indeed fallen since the storm, and rates of home ownership were on the rise. There was talk of innovation, for example, through educational reform in charter schools or the success of high-profile green building projects.

None of this fit with what my parents and I witnessed as we drove around New Orleans that day, or later, as I subsequently settled into life in neighborhoods near where they had lived. Rather than a recovery that addressed the needs of all residents, the social and economic dividing lines seemed redrawn. Statistical analyses may have indicated a population recovery, but this was different from a population *return*; in fact, the demographics of the city were significantly changed. In the year 2000, for example, African Americans made up 66.7 percent of the total population of New Orleans, but by 2008 that percentage had dropped to 60.7 percent. During the same time period, the percentage of whites increased from 26.6 percent to 30.7 percent. Significant growth also occurred in the Hispanic community, where the population increased from 3.1 percent to 4.5 percent (Campanella 2007, 714). Such distinctions were clearly mapped, evident, for example, in the prestorm concentration of poor Blacks in deteriorating public-housing developments and their displacement and exclusion after the storm. This shift was exacerbated by an actual shortage of affordable housing not just because a disproportionate number of housing units in low-income neighborhoods had been damaged but because a large number had been subsequently demolished. Directed by the federal government and pushed forward by the ambitions of an elite group of local leaders with a specific vision for a "new" New Orleans (Arena 2012, 146), the Housing Authority of New Orleans (HANO) destroyed thousands of homes. While promises were made to replace units one-for-one, the emphasis was instead on the construction of mixed-income developments and an expansion of the housing voucher program.[5] Blacks, and poor Blacks in particular, were cast farther aside, their experiences of exclusion contributing to a new and broadly shared sense of grief and anger. Thankfully, this coincided with a new level of collective strength and resolve. No longer confident in the state's ability to provide protection, rescue, or relief, many residents developed their own systems of support within families, neighborhoods, religious institutions, cultural organizations, and other community-based groups.

When we reached my father and stepmother's old neighborhood, we got out of the car and walked around. There really wasn't much to see, a concrete slab where the property had been razed, a few pieces of parquet floor still visible, a short set of stone steps leading from the slab to the sidewalk along the park. I remembered the tasteful three-story townhouse they had purchased new in 1983. The land was part of a small city block that included several other townhouses, a larger home in the center, and a park with a small playground that stretched the width of the block along Napoleon Avenue.

As a child, I had visited them often. My brothers and I took over the second bedroom and upstairs loft, where we stretched out on cots and looked through our father's papers, records, and things. At night, from the back window, we could hear the trickle of the fountain in our neighbor's garden. It lulled us to sleep above a small oasis of banana trees and bougainvillea. During the day, we stepped out the front door and into the park to play on the swings, then headed up the street to St. Charles Avenue with pocket change for candy from the K&B drugstore. We usually went this direction, crossing St. Charles and walking to Magazine Street or taking the streetcar farther Uptown to the park and zoo or downtown to the French Quarter. We rarely went the other way, at least not on foot, toward Freret Street and South Claiborne Avenue or across Napoleon and into the Milan neighborhood. In those directions, things felt slightly different—there were certainly less amenities, the houses seemed smaller and in need of repair, and the people we encountered, hanging about on porches or on the corner, seemed to watch and identify us as outsiders in ways that made me uncomfortable.

As I got older, I understood just how on the edge we were situated, between the predominantly wealthy and white communities that extended farther Uptown, hugging close to St. Charles, and the mostly poor and Black neighborhoods, Uptown but back-of-town, that sloped down and away toward South Claiborne. In many ways, middle-class African American families like ours had a foot in both worlds. We were connected to the social life that revolved around the university where my father taught, but we were also forever tied through history, identity, family, religion, and other legacies to the Black community found across the city—from Broadmoor to the Tremé to New Orleans East. In the wake of the storm, this meant that we would drive across town to see how various people we knew had made out, but it also meant that most everyone we saw had experienced a level of loss that was closely correlated with race, socioeconomic status, and location. As my father frequently lamented, and as was evident by the slab of concrete that was left of his house, he had not been properly positioned, "not Uptown enough," to escape disaster. Family and friends in other areas, lower lying and farther away, had fared much worse.

The Least Bad Place in the Swamp

To understand these distinctions and their connection to urban vulnerability, some history is necessary about New Orleans and the people who settled in, or were relegated to, its margins. The record is centuries long, beginning in the late sixteenth and early seventeenth centuries, when

Europeans began to explore and conquer this part of the New World—the French eventually founding the city of New Orleans in 1718. While I focus on a later period of Americanization and Uptown expansion after the Louisiana Purchase of 1803, I set the stage by describing the geographic, social, and political factors that fueled exploration, exploitation, and the building of empires. These processes are at the root of Uptown/back-of-town development, and they make clear the persistence of both social and environmental vulnerability within New Orleans's African American communities.

The 1,243,700-square-mile Mississippi River basin is the largest watershed in the United States. It drains and filters about 41 percent of the continental United States and 15 percent of the North American continent. The outflow discharges along the southeastern coast of Louisiana, with 70 percent discharged via the Mississippi River and the remaining 30 percent via the Atchafalaya River (Campanella 2006, 58). The delta itself is a patchy mix of land and water in constant flux. In seasonal flooding (before man-made levees and floodwalls), the river, rich with sediment from its long journey south, would spill over and spread out, building up protective wetlands. The land, therefore, is some of the newest in the country, a "thin, soft alluvial 'doormat' cast recently out upon the continent's margin" (Campanella 2008, 78). As Herodotus once wrote of the Nile River valley, southeast Louisiana is in many ways a "gift of the river" (Griffiths 1966, 57).

The indigenous societies that formed in the lower delta included the Choctaw, Houma, Natchez, and Chitimacha, and members of these groups were present when European colonizers arrived in the mid-sixteenth century (Powell 2012, 36). Early expeditions included those led by Spain's Hernando de Soto in 1541 and by French explorer René-Robert Cavelier, Sieur de La Salle, who left New France (Canada) and descended the Mississippi River, reaching the Gulf of Mexico in 1682 (8–9). France financed additional expeditions to locate the mouth and ascend the river from the Gulf, with the brothers Pierre Le Moyne, Sieur d'Iberville, and Jean-Baptiste Le Moyne, Sieur de Bienville, arriving in 1699 and establishing a base near present-day Biloxi, Mississippi. The French navigated their way, with the help of the Natchez and the other *petites nations* they encountered, through the distributaries and bayous of the delta to reach the wide expanse of the Mississippi.[6]

Such encounters mark the beginning of a long and fierce competition between those who sought to establish and expand dominion—namely the French, the Spanish, the British, and the Americans—by controlling access to the North American interior. They also mark the start of an equally long period of human exploitation and subjugation as well as environmental degradation, which brought the brutal weight of the colonial enterprise down on Native people, the enslaved Africans who were soon to arrive, poor immigrants, and others who were forced to labor and who fought to survive on increasingly fragile ground.

In 1718 Bienville, under the direction of the Company of the West (soon after the Company of the Indies), founded La Nouvelle Orléans as the capital of the new French colony.[7] The chosen site was the high ground of a natural levee along a crescent-shaped curve of the Mississippi River. By all accounts from settlers, it was a terrible place to build. While slightly elevated above sea level, the land fell off steeply into uninhabitable cypress swamp. It was, however, "the least bad place in the swamp" (Sublette 2008, 11), a navigable and defensible point along the lower Mississippi with access to a portage route that led overland from the river via Bayou St. John to Lake Pontchartrain, offering a valuable shortcut to the Gulf.[8] For France, it was a most advantageous position for the continuation of its empire- and now city-building project.

From Slavery to the Rise of Black New Orleans

I stayed with my parents in Mandeville for just a few weeks, eventually moving to New Orleans and renting a small carriage house. It was halfway Uptown, in the Touro neighborhood, on the river side of Magazine Street. It seemed like a good place to start in a relatively safe and lively neighborhood not far from the people and places I already knew. Locating myself on the map, I dotted a point just a few blocks from the river's edge, where Tchoupitoulas runs alongside the Port of New Orleans. From my porch, I could hear the barges blow their horns as they navigated the wharfs to waiting freight trains and trucks.

My landlords were recent "transplants" to the city by way of Texas and England. A middle-class white couple, he worked at an art gallery in the French Quarter, and she worked as an administrator for an Uptown university. They loved the neighborhood but did not hesitate to list its problems: the "crazy" old woman who lived for years across the street but hadn't returned after Katrina, the "fat cat" contractors coming in to buy houses after the storm "when they don't even live here," the house across the street down by the river where that guy is always drunk in his front yard. "We keep an eye on that," they told me, "but he doesn't really bother us, and we always make sure to say hello when we pass by." Their point was to assure me that I was safe, but they added that if I could, I should try to park as close as I could get to the carriage house, because at night, and a block or two down, closer to Tchoupitoulas, things can get "a little rough."

On the surface at least, the neighborhood appeared diverse, with residents from multiple racial, ethnic, and socioeconomic backgrounds. There were Black and white residents interspersed on my block, and my neighbors on the other side were a large Honduran family. The house across the street was being gutted and renovated by an out-of-state developer, presumably one of those "fat cats" who relied on cheap day labor from the city's newest Latino immigrants. My block, therefore, seemed somewhat of a transition zone—as one traveled toward the river, the average home value went steadily down, and the percentage of non-white residents went up. Heading the other way, across Magazine Street and toward St. Charles Avenue, the opposite occurred.

Still unsure of the direction of my research, I found refuge farther Uptown in Audubon Park, my long walks ending at "The Fly" where the river comes into full and unobstructed view. I discovered much later that this was a reclaimed garbage dump, converted in the late 1960s into a wide park with green fields and trees. It proved to be a good enough place to think, among the hot Sunday barbeque grills, soccer games, and children's birthday parties. The water's edge is right there, just a few yards down a rocky bank, and the barges and tugboats pass by directly in front—so close that crew members wave and call out to the people on the shore.

Some dog walkers pointed out a small trail down to a muddy patch of low trees and a hidden beach. Sitting on washed up railroad ties next to drainage pipes coming out of the ground, I watched the dogs splash in the pale brown water. It smelled a bit there and was not a place to linger after sunset. If one were to follow the river in the opposite direction, however, one would wind slowly around, past the wharfs at the port, past the Central Business District, along the French Quarter, before curving again to the south and east to define the edge of the Marigny, Bywater, and Lower Ninth Ward. Soon after the river takes you out of town, through St. Bernard then Plaquemines parish, heading toward the Gulf. I followed it once by car, picking up Highway 23 and driving as far as the road would allow. At Venice, seventy-five miles from New Orleans, I arrived at the sign that famously welcomes visitors to the "southernmost point in Louisiana" and "the Gateway to the Gulf."

It was through this gateway, in 1719, that the first ships carrying enslaved Africans to the Louisiana territory passed. Under French rule, the colonists sought to build what Lawrence Powell (2012, 61) describes as "a more perfect order on the Mississippi." This was a political, social, and economic grand scheme that depended on a large and controlled labor force. The French brought nearly six thousand Africans to Louisiana and transformed the territory into a plantation- and slave-based society primarily through the cultivation of tobacco and rice (70–71).

The governance of this society came through the development of a strict set of laws and regulations. The French Code Noir of 1724, a modified version of an existing slave code from the French Caribbean colony of Saint-Domingue, set standards of conduct for masters and nonslaveholders alike with the aim of preventing rebellion or the growth of a large population of "free blacks" and mixed-race people. While certainly oppressive, it did neither. As Gwendolyn Midlo Hall (1992, 155) argues, in the harsh conditions of frontier life, desperation frequently transcended "notions of racial and/or cultural and national superiority"; thus, enslaved Africans developed and deployed a set of valuable competencies that aided in their immediate survival if not their eventual liberation. The conditions of slavery in Louisiana, under French and later Spanish rule, therefore, reflected to some degree the overall disorderly structure of early city life in what Hall describes as "an extremely fluid society where a social-racial hierarchy was ill defined and hard to enforce" (128).[9]

In 1762, at the end of the French and Indian War (the North American stage of the Seven Years War), France ceded control of Louisiana (New Orleans and west of the Mississippi River) to Spain in the Treaty of Fontainebleau. This was a quiet and strategic move to halt British expansion in North America and to protect French and Spanish interests in the Caribbean and in New Spain, respectively (Powell 2012, 131–33). Spain's effective administration of Louisiana began in 1769, and the governors, administrators, and ruling elites of the new regime immediately focused their efforts on solidifying the place and prominence of the Spanish empire. As Powell notes, this involved "more than tweaking trade policy or shoring up tobacco prices. A loose-jointed society had to be guided back toward its destiny as a full-blown slave society, which required reviving plantation agriculture and reopening the slave trade" (223). Between 1763 and 1796, therefore, anywhere from eight thousand to nine thousand enslaved Africans were brought to New Orleans (261). Hall (1992, 279) identifies a population increase of enslaved people in lower Louisiana from 4,598 in 1763 to 24,264 in 1800. This was not, however, a steady enterprise; rather, the slave trade under Spanish rule had a "spasmodic character" (Powell 2012, 231) marked by liberalization and decentralization on the one hand and measured curtailment on the other, particularly due to concerns about insurgency.[10]

Evidence of this tension can be seen in Spanish slave laws, which replaced the French Code Noir with Las Siete Partidas (the Seven-Part Code) (Powell 2012, 225). Based on the absolute sovereignty and authority of the Spanish crown, its provisions determined the way in which all royal subjects were to be viewed. As Powell describes it, this "meant that even serfs and slaves, as well as conquered Indians, were vassals of the king and thus deserving of royal protection" (226). Overall this approach fit with a "corporatist conception of society . . . welded to a Catholic doctrine of spiritual equality," which "afforded enslaved Africans a legal personality" and "acknowledged their spiritual equality in the eyes of God" (226). Laws that allowed the enslaved in Louisiana to purchase their freedom, such as *coartación*, thus followed suit, although the practice was already widespread throughout the Spanish empire (226). Such practices, which also included manumission, fueled the growth of New Orleans's population of free blacks from just over 3 percent of the total population in 1771 to 19 percent in 1805 (Hanger 1997, 18).[11]

Not only did the population of free blacks grow larger, it became increasingly organized through social, economic, and cultural activities such as the solidification of kinship and family networks, participation in the militia, investment in businesses and property, and membership in the church (Hanger 1997, 17). In true "spasmodic" form, however, the Spanish government proposed stricter laws to suppress this development and maintain control in a continued campaign for social, economic, and political authority.[12] What nonetheless emerged despite these efforts was a multi- and mixed-race society—a racial order with three main divisions: Spaniards and other Europeans, Native Americans, and enslaved and free people of African descent. This was unique on the North American mainland, where colonial society was otherwise defined by a racial binary of whites and blacks (Powell 2012, 293). Diversity, however, did not mean equality. To find one's place within this society was a treacherous negotiation of a larger system defined by racial hierarchies and a ruling class, permeable as the determinations of racial classification and caste might have seemed.

It is important to note that apart from the policies of the ruling regime and what it did and did not allow, the growth of a free black society in New Orleans stemmed also from the agency of Black people themselves. As Powell makes clear, "Everywhere the ideal was to render slaves mere extensions of their masters' will. The ideal always fell short of reality, for the simple reason that slaves were rational beings whose ingenuity at resisting complete subjugation was something that masters could never defeat" (Powell 2012, 232).[13] As a result, and by the end of

Spanish rule, New Orleans was home to a diverse but increasingly consolidated Black population. Their settlement and governance on the one
hand within strict social and geographic boundaries and the fight for
citizenship and equal rights on the other, especially by those at the bottom of determined hierarchies, would shape the dimensions of urban
life and death in New Orleans in the centuries to come.

Americanization and Uptown/Back-of-Town Expansion

I stayed at the carriage house off Magazine Street for almost a year. I had
planned to stay longer, but I did not request a lease extension in time,
and my landlords offered the place to a friend of theirs who needed,
for health reasons, to move out of his FEMA trailer. So I rented another
apartment, the front part of a two-story "camelback" house. Located on
Saratoga Street just off of Napoleon Avenue, it was around the corner
from where my father and stepmother's house had stood. I wondered
initially how it would be to live in the shadow of flood and fire, but I
instantly felt at home. Some of the old neighbors were still there, and
they remembered and welcomed me warmly as I settled into familiar but
forever changed surroundings.

One neighbor, Mrs. Thomas, gave me a bit of history about the land
on which my parents' home had been located at the edge of the park
that still remained. The entire property had once housed a Catholic
school named Ecole Classique, established in 1956. When the school relocated, moving in 1979 to Metairie on the heels of suburbanization and
white flight, the land was sold and redeveloped into residential properties, with some open green space preserved in the front. The entire area
had flooded during Hurricane Katrina, the water rising to three or four
feet in some places, the height of the porch of my new apartment. I was
now located on the edge of a designated flood zone, a few meters above
sea level, just as my father and stepmother had been, with the elevation
rising and falling around me.

The concentration of African Americans in this area and the conditions of vulnerability they disproportionately face is a distinctly American story. In the late 1700s, after the American Revolution, many citizens
of the new republic moved west to the Louisiana territory. They were
lured by the Mississippi, recognizing the river as an essential waterway
for commerce and an important link between the North American interior and growing overseas markets. New Orleans was the epicenter of this
exchange. However, in 1800 Napoleon Bonaparte, First Consul of France,

convinced Spain to retrocede Louisiana to France. The move came as a surprise to the United States, then under the leadership of Thomas Jefferson, who failed to anticipate Bonaparte's vision of Louisiana, and New Orleans in particular, as the breadbasket for France's Caribbean exploits (Powell 2012, 317). The Americans naturally opposed a French stronghold west of the Mississippi, and Jefferson sent envoys to negotiate the purchase of the territory. It was the Haitian Revolution against the French (1791–1803), however, that proved to be the more persuasive event. After losing the lucrative Saint-Domingue in what would later be recognized as the largest and most successful rebellion by enslaved Africans in the Western Hemisphere, Bonaparte's position in the New World was weakened, and his need for Louisiana diminished. The Louisiana Purchase took place in 1803.

The Americans focused immediately on building wealth, meeting labor needs, and governing Louisiana's tri-caste population. In New Orleans a new American sector, the Faubourg Sainte Marie, developed upriver. The plantations that were based there supported Louisiana's transformation into a monoculture based on the production of sugar. As historian Rebecca Scott (2005, 11) describes it, this was "a more rigorous calculus of profitability" to which "the improvisations of the agricultural system under French and Spanish rule gave way after the U.S. Purchase of 1803." The transformation also increased the American territory's dependence on slave labor. While at the time importing slaves directly from Africa was prohibited, because of continued fears of insurrection, an act of government in 1805 paved the way for the domestic trade, allowing for their importation from anywhere inside the United States. Thus, approximately eight thousand more people were brought to Louisiana in the first three years of American rule (Powell 2012, 261).[14]

Louisiana was ratified as a state in 1812, and in the decades preceding the Civil War, "Louisiana's legislators systematically tightened the constraints on people of African descent, slave and free, rural and urban" (Scott 2005, 16). For example, in 1806 the territorial legislature enacted the Crimes and Offenses Act. This was part of a new slave code that included some of the strictest measures from the previous slave codes of Louisiana and other territories, making it "the most repressive slave code in New Orleans history to that point in time" (Powell 2012, 332). It gave slaveholders complete authority, abolished the right of emancipation, and severely restricted manumission. The in-migration of free blacks was also prohibited in order to curtail the growth of this already established population (333).

Urban expansion proceeded in ways that reinforced these social hierarchies, inscribing them into the landscape itself. The American sector accommodated wealthy governors and elites on the highest and driest land, with estates that both mirrored and sought to rival the aesthetics of the French Quarter (Spain 1979, 87). Guided by a plan for development created in 1806 by Barthélemy Lafon, deputy surveyor of Orleans Parish, land from existing sugar plantations was gradually parceled off and sold. Lafon's design was inspired by Greek mythology, and the new sector was a classical space complete with wide boulevards (nine named for the Greek muses), public squares, and parks.

The housing needs of the enslaved and the poor could not be ignored, so dependent were the elites on the labor they provided. Lafon's plan included, therefore, a system of canals to drain the swampland that sat "behind" and below the American sector. The land there was permeable and soft but nonetheless deemed suitable for residential expansion.[15] While such engineering drove urban growth, it also facilitated the relegation of poor Blacks and others to the least desirable locations. Whites retained control of the best resources—staking claim to land that was low nuisance (e.g., less pollution or noise), high amenity (access to transportation and services), and low risk (elevated and less likely to flood). Poor people, including laborers, immigrants, and after 1865, emancipated slaves and their descendants, were relegated to the city's margins. They settled, for example, along the riverbank, where they were subject to noise, pollution, and greater risk of disease. They inhabited the narrow "shotgun" rental properties that were built in the newly drained backswamp, slightly elevated on brick piers but in close proximity to industrial canals and floodwalls (Campanella 2007, 706–7). The end result was the social and geographic stratification of society, "with the poor of all races and people of color of all classes often occupying lowlands in the city" (Kelman 2007, 702–3). Residents there, in areas that became known as "back-of-town," built a community for themselves, but they struggled to survive on vulnerable terrain in a city and nation that were dependent on their services but reluctant to grant them citizenship or equal rights (Spain 1979, 89; Warner 2001, 328).

Settlement and Citizenship

From the vantage point of my apartment on Saratoga Street, the city felt familiar, but the course of daily life seemed much less certain than I had remembered. The conditions that once seemed confined to specific neighborhoods, such as poverty and violence, now spilled over, as if to remind those with one foot out the door that they were not as free as they might imagine. Everywhere I went, I got a different set of directions for how to stay safe. Accordingly, my new neighbors advised me to follow specific travel routes, stay away from certain places, park as close to the house as I could get, and keep the doors and windows locked at night.

There was a vacant house next door to my apartment that gave me, and my neighbors, some concern. Mrs. Cotton owned the place; she was an elderly African American woman who, before Katrina, had been a fixture in the community. Too frail to return after evacuating, her house fell into disrepair after the storm. Evangelists from Jehovah's Witness stopped by regularly, leaving pamphlets in the crack of the screen door. One day a homeless and mentally ill man broke into the house and claimed it for his own, declaring to anyone who approached him that the house was a gift from God. Someone called the police, and the man was taken away, most likely to jail given the shortage of mental health beds. A few of the neighbors came together after that, bought plywood, and boarded up the windows. They were quick about it, no need to discuss, and then everyone went home.

Such tensions were common in a neighborhood with a mix of owner-occupied homes, rentals, abandoned structures, and razed lots. Shortly after I moved in, James, my neighbor on the other side, gave me the lay of the land, describing who was who on our block. He framed it all in terms of safety—reporting on each situation in a way that was alarming but really meant to put me at ease. He sat on his porch, and I on mine, while he pointed around in various directions, a cigarette in his hand.

That man who lives over there? He is heavily armed. He was shooting at people after Katrina who were trying to loot. And right there? That guy has a huge drinking problem. Have you ever been into his house? It's a total wreck. He was doing pretty good for a while until his girlfriend committed suicide. Were you here that night he found out? [I was.] He was out in the middle of the street at two a.m. yelling and screaming. I finally had to come out here and yell at him to shut up. And that woman who lives down there? Well her son is a very famous drug dealer around here, so nobody messes with her. Matter of fact this whole block, from that house over there to that house down there is *protected*. Ain't *nothing* going to happen to you here.

It was not exactly the most comforting of reassurances. On another day, James's nine-year-old daughter showed me how easy it was to stand on the garbage can, jump over the iron fence, and land on my porch in front of the door. "A swift kick and you'd be in," she had said. I was not amused and looked into getting an alarm system I could not afford. Instead, I kept an eye on the crime maps, charting the red dots (indicating a murder site) close to my home. During my time there, the closest that violence came was five blocks away. From my perspective this was evidence of crime in the neighborhood, but my neighbors, who assessed safety block by block, declared that we were fine.

Still, I could not shake a general feeling of insecurity—made worse each time I heard an argument on the street, a car speeding by, or a gunshot. Indeed, as time went on I began to notice an uptick in drug trafficking on the corner, just a few doors down. Two or three young men stationed themselves there each night, talking on cell phones, standing in the middle of the street, peering in at the drivers in cars rolling slowly by. When I passed them in my own car coming home, I was already in the process of slowing down and they watched me carefully. It was not until they saw me park and head through the gate and up the stairs to my front door that they turned away, no longer interested. It was a welcome dismissal: "Oh ok, she lives there." Despite these and other anxieties, it was here, in my father's old neighborhood, that I was resolved to stay.

This sense of insecurity and the threat of danger, though it can often appear to be internally generated, has in fact a long history. Life in Uptown/back-of-town neighborhoods, especially for Black residents, has always been an uncertain struggle—for freedom, equality, security, and other rights, according to the conditions and needs of the day. Even on Saratoga Street, the conversations and interactions I had suggested a lingering concern—reflected by an instinct to fiercely safeguard, in whatever way possible, that which one had been able to achieve or acquire. Nothing was guaranteed, as the flood and fire had certainly proved, and as the continuing violence in the city also made clear. It could all be taken away at any moment. Some people even saw this insecurity as the reason behind the *joie de vivre* for which New Orleans was also known. As one resident explained, "We are all living in a place where we know it could all be gone in an instant, and that lends itself to loving passionately what you have because you may not get to keep it. . . . It creates a unique sense of community." It also seemed to warrant, however, a steady vigilance that caused much stress, especially for those who knew that security was false, when it was otherwise determined that one didn't really belong.

Although the Thirteenth Amendment abolished slavery in 1865, at the close of the Civil War, in Louisiana the rights of now "free laborers" remained uncertain, part of a larger debate on Black citizenship there and across the nation. At the center of this debate was the issue of suffrage. Black activist groups in New Orleans took up the cause; their viewpoints developed in two radical newspapers, *L'Union* and *La Tribune*, both started by Creoles of color based in the Tremé (DeVore 2015, 6–7). Out of this activism, the Republican Party of Louisiana was established (Scott 2005, 39).

White supremacists vehemently opposed this mobilization and terrorized Black Republicans and other citizens in armed bands or "militia" in New Orleans and around the state. Although the United States Congress passed the Civil Rights Act of 1866, granting citizenship and equal rights to all male persons in the United Sates "without distinction of race or color, or previous condition of slavery or involuntary servitude," in Louisiana Black citizens still fighting for the right to vote were attacked and killed.[16] At the national level, however, and aided by white northerners, the Republican Party took control of the House of Representatives and the Senate. When state elections for the new Constitutional Convention took place in Louisiana in 1867, Republicans won "in nearly every district, with roughly half of the ninety-eight seats . . . [going] to candidates of some African ancestry" (Scott 2005, 41). Importantly, the state constitution, which was ratified in April 1868, "granted suffrage to all men who had been resident in the state for a year, and in the parish for ten days, except for those explicitly disfranchised for crime or sedition by the constitution itself" (45). That same year, in July, the Fourteenth Amendment to the Constitution was ratified, granting citizenship to "all persons born or naturalized in the United States," including former slaves. The Fifteenth Amendment, ratified in 1870, granted African American men the right to vote; however, the states could institute specific voter qualifications such as literacy tests, and they did so in Louisiana and other places.

Opposed to these advancements, white supremacists continued to terrorize. The "White League," formed in Louisiana in 1874, was a paramilitary group affiliated with the Democratic Party, whose members engaged in brutal acts of violence to protect social hierarchies. As Scott (2005, 87) argues, "the Democrats of Louisiana knew the role they wished the descendants of formerly enslaved workers to play. Black men and women were to remain *labor*. They were to offer their strength and stamina where it was needed, making no claims on a civic identity" (emphasis in original).[17] The mandating of racial segregation in public places would reinforce this hierarchy, and in 1890 the Louisiana legislature passed the Separate Car Act, requiring railroad companies to provide separate accommodations for Black and white passengers. Afro-Creole and other activists fought against such legislation, seeking to prove its unconstitutionality under the law (Scott, 2005, 75). Based largely in the Tremé, they formed a Committee of Citizens to challenge the law in the courts, and a legal suit developed that was anchored in a highly orchestrated act of civil disobedience. In 1896, Homer Plessy, a man of mixed-raced ancestry, boarded a first-class train car, sat in the whites only section, and refused to move when ordered to do so. The case, which challenged the constitutionality of the Separate Car Act went to the United States Supreme Court, but the subsequent ruling upheld segregation laws requiring "separate but equal" public facilities.

The impact of this judgement was nothing short of devastating. Although a series of judicial challenges ensued, Louisiana's advance toward the social and now political death of African Americans could not be thwarted (Scott 2005, 190). As Scott describes it, "if Plessy v. Ferguson had signaled the final repudiation of the 1868 ideal of equal 'public rights,' the new state Constitutional Convention promised political death" (161) through vote suppression based on literacy and property requirements, with voting in particular confirmed by state and federal courts as a *privilege* rather than a *right* of citizenship (192). Such rulings marked the start of the Jim Crow era, with society governed by an all-encompassing set of segregation statutes that sought to circumscribe if not prevent the ascendance of African American life.[18]

The Racialization of Space and the Generational Curse

The segregation statutes put in place during the Jim Crow era were all encompassing, establishing both the social and spatial dimensions of racial hierarchies. They coincided with, and in many ways directed, the formation and subsequent marginalization of poor Black neighborhoods through the first half of the twentieth century. After Reconstruction, in the late 1800s and early 1900s, the clustered settlement of African Americans in New Orleans proceeded, and it was especially concentrated in newly drained Uptown/back-of-town areas. Black settlement thus switched from backyard or alley-based patterns of residence (on or close to plantations) to the relegation of formerly enslaved people to vulnerable (low lying) and otherwise precarious places (Spain 1979, 83). This was a state-driven project, a racialization of space enacted through the landscape and enforced in law and social policy, and it marked the rise and fall of Black neighborhoods like Central City.

In the early part of the twentieth century, Central City was a relatively stable low-income and working-class community with African

Americans and poor immigrants (Sicilians, Irish, Germans, and eastern Europeans) sharing a dense but vibrant space (Campanella 2006, 272). Dryades Street became an important commercial corridor with over two hundred businesses and other establishments. It was here that Blacks could shop with less harassment than they encountered in other areas. While a 1929 census revealed that African Americans in New Orleans were predominantly employed in unskilled service jobs, it noted also the rise of a professional class made up of teachers, ministers, midwives, and doctors. Black businesses included drugstores, insurance companies, stenographers, automotive service providers, and undertakers. Some dividing lines nonetheless remained. For example, Jewish retailers were primarily established in the heart of the Dryades corridor among a range of white Catholic and Protestant religious and educational institutions, while "thousands of poor blacks, many of them emigrants from Louisiana plantations following emancipation, settled on the 'woods side' of the street" (Campanella 2006, 270). In addition, even though Black youth were being educated, there was only one high school that they could attend, McDonogh No. 35, which opened in 1917. It remained the only option until 1942 (Medley 2014, 121).

These divisions were still evident at the dawn of the twenty-first century as I made the drive, on New Year's Day, to the vigil that Pastor Samuel had organized. I traveled past my father's razed property, past the Freret Street neighborhood and Baptist Hospital, and then down the Claiborne Avenue corridor. Claiborne had actually been one of the first roads to extend through the backswamp, originally surveyed and built with a drainage canal down its center. The canal was covered over to accommodate the streetcar, and the streetcar route was later discontinued, converted to a bus route in 1953. However, the wide expanse remained, and it was here that I stood, with Pastor Samuel, Danielle, and the others, beneath the monument to King.[19] The occasion, a vigil that sought to raise awareness about the violent conditions that were now characteristic of the surrounding Black community, was a powerful but still anxious reflection on the development, settlement, and marginalization of back-of-town neighborhoods. But it was also a hopeful show of strength by those still fighting for equality, justice, and peace, including the clergy and parishioners who organized the event and the residents who joined them at the start of a new year.

After the Federal Housing Act of 1937, the marginalization of poor Blacks intensified with the building of several public-housing projects. In New Orleans the first five to open, in 1941, were the St. Thomas Housing Development, the C. J. Peete Housing Development (Magnolia Projects), the Iberville Public Housing Development, the Lafitte Projects, and the B. W. Cooper Projects (Calliope Projects) (Arena 2012, xxxiv). These projects were initially racially segregated—St. Thomas and Iberville were all-white developments—however, by the early 1970s they were almost exclusively inhabited by low-income African American renters (xxxiv). Three projects were located in Central City—B. W. Cooper, C. J. Peete, and the Guste Homes (Melpomene Projects), which opened in 1963.

The concentration of poor Blacks in these developments resulted from a series of policy interventions at the municipal, state, and federal level. Urban renewal initiatives, launched in New Orleans and across the United States during the 1950s, 60s, and 70s, often disrupted Black neighborhoods by displacing people and sending them into public housing as highways, entertainment complexes, and other facilities were built (Arena 2012, xxii; Spain 1979, 94). Public-housing occupancy rates in New Orleans steadily increased throughout the 1970s reaching approximately 60,000 residents at their peak (20 percent of the city's total African American population) (Arena 2012, xxxiii).[20]

Despite their density, and frequently because of it, these developments were increasingly cordoned off through discriminatory practices in housing, employment, and the distribution of resources. For example, government-sponsored corporations, with the help of appraisers and realtors, made determinations of neighborhood risk, "redlining" Black communities and keeping investors out of the area. When combined with racist lending practices, it became difficult if not impossible for many Blacks to buy or maintain property.[21] Housing conditions and infrastructure thus deteriorated, and levels of unemployment, poverty, crime, and associated violence rose.[22]

The broad disinvestment from a now defined Black "ghetto" thus proceeded. Wealthy families and business owners, most of them white and wary of declining property values, began to leave the area. They traveled along new, elevated freeways away from the city center and into neighboring parishes (Fussell 2007). In 1940, for example, the urban population of New Orleans was approximately 70 percent white, but by 1990 that figure had dropped to about 30 percent (Mosher, Keim, and Franques 1995, 507). The demographics of commercial centers like Dryades Street subsequently changed as businesses closed or relocated to more prominent and lucrative environs (Medley 2001). Sociologist Elijah Anderson (2008, 5) describes the effect as a social and economic collapse, "wrought in the inner city by suburban decentralization, urban deindustrialization, and globalization."

Federal cuts to public housing began in the late 1970s under the Carter administration and gained traction in the early 1980s under the Reagan administration. In what was a steady trend toward deconcentration and privatization, the Department of Housing and Urban Development (HUD) budget was slashed and the government shifted course—expanding voucher programs, subsidizing the renting of privately owned apartments, and increasing the availability of low-income housing tax credits. In New Orleans, around the same time, and ironically under the leadership of Ernest N. Dutch Morial, the city's first African American mayor, the result of these programs was a new round of "Negro removal" (Arena 2012, 5). Loyal to his mostly Black constituents but still beholden to the white elite, Morial pursued an agenda grounded in public-private partnerships that sought to dismantle public housing, particularly in areas that were gentrifying or deemed valuable for historic preservation and tourism (3–5).

Many of the residents I met in Central City had lived in public housing at one point or another. Danielle, for example, had spent part of her childhood in the Melpomene projects during the 1970s and at the height of Black occupancy. The testimony she had begun to share, while very personal, was thus part of a larger generational story that had its roots in the history of the Black urban delta, developed through enterprise and the racialization of space substantiated by multiple forms of violence and handed down to those who still found themselves vulnerable in the current moment and condition. A member of Liberty Street since childhood, she was baptized in the church in the late 1960s at the age of nine. Her path to the salvation she claimed as an adult, however, had been difficult and divergent—challenged, as it was for many Black women, by poverty, poor education, teenage pregnancy, substance abuse, and other hardships. As she described it,

My dad came home from Angola [Louisiana State Penitentiary] when I was like eleven. And I had a mom that, you know she was my mother that's all she didn't really raise me. My grandmother raised me. When my dad came home I started hanging out with his family. . . . There was one cousin that I was crazy about and she and I, you know, we just got out of hand. We thought we were grown and stopped coming inside on time and just following the wrong crowd. . . . When I made fifteen years old I got pregnant with Rock, wound up having another baby like eighteen months after that, raised them up by myself. I didn't finish high school. I lived my life the way I saw fit to survive. . . . I thought that was the way to live, because I really wasn't taught any different.

Conditions in low-income communities deteriorated to such a point that social problems seemed nearly detached from their structural causes. This was particularly true in the 1980s and 1990s, when the per capita rate of violent crime skyrocketed after the introduction of crack cocaine into urban markets (Grogger and Willis 2000), exacerbated by the easy access to weapons that Louisiana's lax gun laws afforded. Many people died, and those who remained were met with the full force of the state through policing and incarceration as the criminalization of poor Blacks was institutionalized. African American neighborhoods and residents were thus further devalued.

In the early 1990s the Clinton administration called for the dismantling of "severely distressed" public housing, further emphasizing the shift to mixed-income housing communities via the HOPE VI program (Arena 2012, 89). Officials frequently targeted high-rise projects, which in the public imaginary "signified black welfare dependency, crime, and much of what was perceived as wrong about urban America" (xxii). As Arena argues, demolition "signaled, symbolically and physically, the 'taking back' of the city from, in particular, poor African Americans, allowing for the 're-imaging' of cities critical for increased flows of investment" (xxii). Between the mid-1990s and 2010, therefore, federal and local housing authorities tore down "over 400 public housing projects, eliminating approximately 200,000 apartments out of an original stock of 2.4 million" (xxii). In New Orleans, housing projects such as St. Thomas were demolished and then redeveloped into mixed-income dwellings, with the majority of the original tenants replaced by those who could meet the city's strict eligibility requirements.[23]

Despite the predicted outcomes for poor Black women in such circumstances, Danielle did her best to raise her family. She secured housing and sent her children to school. She made sure that they were baptized in the church. Her face brightened as she remembered her eldest son's innate curiosity about the world. "Rock was very smart in school," she recalled. "He always wanted something out of life. He wanted to be graduated. He was always the type of child to ask questions that I didn't have the answer for . . . When other kids would do things [activities], he used to always be *thinking* on something."

The family could not, however, rise above their circumstances. As time went on, Danielle became involved with the drugs that were rampant in her community, first as a dealer and then a user. She became addicted to crack cocaine by the age of twenty-six. She didn't go looking for drugs, she reported; they were literally all around her. Once offered, they became a reliable source of income, and then a substance that for a time she could not live without, given the quick and gripping hold they had on her mind and body.

I started smoking marijuana, going out with my friends. And when I was twenty-six years old I got hooked on drugs. I was smoking crack cocaine and I used drugs for five years. . . .

Being a drug addict is nothing nice to be. You want to walk straight . . . you can't. And back then I didn't know I had a disease; I just thought I was just crazy off crack. . . . And I was, cause I just was gone . . . my children were suffering, not eating properly. I was on probation. I almost lost my children to the system. I almost lost my life.

She paused to lament the impact on her family, community, and city. Drugs and guns seemed to be everywhere—in the housing projects, on the street, at the corner store, in the hands of friends and family members. Everyone was involved, at the very least by proximity. While Danielle was still coming to terms with her own history, she felt frustrated by the bad choices young people were continuing to make. "These kids today don't want to work . . . that's how my son was," she told me. I interjected, commenting on the state of education and the lack of jobs. Danielle agreed but was insistent that young people "don't have to go that way." To her, participation in the drug trade was largely a choice, "the easy way to go."

I was reluctant to fault them all. To me, choice suggested the existence of a viable alternative, and I was not convinced that one was consistently available. Even Danielle, who at the time was celebrating twenty-one years of sobriety, grappled with the choices she had made, demonstrating how the easy way was in some cases the only way. Going back to her own family history, in the midst of a low-income and cordoned-off Black community, she described a "generational curse," revealing not only the limited options she had been presented with but her continued feeling of failure for seeing no other way but "the easy way." It was a tricky situation, where the burden of recovery was intensified by the invisibility of structural forces and causes. "I am a prime example of blaming the parents," she said,

because I did sell drugs. Because someone brought me drugs, *manipulated* me [saying] "Here. This to make money with. Help you pay your bills." I was like, "*What* is *this*?!" "This is not to use," he told me. "This is to sell and make money." And I called some friends, "I got some drugs, $25 a bag." Not annoying, just ease in on you, that's how it do. And you ain't got no job, are not thinking of the consequences, you gonna fall into that trap. Boom. There it is. That's how it go.

Danielle paused again, and then added the following, shaking her head in remorse.

But I ask myself a question, why didn't I tell him [the person who gave her the drugs] that I don't want that in my life? Because that's all I knew, because that's all my mama knew . . . [she] sold drugs. Now my grandmother didn't do it. So, where she [my mama] get it from? She picked it up out in the streets. She brought it home to me, and then *the generational curse*. My dad used to pop pills and he used to have me to go make the coffee . . . "Go in there and make Daddy some coffee." Get the coffee and drink it. "Get me two [pills] woman," standing right there in front of me. Who you blame? The parent.

Danielle's inclination to blame the parent reflects a broader view, common in the press and the public sphere, that sees the high incidence of drug trafficking, substance abuse, and associated violence in neighborhoods like Central City as a failure of racial uplift, reflecting more specifically an inherent weakness in the Black person, family, and community. Such perceptions remain quite strong, infiltrating the minds of local residents, despite what we now know about structural racism and violence in the development and decline of the inner city. Danielle recognized the larger forces that were behind the suffering in her community, and she understood first hand their impact on generations of Black families. However, she did not fully connect the "generational curse" she identified to these same forces, believing instead that people were mostly responsible for their own actions, could choose to go another way, and were subject to blame when they failed to do so. It was a situation that also revealed Danielle's faith and commitment to the church as a site of salvation and redemption. For as she questioned her own resolve, as she identified her mother and father as negative influences, and as she bemoaned the choices she and then her children made, she remembered with mythic admiration and a sense of proof her faithful aunt and grandmother who had risen above, in church, and with strength and direction from God. It would be to God and to church that Danielle would later return.

The Black Urban Delta as a Space of Death and Transformation

In the quote that opens this chapter, Lafcadio Hearn describes his fascination with a simultaneously "beautiful" and "dead South," one in which he is "resolved to live" ([1907] 2007, 42–43). Such resolve certainly inspired my own desire to live and work in New Orleans, but it more fundamentally referenced a faithful perseverance that seemed to direct the people of this down but determined city. As I witnessed the work of clergy and parishioners at Liberty Street and in diverse religious communities around the city, I began to understand not only how conditions of vulnerability and violence in the "dead South" emerge but how people live within and through these conditions and how this resolve might translate to the recovery of Black lives, families, and communities. The analytical framework of the Black urban delta that I develop here thus sets this small cast of individuals within a broader historical context, one formed through the exploits of empire, the atrocities and legacies of slavery, and the negative impact of urban expansion, settlement, segregation, and decline. But the Black urban delta also invites us to think forward, about the ways in which lives and deaths are nonetheless made meaningful through the formation of distinct belief systems and practices; in the building of social networks; in the development of just economies; and in the ongoing fight for freedom and equality.

TWO

"Twelve Murders and Two Victims?": Asserting Black Social and Spiritual Value

You know one thing about murder in this city and in all cities where violent crime is high is that people think in terms of the murder rate: how many victims there are rather than *who* they are. They also tend to make the victims anonymous, especially if they are poor, and they seem to dismiss or even justify the death depending on what the victim was doing. **FATHER RICHARD**

New Orleans has long been known as a violent city, and homicide in the form of gun violence is the primary reason—the per capita murder rate has been seven to eight times higher than the national average for at least the last three decades (Landrieu 2012). In the years immediately following Hurricane Katrina, however, the nature of homicide felt different—the killing was less predictable, spilling outside of its usual location in poor Black neighborhoods, and the acts themselves seemed more brutal than they perhaps had been before. The shift was especially alarming for those who were unaccustomed to violence so close at hand and for all residents still contending with the trauma of disaster, with Hurricane Katrina a recent and still painful memory.

One resident, a white woman who lived in the Marigny, just outside the French Quarter, gave her perspective. She described violence the first year after Katrina as "not so bad" but as being "much worse the second and third year." "It does seem to be reaching some kind of crescendo," she commented. "Especially if it's not somebody who you would expect to be involved in murder, or drug trafficking, or whatever it is that somebody has got out there. It's hard to believe that a person can just get ripped out like that." Another resident, a Black woman who lived on the other side of the Quarter in the Tremé, referred to the current condition as "a season of loss." "We have always had a high rate of murders," she said. "But I believe that coming back from Katrina we are so sensitive now. We aren't the same. We left out of here one way, and we came back as people who have suffered a lot of loss." These diverse perspectives revealed a nonetheless shared concern; a 2009 survey found that the majority of residents (58 percent) described crime as a "citywide epidemic that affects all residents" with more than two out of three residents saying that they feared for their own personal safety.[1]

The particular perception of a "crescendo" of violence and the sense of a person being "ripped out" had much to do with a string of murders from late December 2006 into the early part of 2007 in which two prominent residents, in these same two neighborhoods, were killed. On Thursday, December 28, 2006, Dinerral Shavers was murdered in the Tremé. Shavers was a New Orleans native, a twenty-five-year-old African American man who was a musician, teacher, and founding member of the Hot 8 Brass Band. He had picked up his family members and was driving home when the car was targeted in a drive-by shooting, the bullets reportedly intended for Shavers's fifteen-year-old stepson who was seated in the back. Just one week later, on Thursday, January 4, 2007, Helen Hill was murdered when an intruder broke into her Marigny home. Hill, a thirty-six-year-old white woman, was a local filmmaker and activist. She and her family had lived in New Orleans since 2000, but they had recently returned, having evacuated before the storm, to be part of a difficult but hopeful recovery.

By all accounts these were not your typical victims. Shavers and Hill were well-known members of the local arts community committed to work that uplifted the city and its inhabitants. As such they did not fit the profile of a homicide victim in New Orleans, namely a poor, young, Black man most likely doing something illegal at the time of his death. The loss of these "innocent" individuals and the now out-of-bounds state of violence it confirmed thus sparked a huge response. A group of family members and friends of Shavers began to organize shortly after his death; their work intensified when Hill's death occurred. Several groups then came together, including a newly formed organization named SilenceIsViolence, to organize a March for Survival, which took place on

January 11, 2007. Several thousand participants, the majority of whom were white despite the fact that New Orleans remained a majority Black city, converged on city hall. Their collective demands included the resignation of Mayor C. Ray Nagin as well as the chief of police and the district attorney, who were among the officials in attendance.

While the size of the march was certainly impressive, many residents were put off by the timing and chose not to attend. The members of poor Black communities, for example, were already familiar with such conditions—they had been mobilizing against them for decades. What was it about this moment that had brought out thousands of residents from across the city? They already knew the answer, feeling certain that it was the expansion of violence into the city's supposed safe havens, the artistic and cultural realms where whites felt at home. While the deaths of Shavers and Hill were certainly tragic, they bookended what had been a violent week in which ten other people had been killed. While the participants in the march were demonstrating on behalf of all those whose lives had been taken, it was also true that the names of the other victims were not well known. Among the dead, however, and in addition to Shavers and Hill, were Larry Glover, Corey Hayes, Cedric Johnson, Hilary Campbell Jr., Randall Thomas, and Kevin Williams.[2]

I began my fieldwork just four months after the march, stepping into an active debate about the problem of violence and following old and new conversations about the value of Black lives. Whose lives mattered and whose did not? Who was worthy of mourning and mobilization and who was cast aside—dismissed or demonized in a larger system that criminalized the usual suspects? In the extended aftermath of disaster, therefore, another field of action emerged not just for mobilization against a level of violence that now seemed widespread but for the necessary grounding of this work in the assertion of Black humanity. These aims were articulated most clearly within the religious community, where the interconnected nature of human life, the divine sources of knowledge and strength, and the extension of social justice work into forgotten places were key components. In this chapter I examine this work at several key sites, tracing the frameworks for social and moral recovery that ultimately came into view.

Religious Pathways

It was a challenging time to be in New Orleans. Residents were trying to pick up the pieces and begin again while grieving for who and what had been lost. When violent crime returned and intensified, as it did despite the efforts of public officials, developers, and others to keep it (and those associated with it) at bay, it was almost too much to bear. A newly inspired approach to recovery seemed desperately needed not just to restore a sense of security but to consider, thoughtfully, the way forward. For many people in a highly religious city, churches and other places of worship became the moral think tanks of the day. Yet while the concern about violence was widely shared, the specific problem of homicide triggered a diverse set of responses from religious leaders and practitioners. For some, it confirmed a morally corrupt society in need of cleansing and conversion. For others, it signaled the continuation of suffering and the need for intervention as part of a broad social recovery that was both possible and imminent.

My fieldwork thus proceeded in uncertain but increasingly deliberate steps through a diverse religious landscape. I spent time with a group of Catholics praying for peace at an Uptown Marian shrine. On the other side of town in the Bywater, I learned about anticrime ceremonies at a Vodou temple that called on the *Lwa* (spirit) Ogou for protection, swift justice, and the restoration of balance. I met with clergy and parishioners at an Episcopal church in the Tremé, where a ministry worked to recognize *all* victims of violence regardless of their identity, social status, or criminal history. I learned through many additional encounters with individual practitioners, spiritual advisors, and others of various faiths and traditions.

By the time I reached Liberty Street Baptist Church in Central City—although in retrospect perhaps that's where I should have started given the church's long history of work on these issues—I had a rough sketch of the city's religious foundations, which made clear the need for and the possibilities of a sacred Black humanity. While Liberty Street, which became the primary site for my research, is the subject of the book's next section, this chapter paves the way by describing the larger social and religious context that framed my navigation of the Crescent City. Before delving into the details, I discuss how homicide in New Orleans has been historically measured and located. I then explore how scholars have tried to unpack violence as a category and how the category continues to be reified, theoretically and in everyday life.

Homicide as Measure, Category, and Condition

The classification of New Orleans as a violent city, apart from perception and experience, is a matter of some calculation. Municipalities keep track of the incidence of specific crimes, using that information to determine per capita rates and sharing data with government agencies. By tracking per capita homicide rates in particular (number of deaths per hundred thousand residents), New Orleans has been consistently identified as a US "murder capital." As mentioned in the introduction to this book, the city experienced an abrupt rise in violent crime over a twenty-five-year period, from around 1970 to 1995, that coincided with a rise in drug trafficking. Homicide rates rose during this period by a staggering 329 percent (Currie 1998, 20).

After Hurricane Katrina, the population change that followed the mass evacuation of thousands of residents brought about a quick and sharp decline in rates of all violent crime. Homicide rates, however, remained well above the national average. According to the FBI's Uniform Crime Report, in 2005 there were 210 homicides, which translated to a per capita rate of 46.13 compared to the national average of 5.6. In 2006, the year after Katrina, there were 162 homicides, which gave a rate of 37.57 compared to the national rate of 5.8. The number rose again the following year in 2007 to pre-Katrina levels, with 209 people killed, even though the population was half the size of what it had been before the storm. This translated to a rate of 94.74, compared to the national rate for that year of 5.7. The number and rate of homicides then fell in 2008 and 2009 with 179 (63.60) and 174 (51.72) murders respectively. City officials were quick to note the downward trend; it is important also to note that rates actually increased in certain areas as the location of the drug trade and other illegal activities shifted across the postdisaster landscape (Walsh 2010).

Studies of violent crime further locate homicide within poor African American communities. A study of homicide in New Orleans over a two-year period (2009–2010) found that the majority of victims were male (86.5 percent), African American (91.5 percent), and young (more than 50 percent aged twenty-seven or younger at the time of death). The offenders were even more homogenous (95.1 percent male, 97.1 percent African American, and 50 percent aged twenty-three or younger). The study also found that most of the killings occurred on the street and in low-income residential areas, with drug-related (29 percent) and revenge killing (24 percent) the primary motivators. Gun violence also prevailed in 78 percent of studied cases (Wellford, Bond, and Goodison 2011).

The statistical locating of homicide in poor Black communities frequently translates into the classification of violence as an *inherent* condition of Black urban life. This process has deep historical roots, but it has been fueled most recently by the US "War on Drugs," with whole communities identified as "drugscapes," places where drug use and other social problems are located and imagined (Tempalski and McQuie 2009, 7). Such identification places the blame on drug-using or drug-selling individuals in predominantly poor communities of color "for a range of social ills, such as violence, crime, disease, and urban decay" (7), thus concealing the influence of racist and increasingly neoliberal spatial politics and economies.

Beyond the Category and Back Again

An important scholarly inquiry sheds light on the process and effect of these determinations. In *The Condemnation of Blackness* (2010), Khalil Gibran Muhammad meticulously traces the statistical formation of Black criminality as a modern invention at work from the late 1800s forward. Muhammad explains how crime statistics work to refashion Blackness, reinforcing a racial category of inferiority in opposition to whiteness (5). As Muhammad argues, "The idea of black criminality was crucial to the making of modern urban America. In nearly every sphere of life it impacted how people defined fundamental differences between native whites, immigrants, and blacks" (273). Such historical knowledge helps to counter continuing processes of criminalization, reminding us that crime statistics "have always been interpreted, and made meaningful, in a broader political, economic, and social context in which race mattered" (277).

Beckett and Sasson contribute by identifying four interrelated factors that produce high rates of homicide in the inner city. These are "the ubiquity of guns, comparatively high levels of social and racial inequality and the concentrated urban poverty with which they are associated, the drug (and especially crack) trade, and a code of the streets that prizes respect and deference above all else" (Beckett and Sasson 2004, 43). Each of these factors is relevant in New Orleans. For example, a 2012 Congressional Research Service report determined that in the year 2009 there were more than 300 million civilian firearms in circulation, up from 200 million just five years earlier. Access to guns is greater in states like Louisiana, where less restrictive gun laws correlate, not surprisingly, with higher rates of violence (Fleegler et al. 2013; Parsons and Weigend 2016, 1). Louisiana, in fact, has the highest level of gun violence in the nation (Parsons and Weigend 2016) as well as one of the highest poverty rates, with poverty concentrated in historically Black neighborhoods.[3] Beckett and Sasson describe these as "socially dislocated" neighborhoods, an identifier that refers to neighborhood conditions rather than demographics. As they state, "it is the degree to which a neighborhood suffers from poverty-related social dislocation, not its racial composition, that helps to explain its homicide rate" (Beckett and Sasson 2004, 35), though clearly poverty and race are linked.

The third factor is the drug trade, especially following the introduction of crack cocaine in urban markets beginning in the 1980s. The Gulf Coast is designated as a high-intensity drug trafficking area (HIDTA), with a 2011 report from the United States Office of National Drug Control Policy identifying cocaine as the principal threat along with the trafficking and abuse of methamphetamine, heroin, and marijuana as additional threats in major cities like New Orleans.[4] Finally, Beckett and Sasson refer to a code of the streets based on a sense of entitlement, a quest for power, a demand for respect, and an obligation to retaliate in the face of affront (Beckett and Sasson 2004, 41; see also Anderson 1990, Bourgois 1995). In New Orleans, such a code also reflects the complex relations residents have with members of law enforcement and the criminal justice system, manifesting, for example, in the form of silence in the aftermath of violence due to fear of reprisal and the general perception of an oppressive, corrupt, and ineffective state authority.

Despite this analysis, the characterization of homicide as a condition of Black urban life persists, revealing the negative determinations of human value that still underlie its process. If not in statistical form, it is on the local news, where crime maps show the location of attacks and where the Black faces of the perpetrator and victim, if known, are front and center. Residents in New Orleans paid close attention to these reports to track the violence inside and outside of their communities. What some of them also realized, however, was the broader and more systematic tracking of Black criminality with the perpetrators and the victims cast in the same negative light. When reporting a homicide, for example, the New Orleans Police Department (NOPD) would include the perpetrator's as well as the *victim's* "rap sheet," if one existed, driving home the message that this was business as usual for a deviant population. This release of information was a matter of policy until the practice was discontinued in 2012.[5] Such practices were added injury, especially for family members of the deceased, who mourned their loved ones alongside a public narrative that implied, crudely, that the world was better off. Situations like this reveal the multiple "locations" of violence, with crime and criminalization operating as "forms, experiences and modes of expression used to manage the social nexuses of power" (Parnell and Kane 2003, 1). Awareness of these locations is especially important in the context of social and political upheaval when power is rearranged and when "people brought together through these processes experience them differently, reasserting perceived essential differences among themselves (as race, ethnicity, gender, morality, and humanity) in changing circumstances" (1).

Within religious communities, power was understood in broader terms. Responses to violence thus had multiple dimensions and were not restricted to earthly and human realms. Some even saw the persistence of violence in the critical moment as an urgent call to battle, with religious teachings and practices serving as shields or weapons in the crafting of a peaceful and just society. I turn now to the encounters I was privileged to have through which these various approaches were made clear.

The Peace Prayer Group

"You have to start with the Ursulines and Our Lady of Prompt Succor," Mrs. LeBlanc was saying, her eyes lighting up. "She's the patroness and protector of the city, and around here people pray to her whenever there's a problem . . . Our Lady was surely watching over us when Katrina hit, because the storm actually *missed* New Orleans. It was *human* error that caused the levees to break, and that is what gave us so much trouble."

Sitting in the front parlor of the large blue house that she was soon to vacate, Mrs. LeBlanc spoke with authority about the subject. "We used to pray to Prompt Succor in school," she continued, telling my parents and I, who had come to pay her a visit, how the Blessed Mother had been a divine source of comfort in times of trouble. Mrs. LeBlanc's devotion remained strong. Our Lady continued to watch over her as she settled her affairs and prepared to move to Houston. She and my parents had been neighbors for years, but their house was gone, her house was empty, and she was tired. Her children and grandchildren were waiting for her in Texas. "Go to the shrine," she said, offering me one last bit of advice for the research I was starting, "and you will find out everything you need to know."

I went a few days later to the shrine far Uptown, climbing the short set of stairs and entering through two heavy doors. The interior was spacious, with a high arched ceiling and a center aisle leading past rows of pews up to the altar, which sat in front of an intricately carved stone wall. Positioned high on a pedestal, above the altar and jutting out from this wall, was a carved wooden statue of Our Lady. She stood several feet high with the baby Jesus in her arms; they were both adorned with jeweled crowns and were brightly illuminated.

Mass was not in session, and so I looked around, stopping by a table near the front door to take some literature. I noticed then a small blue flyer that read "Our Lady Peace Prayer Group. Come Pray with us New Orleans, for Peace, Recovery, and Conversions." The details announced when and where the group would meet—once a month at the shrine— and at the bottom of the flyer was the following: "Please join us in our effort to renew our group, which began June 1995, until 'Katrina.' New Orleans needs our prayers! Come and bring a friend."

With just a few inquiries, I was able to get in touch with the organizer of the group to ask about their purpose and activity. Why did New Orleans need prayers? What conditions of the city prompted the call for peace, recovery, and religious conversion? What favor and intercession, from the Blessed Mother, did they ask for and receive? Donna, one of the founding members, gave me first some history on the group's formation in 1995 in response to the alarmingly high incidence of homicide at the time. As she explained, "The murder rate here was about one per day, something like over 300 murders per year, and no one was dealing with it." She hesitated, qualifying her statement, "I mean the police were trying. There was a new police chief, Pennington, who was trying to improve things, but he eventually went to Atlanta.[6] The situation was so far gone, that prayer was the only thing we could do."

A small group of friends came together, meeting initially in Donna's home. "There were about ten of us, we were all friends who had gone to college together," she recalled. "We wanted to have a day of prayer for peace, for stopping the violence. So, we started to meet regularly." As the number of attendees grew, a larger space became necessary, and a local priest suggested that the group move to the shrine, given Our Lady of Prompt Succor's designation as the patroness of the city. The Ursuline Sisters agreed to host, and they all settled in, praying not just for an end to the violence but for the creation, as one participant put it, of "a city that will be pleasing to God."

New Orleans is a famously Catholic town. From the first days of the colonial enterprise, settlers and traders were required to meet specific religious obligations, including the employment of priests who were in turn responsible for the religious conversion of the local population (Hennesey 1981, 32). Female religious orders were also recruited primarily to supply nuns who would establish schools for girls and young women. In an agreement between the Company of the Indies and the Ursuline Sisters in Rouen, France, six Ursuline nuns arrived in New Orleans in 1727.[7] Their tasks included "hospital nursing, teaching both white and black girls, hospitality for young women who came from France in search of husbands, and care also for 'correction girls' sent to the colony. For these services the Company gave the Ursulines a house, eight arpents of land, and eight black slaves." They established a convent in the Vieux Carré and set about their work and charitable activities (32).

Struggling to sustain the local order through the early part of the nineteenth century, the Ursulines in New Orleans wrote to France requesting additional personnel. Sister St. Michel Gensoul responded to the call. However, she required permission from the pope in order to travel, a difficult and lengthy process given the civil unrest in France at the time. She prayed, therefore, to the Virgin Mary that permission be swiftly granted—promising that if it were, she would honor the Blessed Mother in New Orleans as Our Lady of Prompt Succor (*Secours*). When Pope Pius the Seventh did indeed grant approval, Sister St. Michel had a statue of the Blessed Mother carved and dedicated, which she brought to New Orleans in December 1810. There, Our Lady was enshrined in the chapel within the French Quarter convent, and a community of devotees grew around her, especially after several additional miracles were attributed to her grace (Heaney 1993; Clark 2007). From its original location in the French Quarter, the convent and shrine then moved—first downriver in 1818 to land in the newly developed Creole faubourgs, then Uptown in 1912. In 1928, at the request of the archbishop of New Orleans and the bishops of Alexandria and Lafayette, the Holy See approved the selection of Our Lady of Prompt Succor as the patroness of New Orleans and Louisiana.

The shrine proved to be the perfect home for the peace prayer group, and the monthly meetings grew in size. At one point there were several hundred people attending, but the number eventually settled at about thirty-five. After Hurricane Katrina, the group temporarily disbanded, and it was slowly reorganizing in the spring of 2007 when I arrived. There were about ten to fifteen people at each session I attended, and the majority were elderly white Catholic women, most from the well-to-do neighborhoods that surrounded the religious campus. Slightly discouraged by the low turnout, members were no less committed to the group's overall purpose. Donna shared a verse that she found helpful in this regard, "the one where the Lord says, 'For where two or three are gathered together in my name, I am there among them.'" "Whenever we have a bad turnout," she said, "the nuns remind me of that."

As group members entered the shrine, they came upon a small table placed deliberately in the center of the main aisle. There they found copies of the prayers to be read and a basket for placing petitions and donations. They made their way to seats among the pews, sitting spaced apart and toward the front when the group was small. They sat quietly, or knelt to pray before the meeting began. At a certain time, the appointed leader approached the pulpit to welcome everyone and make announcements. Members who were unable to attend or were in need of special prayers were then acknowledged. This included any recent deaths within the community. "Please remember all of these people in your prayers," the leader would say. After a brief period of silence, the prayers for peace began.

There was a distinct rhythm to the prayer here, a steady rolling murmur punctuated only by slight changes in pitch and voice, subdued but not without feeling. In the first prayer, the "Miracle Prayer," members pledged their devotion, acknowledging their sins and asking for forgiveness as well as the capacity to forgive others. They placed their attention first and foremost on human frailties—their own (and others') shortcomings and the need for healing and strength: "Mary, my mother, and all the saints: Heal me, change me, strengthen me in body, soul and spirit."

This was an important foundation for the next prayer, "To Whom Shall We Go?," which focused on the specific problem of violence in New Orleans:

TO WHOM SHALL WE GO?
God of goodness,
You know that the violence in our community is out of control.
It is taking our helpless and innocent ones, it is taking our children.
And, we confess that beyond the violence of the streets,
    is the violence in our own hearts.
We contribute to a culture of violence whenever we give in to hatred,
    fear, indifference, and our own self satisfaction.

It seems that we are growing numb
    to the suffering, the loss, the indignity done to our sisters
    and brothers and to our earth.
But in our hearts, and in the heart of our community,
    help us to value life and beauty over instant satisfaction,
    and to value sharing over greed.

Empower us to acknowledge and affirm our children, our spouses,
    our neighbors and see respectful solutions to our conflicts.
Create through us a world where it is easier to be good.

Your spirit, given to us, is not timid.
Therefore each of us can do something, person by person,
     family by family, community by community, to realize
that we are one—one body, one people, one earth.
By your design, we thrive or we perish together.

Holy One, give us the grace of hope
     Give us dedication to goodness and truth
as we seek to restore our community to wholeness and life.
Enable us in this way,
     to take back our city from the violence and crippling fear
     we find in our midst
Trusting that your desire for us is peace and not disaster,
     we pray this in your name. Amen.

The prayer had strong resonance in the wake of Hurricane Katrina, given the return and intensification of violence, and it gave some indication of group members' views and desires. While they believed that violence was "out of control," its location was generalized and nonspecific, with reference to "*our* community" and "*our* helpless and innocent ones . . . *our* children." It was an interesting and somewhat puzzling stance in a city where violence was typically characterized as a Black problem even though its reach and impact had broadened after the storm. As my conversations with group members deepened, however, I came to understand the rationale for this view. First, given the devotion members had to Our Lady, the patroness of New Orleans, they considered the "community" to be the entire city and all its inhabitants over which the Blessed Mother unquestionably presided. While this seemed unifying, it also allowed members to position themselves as concerned citizens without having to identify a particular neighborhood or population as the site or cause of the problem. When speaking about the location of violence, for example, Donna made a point to say, "I'm not talking about any one group—no race, or age group. It's across the board."

Group members also saw themselves as contributors to the violence, acknowledging, for example, "the violence in our own hearts." This was a deeply personal and challenging admission, and members acknowledged that they were "going numb" to the suffering and loss that was, in reality, more directly affecting their "brothers and sisters" in other places. The path toward peace, therefore, lay in the healing and redemption of self, in the renouncement of evil, and in the capacity to act and bring about change. As stated in the prayer, "each of us can do something, person by person, family by family, community by community, to realize that we are one— one body, one people, one earth." Such action was further grounded in the formation and strengthening of relationships, in service, and in fostering unity to ultimately take back the city from "violence and crippling fear."

This vision, however, was ultimately dependent on divine interven- tion. Members prayed not only for support but for the greater transforma- tion of self and society that was ultimately made possible by God's will. As one member described it, "Sometimes things seem dark and you wish things weren't the way they were . . . But in the long run you know that God is in charge, and that we can change things by prayer. I am a firm believer in that." Prayer was individually transformative, but its power was collective: "People ask me, 'What do you think your prayer does?' Well I think not just my prayer, but my prayer joined with many other people who are praying, I think that it does change things." While it was ultimately up to God whether they would "thrive or perish together," they continued to worship, trusting that God's desire for them, as a city and people, was "peace and not disaster."

The change that group members sought was further dependent on the moral and spiritual conversion of sinners and nonbelievers. As an- other member explained, "For years my prayer has been for the conver- sion of sinners and the salvation of souls because I consider that that was a tremendous gift for me and I would like that for the whole world. I would like for them all to fall in love with the Lord because if they did then we wouldn't have the problems that we've had." Immediately following the recitation of the prayer to end violence, therefore, group members recited a prayer for religious conversion. It read, in part,

Loving Mother, deliver us from the tide of evil threatening to drown our city by as- sisting us in reversing our rush to depravity which is daily becoming more violent and inhuman. Lead us in renouncing the false understanding of freedom which justifies every moral aberration by helping us repudiate styles that are increasingly indecent and provocative, opposing the press which publicizes evil, and combating entertainment which ruins morals. . . .

Just as you are the Woman Clothed in the Sun standing on the crescent moon crush- ing the head of the serpent, so we invite you to rest your feet on the Crescent City and crush the head of Satan. We pray for a New Pentecost that the conversion of our city may be the first radiant jewel crowning the triumph of your Immaculate Heart.

Donna put this prayer into context. "You can't get peace and cooperation and a decent lifestyle unless people have in their heads the right attitude," she said. This stood in contrast to a lifestyle of sin that cast New Orleans in a negative light: "People pride themselves on shocking you. It's a little quirk, a contentious way of interacting that has developed in the last thirty years or so, and now it's part of our personality. This has had a big effect on the community." Donna cited the media, as well as poor church attendance, as being partly to blame. "The children aren't getting any values, and instead it's all about money and who can look the sexiest," she said. "People here claim that this is part of our culture, that New Orleans is a place where anything goes. They act as if it's a positive thing but it's not. I mean you have to have some rules, ways of proper speech, guidelines for communication and helping people." She paused to make it clear, again and as seemed necessary, that these assessments were *not* about a particular segment of the population.

While religious conversion had been part of the group's purpose from the beginning, members identified the post-Katrina period as an opportune moment for such change to occur. One member spoke about how the word *Katrina*, taken from the Greek *katharos*, means "pure," "cleansed," and "free from corruption." As she stated, "We needed a catharsis, and Katrina delivered." "But of course, you don't want to see people suffer," she added. It was again through prayer that members believed they could best support this change—thus, they prayed for the "crushing" of evil, and they asserted the morals they believed necessary (in themselves and in others) for a holy city. "We've all been put here for a special reason, and the main thing is to cooperate" this same member stated. "And I continue to pray to Our Lady's intercession that our city will be rebuilt, that she'll continue to help in the rebuilding, and that in the end . . . we will all live as God wants us to live. That's my hope and my dream."

This emphasis on sin and conversion, on the "catharsis" brought by Katrina, made clear the religious conservatism that underlay the group's more palatable focus on prayer for peace. Some members of the group were active in other organizations, such as the Crusade for the Conversion of Greater New Orleans, where the focus on moral depravity and cleansing was more explicitly stated. Members of the peace prayer group were reluctant to discuss these affiliations in detail—they worried they might identify the group as "political," inviting attention and pushback from the otherwise irreverent city they perceived. A frequent leader of the monthly meetings stated emphatically, "I always try to stay nonpolitical, because we are *praying*—so we are *not* identified as a political movement." Their actions, however, were not always as clear; the group had already been featured in the press and on a local Christian television program. At one point, they even invited a public official, Mayor Ray Nagin, to come to the shrine and pray with them. I asked this same member about these interactions. "When we invited Nagin, it was to *pray* for him to help our city. It was not a political rally," she explained. "Later someone suggested that we invite the chief of police and people from the fire department. But we decided not to do that . . . We try to keep things noncontroversial so we can pray."

Her answer revealed the fine line that members of the peace prayer group walked. Deeply concerned about the persistence of violence in New Orleans, they saw its roots in the moral failings of its people. They were very cautious, however, about singling out a particular group. Instead, they implicated themselves as part of the problem and the solution, with a perspective of "community" into which everyone could fit. This made the specific dimensions of violence harder to see—structural, social, or otherwise—and it glossed over its development and impact in poor Black communities. The negative implications of this, however, did not deter— as indicated by the intensity with which they carried out their work. Thus, they continued to pray, building on a well-established religious platform dating back to the founding of New Orleans, for a city that would one day be "pleasing to God."

Vodou and the Restoration of Balance

One afternoon, while perusing the community bulletin board at a local coffee shop, a colorful flyer caught my attention, announcing an upcoming "protection ceremony" for New Orleans. This was an annual event organized by a local Vodou society (*sosyete*), and the flyer stood out because of the image it featured—a Black woman holding a child, both adorned with crowns and brightly illuminated. The woman reminded me of Our Lady of Prompt Succor, but this Blessed Mother had a different feel, with a scarred face and arresting stare. It turned out to be an image of Ezili Danto who, as I would later learn, is a powerful Petwo Lwa in the Haitian Vodou tradition. Ezili Danto is a hardworking woman, a warrior, and thus a fierce protector—especially of women and children, including Anaïs, the daughter in her arms. As the flyer announced, the ceremony would be dedicated to both Ezili Danto and Our Lady of Prompt Succor.[8] As such, it was a powerful summons that reflected the mission and purpose of this particular religious group—to honor and serve the spirit world and to seek their guidance and intervention, especially in times of trouble.

Vodou is a broad term that refers to the Afro-Creole religious traditions of Haiti, traditions that are situated in the contemporary world as part of a larger "cluster of mystical religions with millions of followers . . . most of them in West Africa, the Caribbean and North America" (Fandrich 2006, 126). As Ina Fandrich (2007, 779), a New Orleans based scholar of religion, argues, Vodou is slightly different from the tradition of Voodoo, which refers to "the Afro-Creole counterculture religion of southern Louisiana." The history of Voodoo is thus traced through the arrival of three different groups to the Louisiana territory: people from the Senegal River basin, Mande-speaking people from the Congo River basin, and people from the Bight of Benin (Fandrich 2006, 129). These Africans arrived with their own religious beliefs, traditions, and practices. It was not until after the Haitian Revolution and the arrival in New Orleans of more than ten thousand refugees from Saint-Domingue, beginning in 1809, that Vodou also became influential, with aspects of the Kongolese and Dahomean traditions of Central and West Africa, the Yorùbá tradition from southwestern Nigeria, and indigenous traditions of the Caribbean (782). These various threads were woven into the new forms of African American religion that emerged in Louisiana in the eighteenth and nineteenth centuries.[9] Such history sheds light on the varied interpretations of Vodou and Voodoo that subsequently emerged as devotees developed their practices in distinctly local ways. It also helps us understand the accompanying tensions, as claims of authenticity and authority were made and challenged.[10]

The founder of the sosyete was a Vodou priestess named Martine. Originally from New England, she felt called to New Orleans in the mid 1970s and then spiritually called to Vodou, traveling to Haiti in the mid 1990s for initiation. Upon returning to New Orleans, she continued her work at a small botanica she had opened in her Bywater neighborhood, where she offered religious and spiritual items, supplies, and original artwork for sale. As a white woman of eastern European ancestry practicing a religion with a distinct African history, her establishment was both reflective of the religion's reach and caught up in the dilemmas of cultural ownership that complicated its expansion. Yet her work and dedication to service attracted many practitioners and new initiates. In addition to the botanica, Martine held ceremonies that honored the Lwa in her home, eventually building a peristyle in her backyard to accommodate the sosyete's growing membership.

These ceremonies honored a different Lwa each week and were attended by a consistent group of about fifteen to twenty people. While membership was open to all, the attendees I observed were a fairly homogenous group of young white devotees. Many of them came from the surrounding area, the Bywater and Marigny neighborhoods—places that were known for their shelter and support of creative counterculture. They thus seemed unified by their embrace of free expression, which emboldened their commitment to serve the Lwa and the community. As Martine explained in an interview that took place at the botanica, "Vodou is really about bringing things into balance . . . about healing and good health and getting the energy flowing and all the different elements working together. I know that people out there think of it altogether differently, spell casting and hexing and sticking needles in dolls and all of that, but that [bringing things into balance] is in fact what it is."

The balance that practitioners sought was in response to the perception of a broken and unjust world. This was a view that was informed by the conditions sosyete members witnessed in Haiti and in other places, but it was also in direct response to what they witnessed at home, from the lack of affordable housing to poor access to education, healthcare, and other services. One of the biggest concerns, however, was crime and public safety. "When I first moved to this neighborhood in 1995," Martine recalled, "the Bywater had the highest crime rate for three years in a row . . . It was OK to be out in the day time, but you were out of your mind if you were out at night—I mean I've had guns and knives pulled on me . . . you really had to question your sanity for living here."

The city indeed seemed under siege, with violent crime at its height in the mid-1990s, influenced by large-scale drug trafficking operations and worsened by corruption in law enforcement. As Martine recalled, "The corruption was extreme, and the police were in cahoots, they were warehousing the crack cocaine right down on Chartres Street. Everybody knew who it was . . . It was a very bad time in New Orleans."[11] The problem of violence thus became an important focus of the sosyete's work—the situation was so dire that, as Martine described it, "it was really a case where our only option was to go to a higher power." The sosyete thus began to perform special "anticrime ceremonies," to seek guidance and intervention from the spirit world. They held the first ceremony in 1995, at the corner of Piety and Desire Streets.

The Lwa they believed was most relevant to addressing crime and violence was Ogou, and the ceremonies were performed in his honor. As Martine explained, "Ogou is a warrior God and the God of police. He's big, you know he's a big spirit, and he's really strong and quite scary actually. So, we turn it over to him." She added, "A friend of mine described him as kind of a kick butt urban Lwa from whom no one is exempt. And given the situation at the time, I do believe that it was necessary to say, okay, we've got something stronger here, a Lwa who we can go to who is all about truth and justice, because you guys are fallible humans."

The ceremonies were typically conducted in the evening at a chosen intersection. They were almost exclusively performed in the Bywater, as this was familiar territory, and many residents knew about the group and supported their work. Nonetheless, sosyete members went door-to-door well in advance, talking with residents to explain what would occur. According to Martine, people were generally supportive. "Everyone was really fed up and . . . willing to do something different," she recalled. The collective hope was that a strong message of solidarity and power would be sent and received. "If I were a criminal and the whole neighborhood came out dressed in white and stood on my front doorstep and did a Vodou ceremony saying, 'We know you're doing this, and you know you're doing this, and stop it now,' well it would certainly get my attention," she said. "It's strange to say this, but to some extent it's almost helpful that Vodou has such a horrible reputation and people are so terrified of it. They understand it as something that's genuine and real."

Martine began each ceremony by making a traditional drawing for the Lwa, laying cornmeal down in an intricate pattern (*vévé*) on the ground. This "opened the doors" first for Legba, the gatekeeper, who then opened the doors for the other Lwa and regulated their coming and going. This was followed by a procession of sosyete participants bearing flags (*drapeau*) to "represent the might of the Lwa and their dominion" and to create a pathway that would make the spirit world visible in the human domain. The next step was to make offerings and consecrate ceremonial items, which was followed by more drawing of vévés. As Martine explained, "There are four [Lwa] that are traditionally part of the Rada opening, and they are important because you always want to keep things balanced . . . especially if you're dealing with ferocious forces."[12] Following the fourth vévé, the participants sang a song for all the Lwa, and the Petwo part of the ceremony began.[13] The ceremony then took on a different tone, with whips and firecrackers to chase away negative energy. Participants sang songs, starting with a call to Baron Carrefour, one of the barons of the Gede family (guardians of the dead). As Martine explained, "He is the baron of the crossroads in the Petwo ranks. So, we call on him first and sing for him and then also for Ogou."

Calling on Ogou was a pivotal event. Martine drew the appropriate vévé with cornmeal and gunpowder and lit it on fire. "We also have pots of fire burning so the whole ceremony takes a fierce and fiery turn," she said. Pausing to consider the significance of all of this, she added,

So much about violent crime is about trying to renegotiate power or having a misunderstanding maybe about who gets to own power. Because nobody gets to own it, and there's a real imbalance in our society where people think that to get power you have to take it away from somebody else. So Ogou demonstrates this limitless power, and what we are asking him for is to help us take up that power in a real and healthy way where we know it's ours to share and use for good. It's not like we're trying to hang the bad guys, but we do want to show that we are a community and this is a family. In order to temper ourselves we have to go through the alchemical fire and the alchemical furnace, and we have to go to a higher power to bring reason and order and discipline.

The impact of this on both participants and witnesses was clear. The day after the first anticrime ceremony was held, some people who were known to be involved in criminal activity showed up on Martine's front door step begging for absolution. "They were terrified, absolutely terrified," she said. "And I told them, 'I can't help you. We called up Ogou, so go talk to him.'" She was sympathetic, however, and did not mean to dismiss them so directly. Even though the objective was to seek guidance from the Lwa, she maintained that the intent of the ceremony was not to gain power or control over anyone else.

We're not trying to punish or hurt anybody, and in fact we ask that even the criminals be included in the balance we seek. We're just asking the Lwa to please make us all into better metal. Help us to fix this and show us the way to fix it. My image of all of this is that as a society, if anybody is failing, then we're all failing. So, it isn't about just picking out or imprisoning the people that we don't like, it's about all of us figuring out where the imbalances are and how we combine the elements of ourselves and maybe heat them up or do whatever it takes to make those elements work together. So, there's no vindictiveness involved.

The ceremonies were thus performed to heal and support all members of society—from the participants to the observers to the criminals who sometimes showed up to the police officers who blocked off the intersection to provide security. Martine remembered a particular ceremony that demonstrated the kind of collective participation she hoped for. The police had parked a block away, closing off the intersection to traffic. However, as soon as the drumming started, the officers came closer to see what was going on. In the course of the ceremony, one participant became possessed, "mounted" by Ogou, and began to run around, jumping over a huge fire in the middle of the street. As Martine recalled, "They [the police] didn't know he was possessed, and they were just trying to contain him, and they couldn't hold the guy. There were about four really big detectives, and they couldn't hold onto him. That just blew their minds.

After the ceremony, I usually scoop up the ashes from the fire and the gunpowder and the cornmeal and I put them in gris gris bags that people can wear for protection. All the cops wanted one."

Outside of the Bywater, where the sosyete was less well known, special arrangements had to be made with residents and the authorities before anticrime ceremonies could be performed. Even when ceremonies were requested by the residents of those communities, Martine was concerned about how the group would be received: "Will they embrace this and will we be supported? Or will they freak out and run to the police?" she asked. Successful ceremonies depended on local involvement—a community had to see the need for intervention, and residents had to be open to the idea and practice of Vodou and invested in making things better. The group nonetheless responded when called. As Martine stated, "You just have to be courageous and go out and do it."

In the wake of Hurricane Katrina, residents in the Bywater responded to a new configuration of vulnerability, finding themselves literally surrounded by destruction and death, from the near total loss of the neighboring Lower Ninth Ward to the intensified conditions of violence close at hand. Sosyete members were especially affected following the January 2007 home invasion and murder of Helen Hill, who had lived not far from the peristyle. In addition to participating in public protest, members responded by organizing a series of "neighborhood healing ceremonies." These were not explicitly focused on crime; rather, the group worked to harmonize the energy of specific locations and communities according to the needs of the residents therein.

The new ceremonies, however, also indicated a shift in tactic, with devotion and service performed alongside more familiar and thus less scrutinized projects. Martine remained concerned, especially after the storm, that the group might not be welcome in certain areas, especially if their presence was not explicitly requested. "One of the things about healing is that there is almost no point in doing a healing if somebody hasn't asked for it," she said. "It's not something you can impose on anybody else." "What we're doing is sincere," she continued. "We are really attempting in any way to connect with spirit, and you don't want people rolling their eyes and staring at you or refusing to step in and be part of it." Instead, the group became more directly involved in community organizing, taking the lead in the orchestration of healing initiatives in partnership with nonprofits, city agencies, and other entities. While the ceremonial and devotional aspects of Vodou were not as prominently featured in these activities, the sosyete helped unite a diverse community around a set of shared principles, still centered on healing, honor, mutual respect, and the restoration of balance.

God's Holy Family

On a tree-lined street in the Tremé, Holy Family Episcopal Church stands out for its impressive but welcoming facade, a high-pitched marble-faced edifice with an adjoining courtyard. Affixed to the exterior front wall, however, is a large and rather unusual sign. About six feet high and four feet wide, the sign is positioned next to the main entrance, clearly visible from the street and sidewalk and directly in front of church members and visitors as they make the short turn up the stairs to enter the building. At the top of the sign, when I first encountered it, appeared the following: "'God is our hope and strength. A very present help in trouble,' Psalm 46," followed by the heading "Murder Victims 2008." Below that was a long list of names, rows and rows of all the people who had been killed in the city since the beginning of the year with the date of their death, their age, and the method of their killing: "1/2/08, Terrence Handy, 27, shot. 1/4/08, Jose Francisco Ramos, 44, shot. 1/5/08, Kendrick Quinn, 18, shot." It was an arresting sight, a sobering memorial to the violent loss of life and a powerful public statement by this particular religious community.

Finding my way inside the church one day to inquire about the display, I was put in touch with the priest, Father Richard. "We call it the murder board," he told me when we sat down together. "It's not a terribly pleasant name for it, and it's not a terribly pleasant event. So, I guess it's a little bit 'in your face,' but maybe we need to be that way. It's part of our Victims of Violence ministry."

I asked Father Richard about the history of the ministry, discovering that it was a fairly recent initiative, launched in February 2007, about a year and a half after Hurricane Katrina. I also asked, perhaps too boldly, why the ministry had not begun earlier given the long history of violence in the city and especially in the Tremé, the historically African American neighborhood where the church was located. The Catholics had been praying for peace since 1995, and the Vodou sosyete's anti-crime ceremonies dated to the same period. Father Richard cut my question short, slightly agitated: "Because that's when we started!" he said. "Should we have been doing this in 2003? Yeah. Should we have been acutely aware of it in 2004? Yeah." He paused for a moment, regaining composure.

In July 2005, about a month or so before Katrina, I was sitting in my living room one evening, and the news came on, and there were two or three murders that night. And

I turned around and my wife said "Well, where were they?" And I said, "Oh thank God they weren't in our neighborhood." . . . The very next night a seventeen-year-old boy was murdered twenty-five feet from my front door. At 12 o'clock at night, with automatic weapon fire, a drug deal gone bad. . . . And my view of violence changed after that. I now had ownership, and I realized that a kid getting shot in Central City is as important to me as a kid that gets shot in the 9th ward where I live . . . My awareness as a pastor has been, since that time in 2005, very sensitive toward murder and urban violence.

Father Richard's shift in awareness was reflected in the broader history and development of the church. Holy Family was established in the mid-1800s, during the earliest period of growth for the Protestant Episcopal Church, which began in New Orleans in 1805 with the founding of Christ Church (Reinders [1964] 1989, 117). Originally located near the French Quarter, Holy Family identified itself as a "high church" in the Anglo-Catholic tradition. Its leaders and members were predominantly white, part of the Americanization of the city shortly after the Louisiana Purchase.

Holy Family operated as a mission church until it received parish status in 1869. At that time, the property was sold, and construction began at a new site in the recently developed Faubourg Tremé. The relocated parish attended to the needs of the community through a number of service projects, including a parish school and an orphanage for sick children. By the late 1800s, the church had a membership of several hundred people, which slowly diversified over the next century, correlating with the shifting demographics of the Tremé as a Creole and then predominantly African American community. This was a slow process; one longtime parishioner remembered her family as just one of two Black families when they joined the church in 1972. With Father Richard at the pulpit, the leadership remained predominantly white, but the church now considered itself, according to its own literature, a "house for all nations," a community that was "neither black nor white, straight nor gay, poor nor rich, woman nor man, child nor elder."

Hurricane Katrina dealt a serious blow to Holy Family's social and fiscal stability. In the first year after the storm, the congregation consisted of just twenty-five people. However, membership gradually recovered, with parishioners attracted by new ministries relevant to post-Katrina conditions and concerns. By 2007 attendance for Sunday services had doubled to about forty-five, and by the spring of 2008 it was up to seventy.

One particular concern was the continuation of violence in the post-Katrina period. Many church members participated in the March for Survival that took place in January of 2007, in the wake of a string of murders that included the high-profile and separate killings of artists Dinerral Shavers and Helen Hill. However, while thousands of people had converged on city hall, there were thousands more who chose not to attend. Among them was Claire, a white woman from an Uptown congregation who was in training to become a deacon in the Episcopal Church and was thus temporarily based at Holy Family for her ordination internship. Conversing with me one morning at a local café, Claire described how she felt frustrated by the fact that there had been so many other victims of violence during that same period, but those deaths had not triggered the same response. She saw this as an everyday problem: "Often in the paper I noticed that these other victims were being dismissed."

The articles were buried on the second or third page of the metro section, and it was all dismissed as "druggie killing druggie." A lot of times they would even include a long history of the victim's rap sheet. To me that was missing the point. So I, along with some other people within the church, we were concerned about the ongoing murders and the fact that everybody wasn't getting the same kind of attention that Helen Hill and Dinerral Shavers were getting.

She decided to speak to the priest. "I went to Father Richard and I said we have to do something. We have to have a response to the murders in the communities. But how? How do you solve murder? The roots of it are huge . . . where do you even begin to solve it?" She paused, remembering his response. "He looked at me and said simply, 'We don't have to solve it.' And I went, 'Ohhh . . . we don't have to solve it, we just have to call attention to it! We just have to honor the humanity of the victims, because no matter who they were or what their behavior was, they didn't deserve to die.'"

For Father Richard, the conversation reaffirmed his own shift in awareness and the church's refined mission. As he explained,

I think it was by the grace of God that Claire was put before us with that question—how can we solve this? And I remembered some wisdom that had been passed along to me by a Jesuit social activist. He said that the charism of social justice should not be dependent on the outcome but rather on the transformation that takes place in the doing of social justice. And I shared that with Claire, and she found it extremely liberating. We didn't have to fix it. The burden was lifted off of her, off of all of us. We didn't have to make it all OK. What we could do is become active in the issue, and in our activity, transformations would occur.

The rose ministry was one of the first programs to begin, in February 2007. Claire led the initiative, recruiting her fellow parishioners to participate. "None of this was my idea," she stressed, downplaying her role. "I just put things together. Somebody said, 'This is terrible and what are we going to do?' Someone else said, 'Well we had a march on city hall and the mayor's office, but why don't we march there every week?' My husband said, 'Well if you're going to march to the mayor's office, you ought to take something when you go.'" From this synthesis of ideas, the rose ministry was born. Claire began to assemble weekly lists of the people who had been murdered in the city. Then, with the help of a small team of volunteers, most of them women, she created a bouquet of roses with a flower for each victim. This was delivered to the Mayor's office accompanied by a note and a message of prayer. As Claire recalled, "The note would list each victim by name, age, and how they were killed, and then it would say, 'The people at Holy Family are praying for these victims of murder, for their families, and for you our mayor.' And we delivered that every week. Week after week."

This public yet still very personal response was not just about calling attention to the problem of violence; it was also about the ways in which violence was characterized, its mostly poor Black victims devalued and dismissed in a city where death and mourning seemed hierarchical. Father Richard explained,

You know one thing about murder in this city and in all cities where violent crime is high is that people think in terms of murder rate: how many victims there are rather than *who* they are. They also tend to make the victims anonymous, especially if they are poor, and they seem to dismiss or even justify the death depending on what the victim was doing. Somehow a drug dealer is not nearly as important as Helen Hill because we put social priorities on the value of people. That sounds harsh but it's true.

The intent of the ministry, therefore, was to attend to all the victims of violence by identifying them, sharing the details of their lives, and properly mourning their deaths. As Father Richard put it, in terms that were both familiar and prescriptive, "Certainly our faith teaches us that life is so precious and so valuable, that the unnatural loss of any human being is a loss to all human beings and to the kingdom of God."

To generate the list of victims, clergy and parishioners culled information from a variety of sources, including the local news, community reports, and police records. It was a process that Father Richard described as "dredging," and I asked Claire how she handled it, given the emotional impact. Her response came slowly. "It *is* troubling and it *is* sad, but I have been lucky in that I have been successful in continuing to place it all in God's hands." I pressed for more information, asking whether there was a particular routine or method. "I do it every morning, first thing," she replied. "I get up and I read the paper from cover to cover. Because you can never tell where the article is going to be hidden, it's not always in the obituaries. So, I do that first thing. Then I go exercise. And then I go to work." She paused again, softening. "I've been successful at it, I have to say. And I feel like, I feel . . . see for me it's *hopeful*, it's not depressing. It's because we are *attending* to it in the way that we are meant to. We're supposed to pay attention. So, it's hopeful."

Working alongside Claire was an African American woman named Joan who was also in training for the diaconate. In fact, the two women had been in the same ordination class and were placed in each other's home churches for their internships. Claire came downtown to the Tremé and Joan went up to Claire's home congregation. After the internships were over and each deacon had returned, they continued to work together. The rose ministry thus expanded with new sites of delivery; at one point the women carried flowers to the mayor's office, the NOPD, city council chambers, and the office of the district attorney. Joan described what it was like to deliver the flowers and the deep connection she felt to the deceased. "The first time I was very nervous," she told me. "I almost thought that each rose was a little person, and I was holding each one. You know how you just feel things like that? Well each rose does *represent* a person, and you feel almost like a pallbearer really . . . you know we are carrying these people, these roses."

This way of carrying the victims of violence forward and into the world became central to the other activities that formed the church's ministry. It inspired, for example, the creation of the murder board, which remained affixed to the exterior front wall. Father Richard had been thinking about ways to sustain and keep the ministry in public view, and as Claire recalled, he had asked his fellow clergy "about [creating] something like the Vietnam wall." When encouraged, he came up with the idea for the murder board. "I'll put up a sign," he had said, "and that way everyone coming down the street will see it, tourists will see it, residents will see it, and it can be an embarrassment to this city that we tolerate this!" Clergy members updated the sign each week using a ruler and a marker to write the names and descriptors by hand. At the end of the year, the names were engraved on a large plaque, which was installed along the fence of the courtyard by the parish hall.

To continue this work inside the church itself, a scrapbook was created and kept just past the entrance—open and accessible on a tall podium. As Claire stated, "When the murder board started, I thought we also needed a scrapbook, too, some place where we could put more detailed information about each victim based on the pictures we could find, or articles in the paper. It's one of the first things you see as you enter the church." The display, however, had a more basic directive, as Father Richard stressed, to "remind people" as they arrived for worship "that these are human beings."

The deceased were then named, specifically during the "Prayers for the People" that were offered at each Holy Eucharist service. These prayers, led by an associate priest or deacon, came after the sermon and the recitation of the Nicene Creed and just before the confession of sins, the exchange of peace, and the Holy Communion. An associate priest described the prayers as they took place at Holy Family:

> We do the whole Prayers for the People, everything that's in the prayer book. We pray for the sick, the military, and the church leaders. And the last thing we do is pray for the victims of violence in this city. But not just the victims, we also pray for the families of the victims, for the perpetrators and their families, for the police, and then we read the names, we read the exact same information that's on the murder board.

Reading and listening to the names was a powerful experience. In part, this had to do with the delivery, reflective of the commitment each reader made to treat with dignity the loss of human life. Claire, who often led the prayers at her home congregation, described her approach: "I try to slow it down. I try to always honor the fact that that person was loved. That person has a mother, and that person has a life. So, I try to keep that in mind when I say the names. I try to always say it with feeling, to not just rattle them off." Joan had a similar intent, but she would pause dramatically before reciting the method of death, with a sharpness to her voice that conveyed the shock and outrage she felt at the senseless taking of a life. For example, in one service, at the conclusion of the larger set of prayers, she read,

> We pray for the victims of violence in our city. The families of those killed. The perpetrators and their families. Our police department and all who are affected by these deaths. We remember especially, Herbierto Montoya . . . *shot*! Harold J. Stanwod, 24 . . . *shot*! Durrell Pooler, 23 . . . *shot*! Kendrick Sherman, 18 . . . *shot*! Vernon Johnson, 35 . . . *shot*! Albert Clinton McClebb, Jr., 29 . . . *shot*! *Unidentified male*, 21 . . . *shot*! Derek Lacombe, 20 . . . *shot*!

A deliberately long and uncomfortable period of silence followed except for the sounds of children unsettled and a person coughing in the back. Then Father Richard's voice came forth in chant with the invitation to confess sins. The congregation knelt.

The impact of this work was evident—the ministry had received the attention it desired from the press, and attendance was picking up at church services. Most important, however, was the transformation that seemed to occur at the level of family and community. Father Richard gave an example based on a recent exchange he had been privileged to witness. "Just two days ago I was leaving work and I saw a car stop in the middle of the street and pull over into the driveway," he said. "Three young ladies get out and go up to the murder board, and you can see they are trying to find people. They took pictures with their cell phones. So it's doing something." He paused for a moment. "You know, there's always the possibility of being transformed and changed. And sometimes it's an uncomfortable transformation, but in the end it's good. It's all good. So God is present in all that we do. God's telling us that these are my children whom I love, and you need to approach them in that way. God's in that. At some point if our voices keep speaking, there will be a response."

Love Thy Neighbor as Thyself

In these encounters, across diverse religious groups, a framework for social and spiritual change was starting to emerge. I could see it in the concern about violence that brought people together and in the ways in which each community worked not just to understand the problem but to identify and access both earthly and otherworldly sources of knowledge, healing, power, and justice. In conversation with the members of the Catholic peace prayer group, for example, the complex premises of this work became apparent, with violence seen as a shared condition fueled by sin and moral depravity and repaired through prayer, religious conversion, and the divine intercession of Our Lady. The Vodou sosyete also made clear the connection that exists between the human and spiritual world, with the restoration of balance made possible through devotion to the Lwa despite the tensions that can develop among practitioners regarding belief, the desire to serve, and the hope for broad acceptance and impact.

These frameworks, however, were not sufficient on their own. Even though they affirmed the connection between humans and the divine or spiritual world and saw this as a necessary conduit for social change, they seemed to cast both violence and its solution in nonspecific terms. Their practices thus rang hollow to the extent that they seemed removed, albeit to various degrees, from violence's structural and local formations. For example, they did not sufficiently acknowledge its devastation in poor Black communities nor connect this to the underlying and persistently negative determination of Black life. What was missing, therefore, was a fundamental assertion of a sacred Black humanity—not for its sake alone but as a necessary grounding for a more collective and interrelated framework for human being and becoming. The clergy and parishioners at Holy Family appeared to be headed in this direction despite the relative newness of their ministry. Still, the emphasis remained on honoring all murder victims without sufficient consideration of how social hierarchies, and thus value, could be reconfigured within and especially outside of affected communities.

One additional encounter helped to move my inquiry forward, pointing simultaneously to African American religion and the Black Church as critical spaces for both the origination and continuation of these ideas. It came in the form of a long conversation with Raymond, a well-known African American Vodou priest and spiritual advisor based in New Orleans for many years. Meeting by chance at a local bookstore, he was kind enough to meet me for a drink one afternoon in a small coffee shop at the end of Canal Street. It was an odd place, tucked into the corner of a busy intersection and at the edge of a large cemetery. As I would later learn, Raymond lived right around the corner, alongside the dead, and he strode into the shop to meet me like someone who was already at home.

Our conversation covered a wide terrain. He spoke about his life and spiritual development from his Catholic upbringing to his practice and work in martial arts, his many consultations with spiritual leaders around the world, his own initiation in Haiti, and his current work as a spiritual advisor. What I found most interesting, however, was his conceptualization of religion, and African American religion in particular, which added to my understanding of the space of death in Black New Orleans, the role of religion, and the possibilities of conscious awakening. As Raymond explained,

In reality all religions are belief systems created by a particular people, culture, and consciousness. They may be inspired by the creator, but the creator is more of a spirit, or an energy force, or a state of consciousness. It's not somebody up in the sky taking down notes about what you did good and what you did bad and whether or not you're going to be condemned to hell. That's bullshit to me. Heaven and hell are really conditions of *human* life itself—you don't have to die to go to hell [*laughter*] . . . The Devil is not a little man running around with horns and a little red suit with a pitchfork and a little pointy tail—the Devil is a Lucifer state of consciousness in *mankind* because people do devilish things!

With this view, Raymond saw a need for humans to claim their capacity to both create and alleviate suffering. This did not require a complete rejection of religious authority or belief but rather came about as religious practitioners (and people more broadly, regardless of belief) acknowledged themselves as knowing and powerful beings. While Raymond saw this as a need that applied to the world, it was particularly important in the recovery of African American communities. He was critical, for example, of the emotional intensity that frequently accompanied worship in the Black Church, especially if it did not translate into a viable framework for change in the everyday.

People go to church four or five hours on Sunday, they praise God, they praise Jesus, and they have these emotional services, but the biggest principle they violate in their daily lives is *love thy neighbor as thyself.* Because that same community that goes to church four or five hours on Sunday has some of the worst problems—the drugs, the killing, the overall level of distrust. It's just madness. It makes you question what's going on in the church. Do they need to change their theology?

"I'm not discounting them [Black churches] at all because they are a major focus," he was careful to add, "but it depends on what types of programs they have for helping people. You know, if there is spiritual counseling and outreach services like feeding the hungry and giving donations of material goods."

What Raymond hoped for instead, above and beyond any kind of political, structural, or community-based reform, was a return to consciousness—not necessarily apart from the Black Church but wholly integrated and fundamental to its mission. "I'm not sure how to say this," he began somewhat hesitantly, "but I think Dr. King had good intentions with integration, but integration never really was the answer. We need to integrate amongst ourselves first, and love ourselves, and love and support each other—emotionally, socially, economically, politically." He leaned forward, partly so that I could hear but also partly so that others could not, to protect what might be taken as a controversial remark. "So actually, the plight of African Americans here is not so much to be born again *Christians*, but rather to be born again *Africans*, reclaiming our roots and having an African state of consciousness, which is based on spiritual *consciousness* rather than a complete *reliance* on spirit." He sat back, satisfied, and smiled. As I would soon discover, this cultivation of spiritual consciousness, through a commitment to love, was not merely a hoped for ideal; it was an active process and pursuit for many seekers, both within and outside of the Black Church.

PART TWO

In Search of Love at Liberty Street

God's Hands (photo by author)

Walk Out There on Faith

I found Candace waiting at the front entrance of the New Orleans Public Library. She had walked over from her downtown office to meet me on her one-hour lunch break, and I had the nerve to arrive ten minutes late, having circled around for too long looking for a place to park. We introduced, she waved aside my apologies, and we entered the building, escaping the heat and in search of a quiet place to talk.

The downtown branch is an open and illuminated space, and rather than offering up a protected corner to which we could retreat, it showed us to one long table, in plain view, at the center of the first main floor. Surrounded by local materials, including historical documents, government publications, and maps, it turned out to be an oddly appropriate place for the story that Candace would tell—of faith, the impact of death, and the work at hand.

We began with the basic details. She told me she was born in Mississippi, "where my people came from," and for this she was proud. But her immediate family had moved to Louisiana when she was three, and she considered New Orleans to be her home. Raised also through the interconnected structures of family, home, and church, as many African Americans in New Orleans were, I asked Candace about her religious upbringing. However, before she further described herself as "a dedicated, active, member" of her church, she told me about Corey, her son who had passed away twelve years ago. "Corey was my firstborn," she said. "My mother and father's first grandchild. So, it's a loss all the way around as far as the family is concerned." Her next sentence, without pause, was the religious identity about which I had asked: "I'm Baptist." She named the well-established church where she and her family were members. These were basic but essential details—they identified Candace as an African American religious woman and grieving mother, on a long journey of faith, at work in the space of death and transformation.

Corey had died a violent death, gunned down on the street like so many other young Black men who went before him and after. "I guess it was just bad association, you know? He never saw wrong in anybody." Candace shook her head, still trying after all these years to understand. "And it never was solved because we have witness problems. But I never give up, you know? And it's just like it happened yesterday." Indeed, her grief was apparent, just below the surface, and then, in the middle of the library, Candace began to cry. Again, she waved aside my concern, refusing my offer to get tissues, water, food, anything, or to find a more suitable time and place for us to talk. Instead she remained where she was, and she continued to speak, the tears now streaming down her face. "No, it's okay . . . I have to do this," she said. "I tell my story."

The Baptist church to which Candace belonged was established in the early part of the twentieth century, part of the Uptown and back-of-town residential expansion that saw the clustered growth of the city's African American population. Then and now, the church supported "a Christ-Centered, Word Based, Holy Ghost driven, culturally conscious, socially aware body of believers . . . called to make a difference in a dismal world." It was through this history and mission that Candace emerged and now moved. She was guided not just by the support that she received from her minister and fellow parishioners but by the trust she placed, questioned, and then reaffirmed in God's ability to keep and sustain her through the battles that characterized the Black Baptist journey—from pain and suffering toward salvation and peace—in this world and in the next. This was not an easy journey, nor was it complete—telling her story was a necessary way forward.

In the immediate wake of Corey's death, Candace had questioned her faith. How could God let something like that happen? "When it first happened, I was so angry with God," she recalled. "I was angry because he took a fine young man who had never been in trouble." She paused, and then qualified the description, "I mean he was involved in stuff that typical twenty-year-olds do. But you know we all go through that . . . and he was beginning to start doing his junior year in college. His father and I did all we could to support him. We would have him drug tested and everything. And so, you know we didn't have blinders on."

The shock and grief caused by Corey's death, despite whatever aware-
ness his parents might have had regarding the perils of life for young
Black men, did more than provoke anger, it made Candace gravely ill.
"I was so sick," she confided. "My heart stopped a couple of times, you
know? I seized and all that. So, I had to be hospitalized off and on a lot.
The psychologist said that I was just sitting in a black box *just really not
caring*. Not even for my other children." Her tears began again. "Because
I felt like you [God] robbed me of my child, you know? And here I am
a *mother*. You have a mother and father who, we did *everything*, you
know? We educated him, we gave him the best. We warned him about
the trouble and all that. But in spite of all that, it still happened to us!"

Given the intensity of her pain, still so evident as we sat together,
Candace's return to the church was remarkable. It happened slowly, she
said, "through counseling, through my minister and just my church
family embracing me. And having a strong family base. And then my
support group." The support group played an especially important role.
It was there, in the company of other grieving women, that Candace
was "brought back." "At first, I went to the support group and I was still
angry," she said. "I didn't open my mouth. I would just sit there and sit
there, thinking I don't know why I'm here and all this kind of stuff. But
something kept drawing me back. And then before you knew it I was
into it, you know? Because it was almost like everybody there has the
same problem . . . they can understand what you're going through. So,
it kind of brought me back. Brought be back where I could deal with it."

She was quick to note, however, that while some measure of healing had
occurred, Corey's death was a loss that she would never get over. "There's
no fix, there's no fix for this. None. This will take me to my grave. No illness in the world will take me. *This* will take me. I almost was there, too,
you know?" In fact, it was at the moment when Candace was faced with
the very real possibility of her own death, just before but without aban-
doning the possibility of her transformation, that she was brought back. It
had to do, she said, with "just being a God-fearing woman and knowing
that I was consuming myself, I was killing myself, and I either had to just
die or find someplace where I could heal with it and get up every day."

And you know I still get angry now. I do. But it was almost like . . . God had to just tell
me, "Look, I told you I'm not leaving you. This is *my* battle. It's not yours." And I just
had to get to the point where I realized that I had to, you know, *walk out there on faith.*
And I just realized that it's okay, if you're going to say you're going to be a Christian,
you're going to have to do this. And stop fighting it. Because I was blocking out bless-
ings, I really was.

I was impressed by her resolve, but Candace was quick to interject, centering God—not herself, her family, the support group, or the church—as the primary catalyst. "It didn't come easy," she said. "Nobody but the grace of God helped me get that done." "Nobody but the grace of God," she repeated before adding, "Church don't make your spirituality you know? Church can give you some tips on holding onto your faith and all. But your trust in God is what really brings it on."

With her faith restored, Candace aligned herself more intentionally with the religious and social mission of the church, working to help others who were struggling through similar circumstances. She had always been an advocate, long before her son was murdered, and this work now continued in ways that revealed the extended link between the Black Baptist Church, social and religious activism, the underrecognized contributions of African American religious women, and the process of healing and change. She fought for gun control, she worked in the criminal justice system, she supported crime victims and their families, she performed outreach services for women and their children, she accompanied people to court and to prisons for restorative justice programs. This work, so helpful for others, was not separate from her own recovery. "It's been good for me, too" she said. "It really has."

Given the continuation of violence in her community, I asked Candace, finally, about the potential transformation, the change that she hoped her work might bring. "There's always hope for change," she replied. "But change is going to take a minute. It's not going to happen like right away. Because you have people out there that is killing casually. They have *no* respect for life. Not theirs and nobody else's. And it just takes one minute to be caught up. I see it every day." It made her work, and the continued telling of her story, that much more important.

I don't have any problems with opening my mouth and telling people "Look. You don't really want to go on that other side." And when I tell people what *I* go through, some people get shot back into reality . . . So that's the reason why I talk about it. Because if I turn *one* around, I feel like I am doing my part . . . And then some people just need somebody to say that they care . . . you tell them, you say, "Look. *I care.* I really do. I really need you to be *somebody*. And you can."

THREE

Somebodies on the Battlefield for the Lord

I am on the battlefield for my Lord,
I'm on the battlefield for my Lord;
And I promised Him that I would serve Him till I die.
I am on the battlefield for my Lord.
SYLVANA BELL AND E. V. BANKS (1946)

The main entrance to Armstrong Park is a grand metal arch-way—a radiating art deco inspired design with Louis Armstrong's name across the top. Especially when illuminated at night, the sign reads like the marquee for a special event, an invitation and gateway to a wondrous new world. It was with this feeling that I entered the park one Saturday morning, in March of 2009, to attend the Yes We Care! rally. Happy that the rain had cleared, I made my way forward on a paved walk-way that skirted around manicured gardens and man-made lagoons. Across the way, a stage was set up in front of the Mahalia Jackson Theater with a podium and some chairs for those who would later speak. For now, people milled around, clustered together in small groups, leaning against trees and railings, chatting and waiting for the event to begin.

The idea for the rally had come from Pastor Samuel, the pastor at Liberty Street Baptist Church. It would launch the church's latest ministry against urban violence, part of a longer legacy of religious work that stretched back, under Samuel's tenure, to the late 1980s. Each ministry had its own approach, suited to the context, and this one was no different. In a place reeling from recent disaster and for a people lifted by recent victory—in the election of Barack Obama as the nation's first Black president—the rally was about what was now possible and required in this the Crescent City. Pastor Samuel drew deliberately on Obama's "Yes We Can" campaign slogan, changing it into a declaration that centered *care* as the essential affirmation for the work ahead. As the church's press release declared, against the public perception that African Americans tolerated or were reticent about the violence that plagued their communities, residents were "coming together to declare that we do care about our friends, our families, our children, and our neighbors." The declaration was coupled with a commitment to nonviolence in the form of a cease-fire agreement—a direct and immediate action to stop the killing. However, this was not strictly an internal campaign; the declaration of care extended outside of the Black community with the hope that those who weren't directly affected by violence would come to view it as a shared condition and concern.

To begin the rally, a high school marching band paraded in, snare drum and tuba keeping time. They were unfortunately separated from the crowd by the lagoon that lay at the steps of the theater, so the sound ricocheted around the park in disjointed delay. The clarity improved when the speeches began, and the people moved forward to listen. Pastor Samuel and a few other representatives from Liberty Street were seated toward the rear of the stage and for the most part they stayed there, taking a literal back seat for what had been billed as an interfaith gathering and community event. The MC thus turned the microphone over to a diverse group of clergy who called for unity and spoke about the change in perspective they believed was necessary to bring into existence the peaceful and beloved society they envisioned. They were joined by a few city officials who also spoke, including the chief of police and the mayor, Ray Nagin, who rallied the crowd with a series of compelling questions and statements: "Where is black love in New Orleans? . . . That's what we need to come back to!"

Interspersed between these speakers were residents who sang songs, recited poems, and gave testimonies of their own experiences. The most moving accounts came from the family members of victims of violence. They shared details about the lives and deaths of their loved ones with the community that surrounded them, easing the burden of loss if only for a moment. The crowd, several hundred by that point, linked arms, prayed, and shouted out praise when moved. They answered the call in more direct ways as well, for example, by signing the cease-fire agreement, which parishioners from Liberty Street circulated on clipboards throughout the park.

At the end of the rally, Pastor Samuel approached the podium. He was not on the program, careful not to allow his name and stature to overshadow the proceedings. However, after a long and emotional afternoon, he was inspired to speak. Taking a folded piece of paper from his breast pocket, he first acknowledged the impact of violence within the community—the suffering that preceded and followed. He then affirmed his own belief in care as the way forward to a brighter day. However, he took this one step further by identifying the people themselves as the instruments of care. For this was not a gathering of passive onlookers. These were specific individuals, church members, and community members who could bring about change. As Pastor Samuel stated toward the end of his remarks,

Since a life taken could never be given back, then surrendering to the sorrowful soliloquy of "it is what it is" is not for us today an option. The question that confronts us is, Who is it that can possibly change what it is to what it can be? Who is it that can cause our sons and daughters to realize that one life is worth more than every ounce of crack that flows across our borders and every bit of cash that flows through our banks? Well I believe . . . [that] when we heard a grieving family member's crime scene cry, calling out "Somebody has to do something or they have to stop the killing," we were hearing the answer but we did not recognize who "somebody" was or who "they" were.

But I am thankful to God today that "they" finally showed up. "They" are right here, in Armstrong Park. I'm glad today that "they" came from the Upper 9th Ward, and "they" came from below the canal, and "they" came from the 7th Ward, and "they" came from Carrollton. "They" came. And I'm glad because a mother has been waiting for you, and a sister has been hoping for you, and a son has been looking for you. Thank God today that "they" showed up!

But we realize that "they" cannot do it by themselves, no. "They" need "somebody" to help them. And the good news is that "somebody" is here also. "Somebody" came from Central City, and "somebody" came from Gert Town, and "somebody" came from Algiers, and "somebody" came from out front of town, and "somebody" came from back-of-town, Uptown, and downtown . . . it was because "they" decided to meet with "somebody" that we are now joined in Armstrong Park. By the grace of God there is nothing we can't do when we come together!

I had heard Pastor Samuel speak before, but never with such intensity, his voice steadily rising until it boomed over the loudspeakers and echoed back across the park. Even from my vantage point, off to the side and behind a small group of people with their arms raised in praise, his message was loud and clear. However, his overall gentle demeanor was not taken over, and he conveyed both a sense of urgency and a genuine compassion for the people, for what they were going through, and for what he believed they were capable of doing.

Afterward, I walked around to see what the impact of his words had been. A woman named Sheila affirmed her own commitment, which was grounded in an unwavering faith in Pastor Samuel and his leadership. "I sit in church and listen," she began. "And when he says we're gonna do something I'm just gonna do it, you know? I'm following behind him. That's all." This work, of course, was more fundamentally guided by a faith in God and a commitment to uphold the church covenant—to glorify His name, to uphold the duties of Christian living, to walk in love, and to spread the Gospel. Danielle, who had stood on the podium with a few others from the support group for grieving mothers, used a familiar refrain to describe her own participation in this and related church ministries. She was simply "on the battlefield for the Lord," here and always, recalling the many occasions where she and other members had gone out into the community holding vigils and performing outreach, "to let the Word be spread that there's enough violence going on."

Somebodies on the Battlefield for the Lord

In this chapter I explore the ways that Blacks in New Orleans worked toward peace by faith in the space of death and transformation (Taussig 1987, 4; Holland 2000, 4). I examine in particular the theology, teachings, and practices that guided this work at Liberty Street, which were reflected so fervently at the Yes We Care! rally—the religious journey that leads one to be on the battlefield for the Lord, the convergence of "they" and "somebody," and the creation of a beloved community based on nonviolence, inscribed in place, and grounded in the care and love of self and other. While many of these tenets can be traced back to the history and lingering influence of a Black social Christianity, here they created an emergent blueprint for social and spiritual being founded first and foremost on a sacred Black humanity and made visible through embodied and relational practice. Much more than the launch of a new ministry, I consider the Yes We Care! rally as a useful lens through which the trajectory of this work is revealed.

Pastor Samuel had effectively rallied the troops, calling participants to Armstrong Park from all directions. Thus, while he rejoiced in the identification of "they" and "somebody," he was more concerned with the cultivation of relatedness that occurred when they got there and its continuation after they left. As he made clear in his closing remarks, those who arrived found their most significant relations already present: "a mother [who] has been waiting for you, and a sister [who] has been hoping for you, and a son [who] has been looking for you." It was a reunion that was both inspirational and essential for change; as Pastor Samuel had concluded, "by the grace of God there is nothing we can't do when we come together!"

This relatedness extended and did not supplant one's connection to God, which made it possible for parishioners like Danielle, a grieving mother who lost her son to violence, to not just converge but to *stay* "on the battlefield for the Lord." When Danielle invoked this familiar refrain, she referenced the journey of the Christian soldier against sin and evil and toward healing, unity, and everlasting peace. The congregation of "they" and "somebody," "on the battlefield for the Lord," was what indicated the way forward—not just in terms of one's own spiritual journey but in the centering of Black humanity in the interconnected city and world to come. Pastor Samuel had spoken about the need for change months before, after Obama's election and just before traveling to Washington, DC, for the inauguration. Responding to my question about the church's plan for new ministries, he had said, "I feel that there's something we have to do that's much grander and on a larger scale . . . I kind of know *what* it is . . . it's the *how* that I'm waiting for . . . we *have* to do this. . . . if we are going to survive as a people." Two months later, the Yes We Care! rally was held.

In the remainder of this chapter, with the rally as a point of departure and return, I examine the conditions, ideas, and moments of an old and new African American religious ideal. While a comprehensive history is beyond the scope of this book, I identify four relevant periods that shed light on current practices. The first period is the rise of the Black Baptist tradition in America from the revivals of the first and second Great Awakenings to the autonomous establishment of Black churches by the mid-1700s and the emergence of a sacred Afro-Baptist cosmos. The second period is the development and influence of the black social gospel in the late 1800s, which brought about a new abolitionist movement anchored in the Black Church and in renewed pursuit of human rights, justice, and the redemption of a still immoral society. This period includes the rise of an elite African American clergy, a group of religious intellectuals who greatly influenced the civil rights leaders of the 1950s and 1960s, especially Martin Luther King Jr. The third period is King's influence on civil rights work in New Orleans from the 1957 incorporation of the Southern Christian Leadership Conference to aspects of his teaching that resonate in current actions and movements. In the fourth and final period, I examine the memorialization of King in New Orleans after his death to illustrate the embodied claiming of space—a practice that has historical roots in African American religious activism but is simultaneously linked to a distinct local tradition of expressive procession.[1]

These historical moments give important context to the continued development of religious ideals within as well as outside of contemporary Black churches. They reveal the concerns and methods of the work, but they also shed light on the ways that religious frameworks are broadly formed and made relevant across contexts and time periods. As Carol Wayne White (2016, 2) asserts, drawing inspiration from W. E. B. Du Bois, to study the religious life of African Americans is "a crucial task in presenting the inventiveness of a people who struggled to inhabit their humanity and eke out a meaningful existence for themselves in harrowing circumstances." The continuation of this work, particularly given the persistence of Black suffering, remains an essential project.

The Rally as Revival

Beneath the trees and before a dynamic set of preachers who would continue until late in the day, the Yes We Care! rally felt in many ways like a religious revival meeting characteristic of the first and especially second Great Awakenings in the early nineteenth century when Protestant enthusiasm spread south and west across the United States. A similar sense of enthusiasm enlivened this more contemporary setting—people had traveled from all directions, and once they arrived they stayed, sustained by the Word. The fact that this was taking place in Armstrong Park was significant, and it gave the event an important sense of homecoming. Not far from where we were standing was Congo Square, the historic market where enslaved Africans gathered for both cultural and economic exchange during the French and Spanish colonial periods. It remained a sacred site for many, with drumming and dancing still performed, prayers still offered, and libations for the ancestors still poured.

The surrounding neighborhood, an area known as the Tremé, began as a racially mixed community with a large concentration of Creoles and free people of color. It would become one of the nation's oldest predominantly African American communities. During the first decades of the twentieth century, however, the city claimed the land around Congo Square, acquiring it through several acts of "slum clearance" in the name of "urban recovery," razing homes, and displacing thousands of poor Black residents.[2] Two municipal structures were then built—the New Orleans Municipal Auditorium, which opened in 1929, and the New Orleans Theater of the Performing Arts, which opened decades later in 1973.[3] A park was established around these buildings, and it opened in 1980, named for Louis Armstrong, the late and legendary jazz musician who remained New Orleans's favorite son.[4]

Despite this recognition of Black arts and culture, the resulting park did not measure up. The themed attractions that were proposed never materialized, leaving a carefully landscaped, frequently gated, and sparsely populated site in the middle of what had been a bustling neighborhood. Nonetheless, local residents continued to claim the park as their own, recognizing its historical significance and using it to stage many events, including festivals, marches, and rallies, when permitted. After Hurricane Katrina, access to the park was further restricted to allow for the painfully slow repair of buildings and grounds. The park reopened in January 2009, just a few months before the Yes We Care! rally. The event felt, therefore, like a revival in more ways than one—the articulation of religious ideals occurring on the heels of disfranchisement and disaster.

Revivals were central to the emergence of the Black Baptist faith, a history best traced through awakenings great and small. According to the Reverend Dr. Leroy Fitts (1985, 19), these include the European struggle for religious freedom in the Old and New Worlds, white American Baptist history, the religious missions formed by Blacks during the period of American slavery, and the emergence of the Black Church. Beginning in Europe, the Protestant Reformation of the sixteenth century was a call for freedom, defined by Witte (2006, 21) as "freedom of the church from the tyranny of the pope, freedom of the individual conscience from canon law and clerical control, [and] freedom of state officials from church power and privilege." These principles were central to a growing Anabaptist tradition, a radical religious movement developed in separated and self-governed communities. Persecuted by political and religious authorities, many separatists were forced to leave Europe, and they searched for refuge and freedom of religion in the New World (Fitts 1985, 22). This is an important antecedent to the American Baptist movement, with European settlers and religious refugees arriving in New England and advocating for "a full, free, and absolute liberty of conscience" (Fitts 1985, 23, see also Lincoln and Mamiya [1990] 2003, 22–23).

Primarily established in northern colonies at the turn of the seventeenth century, Baptist preachers began to travel to other regions following the wave of heightened religious enthusiasm associated with the First Great Awakening (1730–1755). Coinciding also with the expansive growth of the transatlantic slave trade, this period of evangelism was also the beginning of Black Baptist formation through the religious conversion of enslaved Africans across the North American colonies. Three primary patterns are evident—the inclusion of Black worshippers in predominantly white churches, missions allowed by slave owners and led by Black preachers, and the so-called invisible churches that emerged as enslaved Africans found ways to worship within the confines of the plantation-based economy in which they were kept.

The First Baptist Church of Providence Plantations in Rhode Island, for example, a church founded by Roger Williams in 1638, had nineteen Black members within its predominantly white congregation as early as 1762 (Lincoln and Mamiya [1990] 2003, 23). However, while Blacks were admitted to the membership of white churches, they were limited in their privileges and unable to preach (Fitts 1985, 25). Still, their numbers continued to grow as white evangelists advanced southward into new regions of the country, converting both whites and Blacks. This religious work, which continued through the revivals and camp meetings of the Second Great Awakening (1790–1840), had a strong impact on Black religious formation in the southern colonies and states.

The plantation missions that emerged during this period were frequently led by enslaved Black preachers. Some slave owners encouraged this organization by allowing preachers to travel from plantation to plantation to evangelize others. However, it otherwise took place in secret. Such missions, Fitts (1985, 32) argues, "were the antecedents to organized black churches," which were established outright as early as the mid-1700s (32–33).[5] Independent organization was also fueled by the exodus of Black Baptists from white churches due to two primary factors: discriminatory and segregationist policies and a theological awakening among Black Baptist preachers based on "a new anthropological concept of human freedom and dignity" (44).

Some historians, such as Mechal Sobel (1979) in her study of the emergence of an Afro-Baptist faith, argue against the idea that the early Black Church was an "invisible" institution. Independently established from the middle of the eighteenth century, these churches "were often formally organized, with written covenants, written membership rolls, and written minutes" (Sobel 1979, xvii). Existing across the South and in both rural and urban areas, they were led by enslaved and free blacks and were recognized by whites. Their independence, however, was ultimately based not on their autonomy but on the freedom they found in Christ. As Sobel argues, "Their covenants were between themselves and God and did not involve white intermediaries" (xviii). This religious organization, therefore, had less to do with the proselytizing of white Baptists via the revivals of the Great Awakenings and more to do with the desire and development by enslaved Africans themselves of a Black sacred cosmos.[6] By 1865, over two hundred formal Black Baptist churches had been established (xxiv).

The covenant that guided the worshippers of this emerging Afro-Baptist tradition centered on a view of God as omniscient, "both the creator and the redeemer of man," with redemption made possible "through the agency of God's son and his Holy Spirit (or the Word)" (Sobel 1979, 90). Faith in God, however, was not enough; one could only become a member of a Baptist congregation by salvation—through a rebirth in Christ, at which point "one's whole character would be different—godly, sober, rejecting the worldly or profane, and embracing the holy and sacred" (90).

Born-again experiences were part of a spiritual journey in which the believer "traveled to the High God's abode, Heaven, and in knowing the High God came to have His presence in his heart forever after" (Sobel 1979, 101). For Black Baptists, this traveling ("trabelin") then continued—it was a "hard Christian journey" (101) that began long before salvation and would continue long after as new life proceeded. Thankfully, the reborn spirit returned with a number of essential gifts, love and the elimination of fear chief among them, which gave believers a necessary foundation for the cultivation of joy, unity, and peace along the certain but difficult road to the promised land (120–21).

While these beliefs were shared among all Baptists, the Sacred Cosmos that formed the Afro-Baptist tradition focused further on an aspect of salvation that was deeply connected to the social and spiritual needs of Black people. Salvation promised an eternal freedom, but it was not a freedom that depended on emancipation from slavery. Instead, it was God who affirmed the true and eternal spirit of the seeker and freed his or her soul. As Sobel (1979, 117) explains, "The Christian rebirth set blacks free forever. They might remain slaves in body for the rest of their lives, but they were free, in ways their white masters might or might not be. Theirs was a freedom that could not be bought." This belief was not about accommodation or acceptance of one's status as a slave; rather, it was a crucial development and integration of self, "a spiritual wisdom that became the core of their lives" (117). As Sobel states, "Blacks were anxious to be reborn, to put off their slave identities and slave names, and to find a better self, a social self truer to their internal image" (101).

The Go Ye Therefore People

The basic tenets of the Afro-Baptist tradition still rang true for the people who gathered for the Yes We Care! rally. Many saw themselves on the same spiritual journey that extended from salvation, and they were moved forward through the recognition of self and other, the quest for freedom, the battle against sin and evil, and the obligation to spread the Word. One participant, an elderly gentleman named Reginald, who was resting on a bench and looking out over the lagoon, shared his own story of a "hard Christian journey" (Sobel 1979, 101). He came to the rally because he saw it as an important opportunity to commit to the work ahead. However, he admitted that he had not always been so directed, and he smiled and shook his head as he recalled the disdain he had as a youth for religious proselytizers. Then *he* was saved, and he found himself preaching alongside them. "I was changed," he said. "You see, we are saved by the Word not by what we feel or what we think—only by the Word of God. And faith come by hearing. And when you hear the Word of God, then you can't be just a hearer, you must be a doer." Reginald drew directly from Scripture to make this point clear. "It's Matthew 28," he told me. "'Go ye therefore . . . to all parts of the world.'[7] Go ye. So we are the go ye therefore people."

The conversation shifted to the problem of urban violence for which we were all convened. It was a problem that persisted, according to Reginald, because people weren't properly receiving or hearing the Word of God, and so it was religious outreach and education that he especially vowed to continue. "We can't just sit back, we've got to go to *them*," he said. "You'll find some who know you coming, and they'll find themselves to be gone when you get there. And then there are some who will come out and join up with you. You just have to take the bitter with the sweet and keep going."

The cease-fire agreement, which extended directly from the objectives of the rally, was shared in this manner. Parishioners circulated throughout the park, and later in the community, with clipboards, copies, and pens so that people could sign their names. Not only did this force residents into close and immediate conversation, it forced them also to take a stand through a commitment to care and a promise to value and protect human life. The statement read,

Whereas the life of every African American, as well as every other human being, is the product of Divine creation, and whereas the life of every African American has been divinely instilled with purpose and potential, and whereas every African American life is worth more than the sum total of any and all material possessions, and whereas the value of the life of an African American is never diminished because of his/her economic standing, educational status, social state; nor because of his past, present, or future faults or failings, and whereas the invaluable life of an African American taken by violence can never be replaced, and whereas the taking of the life of an African American affects not only the individual whose life is taken, but also the lives of that individual's parents, siblings, children and other family members, and whereas the taking of the life of an African American is an offense against the African American community as well as the entire human race, I do hereby pledge this day that I will never commit the heinous act of murdering another human being.

Going forth into the world for justice and peace has long been a fundamental orientation for the Black Church. Its historical origins are most productively traced to the late nineteenth and early twentieth centuries, when Reconstruction and the rise of Jim Crow came with the sobering realization that a new abolition was required for the survival and advancement of African Americans. A Black social Christianity and the resulting "black social gospel," were thus formed. As Gary Dorrien (2015, 3–4) writes, the black social gospel was more of a movement than a doctrine, based on "a social ethical understanding of the Christian faith. It taught that Christianity has a mission to transform the structures of society in the direction of social justice." While the salvation of individual seekers remained a central objective within many Christian faiths, it was clear, then and now, that society itself was in need of redemption.

The black social gospel, however, is understudied, its contribution and influence "wrongly and strangely overlooked" (Dorrien 2015, 1).[8] This is certainly true in comparison to the white social gospel, whose emergence in the Progressive Era and subsequent aims are well chronicled (2). The black social gospel arose during roughly the same period; however, it was distinct for the connection it maintained to the realities of racial oppression. It supplied, for example "church leaders, intellectuals, and activists to the civil rights movement, advocate[ed] protest activism within reluctant communities and help[ed] to create an alternative public sphere of excluded voices" (2). As Dorrien writes,

The black social gospel affirmed the dignity, sacred personhood, creativity, and moral agency of African Americans and responded to racial oppression. It asked what a new abolitionism should be and what role the churches should play within it. Like the white social gospel, it had numerous ideologies and theologies, but here the trump concern was distinctly given, obvious, and a survival issue: upholding black dignity in the face of racial tyranny. (2)

Dorrien identifies four major moments in the development of the black social gospel from the 1890s forward (2015, 5–7; 2018, 3). The trajectory that I follow here focuses on the third and fourth moments and attempts to connect Black social Christianity, the emergence of the black social gospel and its influence on the civil rights movement, and the development and continuation of progressive religious thought and activism in New Orleans. A key point along this trajectory is the Niagara Movement, which was cofounded in 1905 by W. E. B. Du Bois and William Monroe Trotter. Its members radicalized the black social gospel, calling for "a new abolitionist politics of racial and social justice" (Dorrien 2015, 6), one that went against a more accommodating and conciliatory approach represented at the time by Booker T. Washington. Forcefully demanding equal rights, the Niagara Movement was an important precursor to the National Association for the Advancement of Colored People (NAACP), founded in 1909.

An admittedly selective thread then extends from the Niagara Movement and the NAACP (involving Reverdy C. Ransom, Ida B. Wells-Barnett, Richard R. Wright Jr., and others) to those who saw the development of the black social gospel as requiring both militancy and realism (Nannie H. Burroughs, Adam Clayton Powell Sr., and others) to the religious intellectuals and luminaries who took up the call for "a second great movement of abolition" (Dorrien 2015, 8; especially Mordecai Johnson, Benjamin E. Mays, and Howard Thurman) to the influence they had on Martin Luther King Jr. and the civil rights movement of the 1950s and 1960s. I consider further the influence that King had on Black religious activism in New Orleans, especially with the 1957 founding of the Southern Christian Leadership Conference and its incorporation in New Orleans.[9] The full-fledged black social gospel, as Dorrien (2015, 3) defines it, "combined an emphasis on black dignity and personhood with protest activism for racial justice, a comprehensive social justice agenda, an insistence that authentic Christian faith is incompatible with racial prejudice, an emphasis on the social ethical teaching of Jesus, and an acceptance of modern scholarship and social consciousness."

Uptown Congregations

Beginning in the mid-1800s, Blacks in New Orleans began to organize their own churches separate from the white churches, both Catholic and Protestant, at which they had been granted limited membership. It is important to understand why this organization took place. Black people here were motivated by the same concerns as those across the nation—the denial of their full participation in white religious institutions and their continued realization that only humanistic religious frameworks would support the salvation of an enslaved but about to be free Black population. The larger social and political context was grim, marked by "the collapse of the Reconstruction experiment in 1877, the return of Louisiana to Democratic rule, the rapid resegregation of public schools, the disfranchisement of Black men, the enactment of Jim Crow laws, and the economic depression of 1894," all of which "ushered in a decade of incorrigible and violent conflict between whites and blacks that changed the religious landscape of the city" (Frey 2012, 230).

It is also important to specify where this organization took place, co-inciding as it did with the clustered settlement of Black residents at the dawn of the twentieth century in Uptown but still back-of-town neighbor-hoods (Spain 1979, 93). As historian Sylvia Frey (2012, 231) writes, many of the Black Protestant churches were established "upriver from Canal Street where Americans and the recent immigrant population tended to cluster, thus pressing forward the pattern of forming religious life around ethnic groups, particularly those defined by language."[10] Central City was one such enclave, and the Black churches that were established there were primarily Baptist, Congregationalist, and Methodist.

In 1826, for example, a Black minister by the name of Asa C. Golds-bery organized the First African Baptist Church of New Orleans (Hicks [1914] 1998, 50–51). The church was located on Burgundy Street (near the French Quarter) but it later moved Uptown—first to the corner of Howard and Cypress Street and then to Third Street in Central City (51). By 1867 it was home to approximately five thousand members (Frey 2012, 231). At the state level, in 1865, Black Baptists organized the Loui-siana Southern Baptist Association. Some members, taking issue with the name "Southern Baptist," withdrew from this organization to form the First Free Mission Association (Hicks [1914] 1998, 54). In 1872, these associations and others came together to organize a state convention focused on unification and the adoption of guiding principles for belief, worship, and evangelism. The new structure supported an exponential growth in church membership. As Jacobs and Kaslow (1991, 27) note, by 1883, "Black Baptists claimed some 500 churches, over 70,000 members, and 650 ministers in Louisiana." According to Hicks ([1914] 1998, 55–56), by 1902 there were 125,000 members, 1,200 churches, eleven academies, and one institution of higher education—Leland University.

Attempts at national organization began not in the South but in regions of the North and the West. The American Baptist Missionary Convention, organized in 1840 in New York City, focused on evangelization, education, and racial uplift in New England and the Middle Atlantic states. The Western Colored Baptist Association formed in 1844 out of associations begun in Ohio and Illinois and with a strong focus on abolitionist work. It developed into a "regional grouping known as the Northwestern and Southern Baptist Convention, with representatives from eight states" (Lincoln and Mamiya [1990] 2003, 26–28). Efforts at national consolidation followed, beginning in 1866 with the establishment of the Consolidated American Baptist Missionary Convention and continuing with three organizations: the Baptist Foreign Mission Convention founded in 1880 in Montgomery; the American National Baptist Convention founded in 1886 in St. Louis; and the National Baptist Educational Convention of the U.S.A., formed in 1893 in Washington, DC. These bodies converged in 1895 to form the National Baptist Convention, USA (Pius 1911, 69–70; Fitts 1985, 73–79; Lincoln and Mamiya [1990] 2003, 26–28).

Despite this organization, and as Bennett (2005, 96) argues, "African Americans were far from united on the best approach for advancing racial interests, not only across different denominations but even within the same traditions." A case in point was the National Baptist Convention, USA, which suffered from internal conflict and schism in 1915 because of a controversy over the ownership and operation of the National Baptist Publishing Board. One group rallied around Reverend Roland H. Boyd, who was instrumental in building the publishing board on the basis of his own financial credit and land holdings. This group supported the continued independence of the board and rejected a proposed charter that would give the convention greater control. Boyd and his followers thus withdrew from the National Baptist Convention, USA, and formed the National Baptist Convention of America (NBCA), which was later incorporated in 1987. The NBCA kept the publishing board at the center of its activities while also focusing on domestic social work and foreign service, particularly in developing countries (Glazier 2001, 209).[11]

Within this history, the influence of the black social gospel is clear, especially in the establishment and growth of black churches in New Orleans's Uptown/back-of-town neighborhoods. To better trace this influence, however, a long view of religious activism and social justice work is required, one that situates key approaches and time periods as distinct phases within the broader Black freedom movement. For example, Dorrien (2015, 1) argues for a historical tracing of the civil rights movement that begins in 1884 "with a call for what became the National Afro-American League in 1890," developing through the Niagara Movement of 1905 and the founding of the NAACP in 1909, before "exploding into a historic mass movement" beginning in the mid-1950s. This tracing could arguably begin much earlier with the assertions of humanity and freedom found in the African and Afro-Baptist sacred cosmos during the earliest days of enslavement and resistance in the Americas.

Regardless of which moments are identified, this expanded view confirms the centrality of religion. David Chappell (2004, 97), for example, likens the civil rights movement of the 1950s and 1960s to an old-time revival, one that becomes distinctly oriented toward justice in the form of a battle waged in the here, now, and the hereafter. As Chappell states,

It may be misleading to view the civil rights movement as a social and political event that had religious overtones. The words of many participants suggest that it was, for them, primarily a religious event, whose social and political aspects were, in their minds, secondary or incidental. To take the testimony of intense religious transformation seriously is to consider the civil rights movement as part of the historical tradition of religious revivals, such as the so-called First and Second Great Awakenings, as much as it is part of the tradition of protest movements such as abolitionism, populism, feminism, and the labor movement. (87)

According to Chappell, therefore, one important reason that the civil rights movement succeeded was because "Black southern activists got strength from old-time religion," and they put it to use to "inspire solidarity and self-sacrificial devotion to their cause" (8). Affirming religion as a driving force also supports Dorrien's project to recover the black social gospel and its influence. As Dorrien (2015, 10) argues, "'Religion' goes hand in hand, in the case of the civil rights movement, with local communities, activist organizing, and public intellectual discourse."

Religious activists in Central City organized in response to a range of worsening conditions. While the development and growth of Uptown/ back-of-town neighborhoods in some ways supported the upward mobility of Black residents, it ultimately intensified their vulnerability, with rates of poverty, disease, and mortality for Blacks among the highest in the nation (Jacobs and Kaslow 1991, 33). For Black clergy and others, these were moral issues, ones that required an equally decided moral response. Accordingly, in 1941, an activist and social worker by the name of Ernest J. Wright founded the People's Defense League, partnering in 1943 with the Reverend Abraham Lincoln (A. L.) Davis, pastor of New Zion Baptist Church in New Orleans and founder and president of the Interdenominational Ministerial Alliance (Fairclough [1995] 2008, 211). Together they formed the Louisiana Association for the Progress of Negro Citizens (55). These groups worked on several critical issues facing African Americans (who by 1950 made up roughly a third of the city's population), including police brutality, discrimination, organized labor, and the right to vote.[12]

In *Righteous Lives: Narratives of the New Orleans Civil Rights Movement* (1993), Kim Lacy Rogers traces Black activism in New Orleans by identifying three primary generations: the "integrationists" mobilizing in the wake of the *Brown v. Board of Education* decision (1954–1959), the well-aligned middle-class professionals of the "political generation" (1960–1964), and the students and working-class men and women who made up the "protest generation" (1960–1965). In the first generation, Reverend A. L. Davis joined with other activists to fight against the campaign of Massive Resistance, which was set against the desegregation of schools and other institutions. This work was linked to the objectives of the broader civil rights movement emerging across the nation and led by Black ministers in the South (Rogers 1993, 46; Morris 1984, 82–83).

In January 1957, on the heels of the Montgomery Bus Boycott, Martin Luther King Jr. and several other prominent civil rights leaders convened the Southern Leaders Conference on Transportation and Non-Violent Integration at the Ebenezer Baptist Church in Atlanta, Georgia. Their objective was to coordinate a nonviolent campaign to desegregate buses throughout the South. The "Statement to the South and Nation," issued at that meeting, was a powerful call to action, yet it demonstrated also the extent to which the central tenets of the black social gospel—dignity, sacred personhood, moral agency—remained salient in the ongoing struggle for freedom:

In dedication to this task, we call upon all Negroes in the South and in the nation *to assert their human dignity*. We ask them *to seek justice and reject all injustice*, especially that in themselves. We pray that they will *refuse further cooperation with the evil element which invites them to collude against themselves in return for bits of patronage*. We know that such an assertion may cause them persecution; yet *no matter how great the obstacles and suffering, we urge all Negroes to reject segregation*.

But far beyond this, *we call upon them to accept Christian Love in full knowledge of its power to defy evil.* We call upon them to understand that *non-violence is not a symbol of weakness or cowardice,* but as Jesus demonstrated, *non-violent resistance transforms weakness into strength and heeds courage in face of danger.* We urge them, no matter how great the provocation, to dedicate themselves to this motto: "Not one hair of one head of one white person shall be harmed." (Emphasis in original)[13]

The resonance of the black social gospel at this moment is no accident. The search for a new abolition had extended from the Niagara Movement to an influential second generation of religious intellectuals who were well positioned at Black colleges and universities. Several ordained Baptist clergymen were prominent members of this group, including Mordecai W. Johnson, president of Howard University; Benjamin E. Mays, president of Morehouse College; Howard Thurman, professor at Howard University; and George D. Kelsey, professor at Morehouse College (Dickerson 2005, 219). They shared their theological and other views in a wide variety of national and international settings, including meetings, lectures, sermons, speeches, and published works. This teaching would greatly influence the public theology fashioned by King, whose close mentors included Mays at Morehouse College. King "epitomized the black social gospel at its best and most radical" (Dorrien 2017, 21), emphasizing the sacredness of human personality; the evil of racism and the sinfulness of segregation; the emphasis on nonviolent acts of resistance grounded in absolute love, even for the enemy; the idea that "freedom has no reality apart from power and that power is integral to hope and liberation"; and the development of "the lack of power of black Americans into creative, vital, interpersonal, organized power" as the crafting of a beloved community proceeded (Dorrien 2017, 21; see also Dickerson 2005, 218).

One month after the Southern Leaders Conference on Transportation and Non-Violent Integration in Atlanta, an important follow-up meeting was held in New Orleans. Reverend Davis served as host, welcoming King and other civil rights leaders to New Zion Baptist Church in Central City, where Davis continued to serve as pastor. There, on February 14, 1957, the Southern Christian Leadership Conference (SCLC) was formerly incorporated (Fairclough [1995] 2008, 211). This meeting further galvanized Black ministers and community leaders in New Orleans, who could assert their city as a key site in a now widespread movement as they continued to fight for equality and social justice on both the local and national stage.[14]

For example, members of the Consumers' League of Greater New Orleans, founded in 1959, boycotted stores along Dryades Street in Central

City to protest employment discrimination and low wages (Rogers 1993, 67). Their work inspired the formation of the Coordinating Council of Greater New Orleans (CCGNO), a federation of Black organizations that focused on voter registration and voting rights violations (67). Other activists representing a young and increasingly well-educated cohort of Black men and women founded local chapters of national civil rights organizations, including the Congress of Racial Equality (CORE) and the Student Non-Violent Coordinating Committee (SNCC). They addressed a similar range of issues, from voting rights to housing and employment discrimination. They also lobbied for municipal and federal funding to repair neighborhood infrastructure and to support Black businesses, economic development, and Black political leadership (Fairclough [1995] 2008, 263; Rogers 1993, 76). Collectively, these efforts led to greater political representation, for example, with the 1975 appointment of Reverend Davis to the New Orleans City Council and the 1978 election of Ernest Nathan ("Dutch") Morial as the city's first African American mayor. Perhaps more importantly, they reflected an internal shift, a "spiritual and internal change that developed within people—[about] how Black people came to see themselves," as expressed by civil rights activist Oretha Castle Haley (cited in Rogers 1993, 142–43).

The assassination of King in 1968 was devastating for Black residents in New Orleans as it was for the nation and world. Activists in Central City were determined to honor King's life and legacy, and they did so in ways that also claimed and inscribed the landscape—identifying, inhabiting, and then linking the sites that would preserve the ideals of the movement while paving the way forward for the work to come. In 1973, members of the Consumers' League and the Central City Economic Opportunity Corporation (CCEOC) acquired funds for neighborhood improvements, proposing that one major street, Melpomene Street, be renamed Martin Luther King Jr. Boulevard (Devalcourt 2011, 34). After three years of neighborhood impact studies and extensive lobbying, the city council passed the resolution, but only for the portion of the street that ran through the predominantly African American part of Central City (from Baronne Street to the lake side of South Claiborne) (36).

Encouraged nonetheless, activists commissioned a sculpture in honor of King, which was installed on the neutral ground of the named boulevard, part of a "Freedom Walk" complete with historic markers and benches. The public was generally unhappy with the result—an abstract symbol of unity by artist Frank Hayden, which was a far cry from the literal representation of King they had been expecting. A second sculpture was added later, in 1981, at the opposite end of the boulevard and at the intersection of South Claiborne Avenue. The thirteen-foot sculpture installed there features a bronze bust of King atop a granite pedestal. The base is inscribed with the dates of King's birth and death and the quote "I Have a Dream." The memorial also honors "others who gave their lives for freedom and equality" and lists the names of prominent Black leaders including Medgar Evers and Malcolm X.

This claiming and inscribing of the urban landscape was a key and visible change, but it stemmed from the more personal determinations of identity, value, and capacity of which activists such as Oretha Castle Haley spoke. It thus shifted the internal and external boundaries of the "Black spatial imaginary" (Lipsitz 2011, 13) through a variety of strategies "to turn segregation into congregation, to transform divisiveness into solidarity, to change dehumanization into rehumanization" (19). Not only did the creation of MLK Boulevard, the Freedom Walk, and the King memorial identify the specific sites of this congregation, the routes that residents established between these places defined and broadened the space for this congregation to exist and grow. This happened through everyday movement, action, and interaction, be it a bus trip downtown, a jazz funeral, or a protest march between Central City and Congo Square. In this way, the past, present, and future of Black urban life was slowly etched in the landscape, countering ongoing processes of erasure, and religious activism worked to free the people as it also defined the parameters for the community and city they sought to transform.

Somebodiness

It was thus along familiar routes that the people arrived in Armstrong Park, decades later, for the Yes We Care! rally. They knew the history of the land on which they stood, and they knew that they would not be standing there were it not for the work of those who had come before them. Their gathering remained connected, therefore, to the congregations that shaped Black New Orleans—at Congo Square, at city hall, at the King memorial in Central City, and other places. However, they also understood the continuation of oppression, and they remained vulnerable to violence in a city that was still not vested in their safety and well-being. Thus, guided by faith and a vision for change still necessary in the current moment, they worked to transform themselves, their families and communities, and the city before them. This was why Pastor Samuel had so urgently called them together on the battlefield for the Lord. Despite the circumstances, he remained confident, declaring "by the grace of God there is nothing we can't do when we come together!"

To articulate the next step, the place or state of being where this congregation might lead, Pastor Samuel reached back as he looked forward—with deep gratitude for the frameworks he had inherited and with certainty of their continued relevance in these and future times. The emphasis he placed on "they" and "somebody," for example, seemed a direct extension of Martin Luther King Jr.'s concept of "somebodiness," which implored a sense of value and dignity unquestionably realized for a Black person and human being. As King stated in a 1959 address at the Southern Christian Ministers Conference of Mississippi,

We must maintain a sense of somebodiness and self-respect. One of the great tragedies of the system of segregation is that it so often robs its victims of a sense of dignity and worth. It tends to develop a false sense of inferiority in the segregated. But despite the existence of a system that denies our essential worth, we must have the spiritual audacity to assert our somebodiness. (D. R. Smith 2014, 232)

This sense of self-worth, as fundamental as it was, was only part of King's objective. What King desired, and what Pastor Samuel seemed to continue, was the creation of a beloved community, "a transformed and regenerated human society" (Smith and Zepp [1974] 1998, 130) that would sustain life in the here and now and ever after. As theologian James Cone (1999, 64) argues, "King's goal was not simply the elimination of racism, poverty, and war, but rather the establishment of an integrated community of persons of all races, working together toward the building of the kingdom that he called the 'beloved community.'"

King made the vision for this community clear in an even earlier statement, a 1956 address titled "Facing the Challenge of a New Age," delivered at the First Annual Institute on Nonviolent Social Change and just after the announcement of a US Supreme Court decision on the desegregation of buses in Montgomery, Alabama. Speaking beyond the current circumstances, King declared that the boycott and subsequent ruling were not the end; rather,

the end is reconciliation; the end is redemption; the end is the creation of the beloved community. It is this type of spirit and this type of love that can transform opponents into friends. It is this type of understanding goodwill that will transform the deep gloom of the old age into the exuberant gladness of the new age. It is this love which will bring about miracles in the hearts of men.[15]

Such belief was shortly thereafter established as an official objective of the SCLC. Writing in the SCLC newsletter just after the organization's founding, King stated that the aim and purpose of the organization was "to foster and create the 'beloved community' in America where brotherhood is a reality. . . . SCLC works for integration. Our ultimate goal is genuine intergroup and interpersonal living—*integration*" (Smith and Zepp [1974] 1998, 130). This emphasis on *integration* rather than desegregation, was a significant aspect of the community King sought. Yet it was understood as the most difficult to realize because it depended not on laws but on "a change in attitudes, the loving acceptance of individuals and groups" (131). Such a change required in turn the recognition of the interrelated and interdependent nature of the human family and a commitment to "personal and social relationships that are created by love" (131).[16]

The clergy and parishioners in Armstrong Park embraced this theology and intention. In the space of death, they longed for a beloved community that according to their beliefs could only come through redemption and reconciliation. It required a nonviolent and relational existence, founded on the assertion of Black humanity, that would ultimately, as King (1956) had proclaimed, "transform the deep gloom of the old age into the exuberant gladness of the new age." The deep longing for this new age was palpable. One elder member of Liberty Street, for example, described his view of the violence that still plagued the community. He mourned for the dead, but he was most disheartened by the lack of concern he increasingly witnessed. "Oh, it have changed," he replied sadly, shaking his head. "It have changed."

It have changed from neighbors being neighbors. It have changed from helping people. It used to be that if you see your neighbor was in need you would go to their rescue. And if you were in need, you could go to them. But now if they see you in need they will just talk about you. I believe it's the lack of the Word. They don't want to go to church. And they want to take a gun . . . eye for an eye! Yes, it have changed.

His sentiments were echoed in the speeches that came from the podium as the rally continued, now well into the afternoon. Among the many city officials who took the stage was Mayor Nagin, who called for unity grounded in Black love. Nagin had recently returned from Washington, DC, as had Pastor Samuel, where they had attended Obama's inauguration. He was clearly inspired and used his time before the home crowd to reflect on the moment, the state of the city, and the foundation for recovery he believed was necessary. "Something is missing, ladies and gentlemen," he began.

What's missing in my opinion is black love. Where is black love in New Orleans? Where is the kind of love that you want to stand up with your brothers and sisters regardless of what's going on? Where is black love where you will not hurt your brother and your sister? That's what we need to come back to!

While such comments were rousing, they were also difficult to digest, as they placed both the need and the responsibility for love squarely on the shoulders of the Black community. This might be easily construed as a confirmation that indeed violence was solely a Black problem, caused by Black people and up to them to solve. Yet the religious leaders of this movement remained aware of the structural forces by which violence was also produced, and they did not suggest that those forces were no longer at work, or that resistance against them was no longer necessary. Rather, they believed that a broader change was required based on a love that would transform one's enemy into one's brother or sister and that this transformation had to occur both within and outside of the Black community. Only then could a beloved community based on an interrelatedness that extended across all races, classes, ethnic groups, nations, and religions emerge (Smith and Zepp [1974] 1998, 137). Indeed, as Vincent Harding writes in the introduction to King's book, *Where Do We Go from Here: Chaos or Community?* ([1967] 2010), such a project will only succeed if it is a shared exercise, part of "the recognizable queries that mature human beings persistently pose to themselves—and to their communities—as they explore the way toward their best possibilities" (x). The beloved community is not limited in scale or membership— thus the diverse peoples, communities, and nations of the world were equally called, as King stated on behalf of all creative dissenters, "to a higher destiny, to a new plateau of compassion, to a more noble expression of humaneness" (142).

African American Religious Ideals

As the Yes We Care! rally came to a close, participants retraced their steps along the walkways that skirted the lagoons, finding their way out of Armstrong Park and on to other places. They were tired but full of purpose, their backs warmed by the late afternoon sun. Several days later, I spoke with a few church members from Liberty Street about the event and how successful, in their eyes, it had been. One woman recalled, "There was such a feeling of love between different races and people of all faiths.

We need times like that, where we show our unity. It's an absolute necessity, and for us it was a new beginning, about a new movement that will connect us with other peace movements." She paused, however, as she acknowledged the magnitude of the problem and the difficulty of the task ahead:

But on Sunday, the very next day, there was a shooting right in our neighborhood. So, we all came in that Monday and had a prayer circle at the crime site. So, we know we have our work cut out for us. I mean we can talk and give good speeches but ultimately, we have to show our unity in action. And so, we are going about it. We didn't think it was going to happen so quickly and right in our neighborhood, given all the work we did on the cease-fire, but we are dealing with it. And it's still so refreshing to see so many people coming together, those who have the courage to take that first step.

The journey toward peace by faith thus continued. The rally had brought "they" and "somebody" together, and a great vision for change had been shared, but everyone recognized that the work was far from over. The people would stay on the battlefield for the Lord, continuing to anchor religious formation in the gift of salvation and doing their best to hear and share the Word of God. Each person would strive to recognize his or her true essence, as a valued child of God, understanding that their souls were set free despite the conditions of the world to which they might otherwise be subjected. Individually and collectively, they would rally against evil and sin, motivated by a vision of a world where human worth was nonnegotiable, inherent in one's divine creation, and where people were bound together—a relatedness whose cultivation was grounded in love, care, and the commitment to nonviolence. None of this would be easy—the battlefield was a dangerous place, as the killing shortly after the rally confirmed, and the battle itself was a long Christian walk through many trials and tribulations.

These histories shed light on the direction of religious and social movement in the Crescent City—certainly in New Orleans but more broadly in an urban context that is always in the making and thus open, necessarily, to new ways of being. Carol Wayne White, in her book *Black Lives and Humanity: Toward an African American Religious Naturalism* (2016), poses several important questions, to "consider anew the evolving nature of African American religiosity and its import in the contemporary era." "What might constitute a new African American religious ideal in the twenty-first century?" she asks. "How might one see it emerging from past convictions?" In response, White proposes a sacred and interconnected conceptualization of humanity, a "radical human-ism with religious sensibilities," based on the premise that humans are "interconnected, social, value-laden organisms in constant search of meaning (cognition), enamored of value (beauty, goodness, love), and instilled with a sense of purpose (telos)" (White 2016, 2–3).

White draws from a rich legacy of African American religious and intellectual thought in the development of this ideal, finding its ideas foreshadowed in the writings of Anna Julia Cooper, W. E. B. Du Bois, and James Baldwin. It is an ideal that for White is also furthered by the advancement of science, which confirms with increasing relevance the social and deeply relational nature of existence for humans and other organisms—thus fueling, in both abstract and concrete ways, an exami-nation of what it means to be fully alive. These are profound ideas to explore in contemporary contexts of vulnerability, where social death and physical death are intertwined. Indeed, White argues that the in-evitability of death is what best informs a notion of sacred humanity, where the affirmation of death "becomes the proper point of departure for appreciating the value and meaningfulness of human life" (White 2016, 3, 39).

The African American religious practitioners I encountered in New Or-leans were similarly motivated. The beloved community they envisioned depended in fact on what White describes as an "essential connectivity—with oneself, one's family, the larger human community, myriad local and global ecosystems, and yes, the universe." As White continues, "Reli-giously, this implies love, and love implies concern for the well-being of the beloved" (White 2016, 35). While White's idea of religious naturalism differs from the more familiar and otherworldly terms of African American religious belief, it is through relatedness and love that common ground might be found.

FOUR

THOU SHALT <u>NOT</u> KILL: Commanding Peace in Particular Places

There was this black guy, I could see him coming almost all the way from Simon Bolivar. He walked right down the middle of that neutral ground, all the
way down to Claiborne, came right up to me, looked me dead in the eye,
and said, "This is the safest I have ever felt in my life." I'll never forget that!
PASTOR SAMUEL

"I'll tell you how it all got started," Pastor Samuel was saying. "You see, my goal was reaching people. So I came up
with the idea of putting up these signs around town that
would allow everybody to realize that what is going on as far
as the violence in this city is wrong. And I wanted to make
a statement that first of all it is God who says it is wrong."
He looked up at the display of photographs hanging on the
wall to find one that would illustrate. "So we had a large
billboard made with the words "THOU SHALT <u>NOT</u> KILL,"
and we put that up on Martin Luther King Boulevard, right
at the intersection of Claiborne. . . . We made thousands of
smaller signs, too . . . Here, they looked like this," he said,
taking down a photograph and handing it to me, pointing
out one of the smaller signs tacked to a telephone pole and
congregation members gathered in prayer. It was a distinct
form of religious education, a very visible campaign that
was only part of a broader ministry to bring about an end to
violence by transforming the minds and hearts of residents
within and outside of the Black community.

I was sitting with the pastor in his office at Liberty Street. Arriving in the early afternoon, I had come in the back door of the main church building, stepping around the tail end of the lunch line to reach the stairs leading up to his office. Free meals were served at the church on certain afternoons, and a small crowd, made up mostly of elderly African American men, still lingered at the entrance. They smiled and nodded their hellos. A few younger Latino men greeted me also—most were relative newcomers to a recovering community who relied on Liberty Street for a meal and a place to pray during a long and uncertain workday.

Pastor Samuel had generously carved out time in his schedule to answer my questions, particularly about the church's history and mission and the antiviolence ministries and programs that had been developed since the late 1980s, when his tenure as pastor began. Stepping into his office, I felt as if I had entered a small museum: the wood-paneled walls were nearly covered with photographs, awards, and posters—the most recent addition being a framed poster from Barack Obama's presidential campaign, which was prominently displayed on a side wall with images of other important historical figures. More than a display of the people who inspired the pastor, it was a visual narration of his own religious activism over the years. He featured prominently in many group photos, and his name appeared front and center on awards, certificates, and other records of accomplishment.

Toward a Beloved Community

In this chapter I examine the span of religious work at Liberty Street, focusing on the ministries that Pastor Samuel developed as spiritual leader of the church from 1988 until his untimely death from illness in 2013. This examination sheds light on the work of an African American Baptist church whose members responded to the conditions of Black urban life in the late twentieth and early twenty-first centuries. However, it also traces the emergence of an African American religious ideal, one that extended from the legacy of the black social gospel while it advanced, simultaneously, the frameworks and practices of a sacred and sustainable Black future. As I argue in chapter 3, this religious ideal had several important dimensions. It recognized the value of each person as a child of God, centering salvation, adherence to the Word of God, and the continued battle against evil, moral depravity, and sin as essential organizing principles for a life in Christ. It called people together, understanding congregation as a necessary condition for religious work on the battlefield for the Lord. In doing so it cultivated relatedness, supported by practices of love and care for self and others. The ultimate goal, however, was the creation of a beloved community inspired by the black social gospel but realized through the embodied claiming and reconfiguration of the urban landscape.

Three primary ministries anchored this work. In the THOU SHALT <u>NOT</u> KILL ministry, developed in the mid-1990s, clergy and parishioners worked to educate the community about the religious and moral incorrectness of violence. A decade later, in the wake of Hurricane Katrina, the focus of religious work shifted slightly to address more directly questions of humanity and to assert the value of Black lives in an overlapped context of disaster, displacement, and exclusion. Two ministries that developed after the storm reflect this shift: The ENOUGH ministry brought people from multiple religious groups together in a coalition-based response to violent conditions via public demonstrations, walks, vigils, prayer groups, and other activities. The Yes We Care! ministry, launched in the spring of 2009 and inspired by Barack Obama's Yes We Can! campaign slogan, marked a critical moment—a time of recovery stalled by the continuation of violence after the storm yet inspired by the possibilities of national Black leadership. While I feature the Yes We Care! rally in chapter 3, here I examine the ministries that led to its launch, giving context to the movement it proclaimed.

A Call to Preach

Pastor Samuel's call to the pulpit came in the late 1980s. At the time he was already a dedicated public servant, employed as a New Orleans police officer since 1973. This initial career choice was not unexpected; Pastor Samuel had followed in his father's footsteps, one of the first African American police officers in New Orleans. His grandfather, however, had been a pastor, and he played a subtle but ultimately more significant role in Pastor Samuel's own turn to religious service. Pastor Samuel recalled a specific exchange that illustrated this influence, which occurred early on in his police career.

I was in the police department. For fifteen years. I went on in 1973 and started the academy. And in 1976 a strange thing happened. My grandfather was a pastor, and he was also the president of one of the local seminaries. And one day I was working—I was on duty and I passed by his house. And he was at the kitchen table drinking a cup of coffee. And out of nowhere I said, "You know, I'm thinking about going into the seminary."

He said, "You need to call and talk to the secretary and find out when registration is." And I left and I never thought about it again, until after I was a pastor. I don't know why that happened.

While Pastor Samuel did not anticipate the call to preach, it undoubtedly extended from his upbringing in the Black Baptist community. He attended church in Central City with his grandparents and father, his mother having passed away when he was young. He was drawn in particular by the music, and he sang in the choir. Then years later, while working as a police officer on a local parade route, he met a woman and fellow police officer who invited him to visit her own church (Liberty Street). Accepting the invitation and arriving late one Sunday morning, he took the only seat left, way in the back. He quickly became transfixed, and the spiritual awakening that ensued fueled his career change, seminary training, marriage (to the woman whose invitation to church he had accepted), and eventual church leadership.

From that Sunday, I knew this was where I was supposed to be. . . . I mean I had been in church all my life, and he [the pastor] wasn't preaching any Scriptures different from the ones I'd been reading all my life. But I could *hear* it. The Lord just gave me the capacity to receive that which he had been putting in front of me all my life. But it was more than that. I committed myself to this church that Sunday. . . . [And] after a while I let him [the pastor] know that I believed I had been called to preach.

Under Pastor Samuel's leadership, the size of Liberty Street's congregation grew to some 1,500 members. He continued many of the church's existing ministries and he launched several new initiatives that addressed the changing needs of parishioners and residents in the surrounding community. The list was long and included Vision 2000, a vision that would lead two thousand souls to Christ by the year 2000; Project Love, which fed the hungry; The Lion Tamers, which aided and counseled substance abusers; and homework assistance, summer enrichment, and scholarship programs for youth. These ministries were supported by fundraising as well as investments, namely revenue from real estate holdings including the church structure itself and a newly renovated community development building across the street.

Beginning in the early 1990s, urban violence became an urgent concern. The rate and incidence of homicide in Central City, indeed across New Orleans, was dramatically increasing, primarily because of the cumulative impact of poverty, a corresponding rise in drug trafficking and associated gun violence, and corruption in law enforcement. Church members at Liberty Street were directly affected. As one of the assistant pastors described, "We've had members to get killed with violence in the street, members to get shot up, stuff like that, so we have mothers and brothers and really a lot of our church members who have family members who have fallen victim to the streets." Pastor Samuel agreed, describing the context of violence that surrounded the church by recalling an incident that took place in the mid-1990s. "Matter of fact it was so bad it was like Satan was just upset," he said.

Right outside this church, right outside that back fence, somebody got shot nine times, a young man. One of the deacons called me, I just got home that night. He said "Samuel, I got some bad news. Somebody just got killed outside the back gate." It drained me. I got in my car and drove back over here, and some of the detectives were still out there. And the body was gone and the detective said, "We're not sure if he's going to live." I said, "Not sure if he's going to live?" And they said, "No, he's still alive."

Acknowledging the space of death and transformation as well as the ministry of the church and its impact, he added, "About a month later that guy walked down the aisle and joined this church."

The pastor was careful, however, to situate current ministries at Liberty Street within the long legacy of religious antiviolence and social justice work in New Orleans. As he explained, "When I became pastor the church was already outreach minded and doing a lot of work on the streets, so I just tried to continue and build upon that which had already been established." Even so, his work seemed inspired by a new vision that saw the end to violence as being dependent on a deeper social and moral awakening. The ministries he subsequently developed, therefore, had this awareness in mind, and they relied on a range of strategies to both recover and save the congregation and broader community.

THOU SHALT NOT KILL

In the history of urban violence in New Orleans, the deadliest year on record is 1994, when 424 people were murdered—most of them young, poor, Black men. This gave the city the highest per capita murder rate in the nation. To Pastor Samuel, as well as to many others, this was a moral affront—evidence of Satan's work, as Pastor Samuel had described. The clergy and parishioners of Black churches thus paid close attention to each and every act of violence—mourning and burying the victims, claiming the displaced and the deceased, and doing what they could to conquer evil forces, within and outside of the Black community.

A critical breaking point came when the violence took the lives of neighborhood children in two separate and tragic killings. In May 1994, a nine-year-old boy was killed on Mother's Day, caught in the crossfire of a shooting as he sat with his family at a picnic in the park. A few months later another boy, four years old, was killed by a stray bullet as he sat on the front steps of his house. Within a community now reeling with sorrow and outrage, these deaths triggered a desperate plea for an end to the violence and a response that was organized by several religious and community leaders in Central City, where the children and many of the other victims had lived. In a show of unity and protest, Pastor Samuel joined with other Black clergy in a public funeral procession. They and thousands of concerned citizens walked the increasingly well-worn path that linked back-of-town neighborhoods, from Central City to Armstrong Park, where funeral services were held.

It was shortly after these events that Pastor Samuel rented the large commercial billboard at the intersection of Martin Luther King Jr. Boulevard and South Claiborne Avenue in the heart of Central City. The sign that went up read THOU SHALT <u>NOT</u> KILL. It was a simple but arresting message, rendered in dark capital letters set against a plain white background. There were no other words or images—not even the name of the church. The impact was heightened by the location. Not only was this one of the city's busiest corridors, the billboard looked over the memorial to Martin Luther King Jr., giving extra emphasis to the theology and practice of nonviolence that King's work still inspired.

The inspiration for this action came to Pastor Samuel during a local election. Bombarded by political advertising in the form of signs and posters for this candidate or that, it occurred to him to use the same tactic to fulfill his goal of "reaching people." As he explained,

I don't know which election it was. A local election. And I was living in New Orleans East, and I would drive up here to this church . . . [on the way] I was forced to see so many [campaign] signs that I really didn't want to see. But I just had to keep seeing them. So, I said, well I'm going to put a different sign up . . . People may not want to see it, but, like me, they're going to have to see it when they pass by. And many did.

It was clear, however, that the action was less about the sign and more about the message—not just to say that killing was wrong but to make a statement through the community that "it is *God* who says it is wrong." This was a form of religious and moral education—a commandment—and Pastor Samuel hoped it would have an impact at all levels of society, from adults to young children who were just learning about the world. As he continued,

You know the parents used to make children go to church. That's not happening. Many kids are not taught that, they're not going to be taught it in school. But every day all the kids who had to go past there [the billboard] on their way to school had to read that sign, whether they went to church or not.

The church maintained the billboard for three years, and the investment was great; the rental fee alone was almost $1,000 a month. This was a real test of faith for church administrators as well as parishioners who had to approve and support the project. As Pastor Samuel explained,

It was very difficult. It was a challenge to the faith of the church. Because there are many churches that will pay that kind of price for a sign if the name of the church is going to be up there, picture of the pastor and all that. But just to put a sign that says nothing about you and you're paying almost $1000 a month? That took a lot of faith.

One of the assistant pastors at Liberty Street agreed that faith was key to the success of the ministry. However, this faith was not solely about a trust that church members had in their pastor and his leadership. It was also, fundamentally, about the transformative power of the Word of God. As he explained,

You know, I was thinking that it was special first of all, like a lot of the things that Pastor [Samuel] does, that he had the idea for us to do that. And second of all that he had the faith of just using "THOU SHALT NOT KILL," the Word of God, he had the faith that that could actually change something, you know, to bring about a change in people's hearts and in the community ultimately.

This confidence in the power of God's Word was supported by the responses of residents who saw the sign. Pastor Samuel knew of many individuals who had been spiritually and morally moved, in some cases inspired to choose a nonviolent response in what might have otherwise been a violent altercation. As he described it, "We had people actually come to church and confess that they wanted to take somebody's life, but they kept seeing that sign and chose another way."

However, and despite its positive impact, the billboard eventually came down. This was not a decision that Pastor Samuel made; rather, the advertising agency abruptly canceled the contract, closed the church's account, and returned the sign to its corporate advertising origins. Pastor Samuel recalled how this had happened, triggered by a simple accounting mistake. One of the church officers, the person who took care of the bills every month, was late sending in the monthly payment. "We were late just one time," he explained. "And you know what? The company never said a word. I came to church one morning and I turned the corner and there was something else on that billboard. And everybody started calling me and asking me, 'Why did you take the sign down? Why did you take it down?'" I interrupted, "You mean the company didn't notify you or anything?" Pastor Samuel shook his head,

Oh no, they wanted to get out from under that! I truly believe that the company . . . never thought that I was going to keep the sign past a couple of months or something. And I think they wanted to get out from under that because they could be making a couple of thousand dollars. Some of the billboards in the city are four or five thousand dollars a month! I remember that before I got it, there was a liquor thing, Crown Royal, you know the big purple bag? And I know they pay big bucks. So, I'm sure that after three years, the company had to consider the financial benefits of getting us out of there and getting somebody [else] in.

I wondered out loud about other possible reasons for the termination of Liberty Street's lease, particularly given long-term efforts by city officials and others to promote a positive image of New Orleans. I asked Pastor Samuel whether he thought the billboard company had been under any kind of political pressure. "Oh, I'm sure they got inquiries," he cut in. "I know there were people that were upset about the sign being there, for business purposes and for the image of the city, because they didn't want to give the appearance that we had a problem."

Even though the billboard came down, the THOU SHALT <u>NOT</u> KILL ministry continued on a smaller scale but with expanded reach. Pastor Samuel printed thousands of placard-size signs in the same bold design— dark letters on a white background. Church members placed them up all over town, broadcasting the Word of God in what turned out to be a more accessible format. As one parishioner said, "We were nailing signs down everywhere, and giving so many away because people were saying, 'Well I want one to put in my neighborhood.'" Again, the financial cost to the church was significant, particularly as the signs became very popular. The return from the investment, however, was in the message the signs carried and the nonviolent action they directed. The great potential church members saw in this work, to save a city and its people, made the ministry a worthy project despite the cost.

Nonetheless, there were some who sought to capitalize on its popularity and success, to increase revenue for the church. As Pastor Samuel recalled,

I got a lot of responses from people who came up with all of these crazy ideas (and it's one of the things I always have to be careful of because people have a way of muddying your vision). And there was somebody who wanted to get some of the businesses together, and they wanted to help me put those signs all over the city. But they wanted corporate sponsors, and then put "Popeye's Fried Chicken says THOU SHALT <u>NOT</u> KILL!," "McDonalds says THOU SHALT <u>NOT</u> KILL!"

He finished, laughing and shaking his head at the absurdity of the idea, so contrary to the intent of the ministry, which saw profit not in individual or institutional gain but in the power of God's Word to heal and transform a wounded society.

Congregation members stepped up their own distribution, leaving signs with residents and business owners, nailing them up on boards and telephone poles, and staking them in the ground. Soon they were visible at almost every turn—that is until the city department of sanitation swept through and removed them all. It was a source of much frustration for the pastor: "I was going all the way down that neutral ground—Claiborne, Simon Bolivar, and then up Jackson along the street, putting those signs . . . maybe twenty in a block on each side. And the city came through and took every sign down, took every sign and threw them away—and they were *expensive* too! So, I said, I'll tell you what, *we'll* be the signs."

Thus began a series of weekly public demonstrations. The members of Liberty Street would gather outside, positioning themselves shoulder to shoulder to form a protective barrier around a particular part of the neighborhood. They stood for unity, reflecting the care and commitment they brought to their work, but they also stood for the Word of God, with each person holding a THOU SHALT <u>NOT</u> KILL sign, their bodies as signposts for a great, and now embodied, directive. Pastor Samuel explained the impact: "We've had times when we surrounded all the way from Claiborne to Simon Bolivar and MLK to Felicity . . . holding THOU SHALT <u>NOT</u> KILL signs. During the time we did that, each week . . . we didn't have one murder. Not one." The commitment to this action was impressive; congregation members returned at each session to place themselves on the front lines of their community, defining a physical and symbolic safe zone for themselves and their fellow citizens. One parishioner I spoke with remembered these gatherings as "a sight to behold." The impact was further exemplified by a memorable encounter that Pastor Samuel had on one of those evenings. "There was this black guy, I could see him coming almost all the way from Simon Bolivar," he started.

He walked right down the middle of that neutral ground, all the way down to Claiborne, came right up to me, looked me dead in the eye, and said, "This is the safest I have ever felt in my life." I'll never forget that! He said, "This is the safest I have ever felt, in . . . my . . . *life*." And every one of our members just stood there. They just stood there holding those signs, and it was just awesome.

The THOU SHALT <u>NOT</u> KILL ministry stands out not just for its impact but because it was the first ministry at Liberty Street under Pastor Samuel's leadership that understood religious and moral awakening, through the word of God, as fundamental to the solution of the problem of violence. As such, it marks the beginning of a movement that developed through a series of related ministries and programs, as an African American religious ideal was forged in the Crescent City. However, the ministry is also significant for the strategies and methods of awakening it introduced. One primary mode of action was the claiming and inscribing of the urban landscape through the placing of materials—including the body—on key sites. This facilitated not only the broadcasting of particular commandments but the building of solidarity by marking and then inhabiting the transformed city. The locations for this work were often historically relevant, or they became so—referencing the victories of human progress (the King memorial), the failures (the crime sites to which clergy and parishioners also processed), and the possibilities that new perimeters and safe zones made clear.

In this work, the physical body was a particularly powerful site of interaction. Specific ministries deployed the people themselves, who operated like lay preachers at urban pulpits, sometimes far beyond the boundaries of their own neighborhoods. As M. Shawn Copeland (2010, 2) argues, the body is "a site and mediation of divine revelation" that "shapes human existence as relational and social"; thus, "solidarity is a set of body practices." The parishioners who stood shoulder to shoulder holding THOU SHALT <u>NOT</u> KILL signs certainly understood this, as well as the man who walked down the middle of the street during one of their demonstrations proclaiming, "This is the safest I have ever felt in my life."

Such interaction is further understood through theories of place and placemaking. The mutual constitution of people and place is well established in phenomenological conceptualizations of human dwelling. In this view, places are not fixed and bounded locales; rather, a place is like an event—a convergence of humans, other organisms, and materials. Places thus emerge through the pathways, activities, and movements of everyday life (Casey 1996, 25; Ingold [2009] 2011, 148). Following from this conceptualization, placemaking is a type of "world-building" that is both retrospective and forward thinking, involving simultaneous and frequently site-specific acts of remembering and imagination (Basso 1996, 5). When such acts are grounded through a conceptualization of the sacred (Garbin 2012, 401), placemaking becomes an encompassing and deeply transformative process.

Additional research is required, however, to understand the role that religious placemaking plays in the world-building that occurs during and following periods of crisis or upheaval. In Central City, for example, clergy and parishioners situated themselves as part of the urban landscape itself—inseparable, not subject to removal, and essential to urban recovery, with the reconfigured landscape in turn essential to Black flourishing. Their specific acts of remembrance and imagination point out the important connection between placemaking and place *marking*—in this case through religious and moral inscription. Bruno David and Meredith Wilson, in their edited volume *Inscribed Landscapes: Marking and Making Place* (2002, 7), conceive of place markings "not simply as signs loaded with conscious, intended messages, but rather as the result of relations between people, places, and things that have emerged from historical circumstances." In this way, inscriptions of THOU SHALT <u>NOT</u> KILL became powerful directives for nonviolence in New Orleans, etching moral belief and a relational framework for human being onto the social, spiritual, and physical grounds of the Crescent City.[1]

The Katrina Effect

Religious work at Liberty Street was severely disrupted by Hurricane Katrina in 2005. However, in many respects, the storm was also an important catalyst for the church. It prompted the refinement of religious and moral frameworks for nonviolent recovery based on the postdisaster renewal of Black faith and the vision of a beloved community that clergy and parishioners hoped would finally emerge from the depths of the flooded city. In late August, even before the course and direction of the storm was known, Pastor Samuel felt that the city was in need of prayer, and he believed that the Lord was guiding him to a specific action—an outdoor fast and vigil. As he recalled, "I told a couple of people that the Lord was leading me to do this. Crime . . . violence was up. But I had never done something like that before. I was supposed to start [the vigil] that Monday, one week before Katrina, and stay there until that Friday. That's what I believed."

Pastor Samuel chose a familiar site, beneath the statue at the memorial to Martin Luther King Jr. on the neutral ground of South Claiborne Avenue. The King memorial had, by then, become an important location for the church's public outreach. Not only did it represent the long legacy of religious activism and social justice work in New Orleans and across the nation, it was just steps away from the intersection where the THOU SHALT <u>NOT</u> KILL billboard had been placed a decade before. However, the vigil never happened. Just before it was supposed to start, a prominent pastor in New Orleans passed away, and the family requested that the funeral be held at Liberty Street. Pastor Samuel recalled the chain of events:

The family wanted to have the funeral here. They wanted to have it here that Wednesday, which was the week I was supposed to go out [for the vigil], be out on the street Monday through Friday. But pride crept in and told me several things, because they could have had the funeral here whether I was here or not . . . they were just using the place that had enough space. But pride told me, if you go sit on that corner and as the pastors—because everybody comes up Claiborne—as these pastors and people coming to this funeral see you sitting out there, they are going to say, "Pastor Samuel done lost his mind sitting on the corner," and pride didn't want to be laughed at or looked down on! So, I let *pride* cancel what *God* had led me to do, and I did not do it. The funeral was on Wednesday, we buried him that Thursday, and by Monday this city was just about destroyed. And I always, I mean I'm not saying I could have stopped that [the storm's destruction], but I always felt guilty about not doing what God had led me to do.

Instead, the pastor had busied himself with preparations for the storm, working frantically but ultimately unsuccessfully to get all the members of his congregation to evacuate.

I was on the radio early that morning [Sunday, August 28, the day before the storm made landfall] trying to tell people, "You have to leave town." Later we had about 200 or 250 people come to church . . . then after the service was over, about seventy people said, "Oh no, we're not leaving, we're going to go home and try to ride it out." And I said, "You can't go home, trust me. I'm telling you. You have to leave!" But I couldn't talk them out of it. So, I said, "Well look, if you're not going to leave town then don't stay at home, come back to the church. Go and get your stuff, come back, and I'll stay here with you." And that's what happened.

After the storm, residents tried to come to terms with the destruction and the death toll, working to find stability in the city they still considered home. Their efforts were hampered, however, by the return of violent crime. This was not unexpected, given the scarcities that result from disaster, but it nonetheless felt intensified—the killings were less predictable and certainly seemed closer to home. One of the assistant pastors recalled a particularly violent Sunday in 2006, about seven months after the storm: "There was a gunfight right outside! They were running up the street shooting each other, and the bullets hit our church right when the service was over and people were starting to come out."[2]

The continuing state of violence prompted the refinement of Liberty Street's religious work. In addition to providing support to those in need, for example, by continuing projects that sought to improve neighborhood conditions and working with city officials and law enforcement to improve public safety, the church put out an urgent call for recovery based on the guiding principles of nonviolence, value, relatedness, and love. While these ideals could be perceived as abstract and therefore ineffective given the hardships that people were facing, they were believed to be fundamental not just for recovery but for renewal in the Black community and beyond. I asked Pastor Samuel about this shift. "It was after the storm, when the homicides started back in New Orleans," he explained. "And I just felt we had to get on that."

At the time, it was more manageable. I hate to use that word, but it was an opportunity for us to try to prevent at least that part of New Orleans from coming back. So, I sent out an open invitation to pastors who had made it back in the city. We were prayerfully trying to look for ways to address the situation. And initially we were looking for some kind of statement to be made.

The desire to prevent violence from returning to New Orleans was widely shared in a postdisaster period that was perceived by many, for better or for worse, as an "opportunity" to remake the city. However, the collective response to violence that church members witnessed in the years just after the storm further confirmed the need to address underlying determinations of human value and to elevate Black lives and deaths in particular. A violent string of murders in late 2006 and early 2007, which included the separate deaths of musician Dinerral Shavers and filmmaker Helen Hill, was especially significant in this regard. Pastor Samuel and some of his parishioners participated in the resulting March for Survival in January 2007. The Liberty Street contingent, about one hundred members in all, walked the well-worn path from Central City to city hall. When they arrived, Pastor Samuel took to the podium as an invited speaker.

The statement he gave was a powerful plea for an end to the violence. However, it was also a protest against the continued disregard for the lives and deaths of Black people. While the deaths of Shavers and Hill were unquestionably tragic, clergy and parishioners were cautious about their elevation as catalysts for change. It rendered other deaths, and there had been thousands before them, as common and inconsequential. It was outrageous that the same crowds had not previously appeared. One church member let it be known that this was not the first time that she had marched, nor sadly would it be the last. She had long been showing up, wondering where everybody else was.

Ministries after the storm were thus more intensely focused on Black social and spiritual value with the belief that all persons, in God's holy family, were worthy of care. When asked to testify at a national hearing about the impact of Hurricane Katrina and the obstacles to recovery, Pastor Samuel argued that the only real starting point was to recognize and work against the dehumanization and devaluing of Black people— otherwise the work of disaster recovery would be superficial at best. He was careful to emphasize, however, that this was not solely an ideological change; it required that basic needs such as housing, health care, education, and employment be simultaneously supported.

ENOUGH and the Coalition of Pastors

The first ministry to emerge in the wake of the storm inscribed the urban landscape with a simple and direct message: "ENOUGH." I asked Pastor Samuel for some details about this ministry, beginning with how it had developed. "Just prior to the storm I had made a few posters that said, 'Enough is Enough,'" he said.

And [after the storm] I thought about having more of those made to put out, but another pastor said, "Well, let's just use that one word, 'ENOUGH.'" So that's where that came from. And we did some things. We got out on the street, got as many folks together as we could, and we marched down to Martin Luther King Boulevard putting "ENOUGH" signs out.

These were familiar tactics—the same ones that had fueled the THOU SHALT <u>NOT</u> KILL ministry of the 1990s. The message, sadly, was also familiar—the violence continued and the people had had *enough*.

Yet while "ENOUGH" sounded like the latest rallying cry, it represented a larger effort, led by Black Protestant pastors, to unify, share ideas, and coordinate response, not solely because of the recent rash of murders but because the postdisaster moment made progress seem possible. This was an opportunity to move closer to the inclusive, just, and sustainable city for which they had long been fighting.

Pastor Samuel further understood this work as a response to a spiritual calling, one that was clearly defined in the wake of the storm. As he described it,

The Lord laid on my heart that we had been back in this city and we had not really come together as a Christian community just to say thank you. And the city was starting right back down the same old path, and people's lives were upside down, and everybody was trying to build up, but we were going right back into the deterioration of violence and drugs. I remember praying, and I asked the Lord how could we, after all we saw against the backdrop of Katrina, I mean it wiped out the whole city and we get the *privilege* of being able to come back in, how could folks go right back to doing the same thing?

The answer came unexpectedly, as he was driving across town, in an experience so intense that he had to pull off the highway to settle himself.

I got off the Westbank expressway and pulled into the parking lot of Best Buy. And as clear as the Lord could make it known to me, he told me that the reason why those people went back to doing the same thing the way they was doing before Katrina is because *the church* went back to doing the same thing *it* was doing before Katrina. We were not responding to the issues, we were so busy in our own recovery, our own individual recoveries, our own church congregational recoveries, that if the homicides, or the violence, or the drugs did not affect us personally, if it wasn't our family or a member of our church, we didn't really have time. I just thought that Christians in the city would recognize the need at least to say thank you to God. And to ask and to intercede for those who were going through violence and struggling.

Pastor Samuel paused, as if for effect, and then concluded, "And so I took every penny I had and I rented the Superdome." I paused too, amazed. "I can't imagine how much money it cost to rent the Superdome," I said finally, and Pastor Samuel laughed, slowly shaking his head. "You don't want to know," he said. "But I did it."

The event that was subsequently organized brought together a diverse group of Christian clergy. As Pastor Samuel described it, "the pastors came, in white and black and different denominations . . . and we pushed hard to recognize that there is only *one church* in New Orleans." Attendance was high, confirming a shared interest and willingness to work together. However, what Pastor Samuel remembered most was a gathering that revealed, in no uncertain terms, the challenges of interreligious organizing. "We all realized that we had very little ability to work together," he said sadly. "I'm talking about the Christian community—we had very little ability to work together, it was almost a competition thing." He used his own denomination as an example: "I mean just within the Baptist denomination we have about twenty-five or thirty associations, and all it does is keep us disassociated."

These tensions were a constant source of anxiety for religious leaders who sincerely desired unity but struggled through the politics that seem implicit in coalition building. Pastor Samuel continued,

Any time you start an association or an organization, you have set yourself up for competition with other groups. This was one of our weaknesses—you know, "I don't like the way you are doing it, and I wanted to be in charge but I'm not in charge, so I'll go start my own group. Now I'm in charge and I declare myself president, make myself bishop." Everybody is looking for a position but don't really have the desire in their heart to do something about the problem. Then there's the money thing. Because if you get an organization, then you can get some funding and get this and get that . . . and that's a temptation that often hinders us from being as effective as we could be.[3]

Despite these challenges, the convention at the Superdome led to the formation of a Pastors' Coalition, which continued in the form of weekly prayer meetings and related activities on behalf of the city and its residents. In this effort, Pastor Samuel intentionally took a back seat: "I was not involved in any way in the organizing of it. I went to it, and many of our members went to it . . . I just kind of sat in the back. Stayed hands off. Since I did not plan it . . . I didn't want to get in there and force myself into that."

While he remained deeply committed to coalition building, Pastor Samuel seemed more comfortable at Liberty Street. He was certainly not immune to the thirst for power that caused so much frustration in interreligious organizing, but the struggle against it was more manageable at home. He immersed himself in the administration of the church, in preaching, and in ministry, fighting hard to keep God at the center rather than the desires and potential gains that access to the pulpit might provide. He explained this practice in more depth: "It's a struggle for many, many pastors, anybody really in any kind of position of leadership or spiritual or religious responsibility. Because people look to you and you can kind of forget after a while that it's not about you." He shared a Scripture that helped to guide him through these challenges, a copy of which he kept displayed behind the pulpit.

When I sit, I can see it but the congregation can't . . . And the quote is when those Greeks came and the disciples, and they said, "Sir, we would see Jesus, we want to see Jesus"![4] So when I stand up I can be reminded every time that the people didn't come here to see me. And if they did, well they're in the right place for the wrong reason!

Violence and Vigils

Pastor Samuel felt guilty about canceling the outdoor prayer vigil he believed that God had directed him to perform. Nearly three years later he finally answered the call, holding a similar event over the New Year's Day holiday, beginning on New Year's Eve in 2008. It was just a few months after Obama's election and the pastor was inspired, no longer concerned about who would see him beneath the King monument and what they might say. Instead, the action felt appropriate for the time—an opportunity to reflect on current conditions and commit to change at the dawn of a new year.

In many ways, the vigil extended from the aims of the ENOUGH ministry to give thanks for what remained and to begin anew. However, while that effort was mired in religious politics, the vigil had a deeply personal feel even though Pastor Samuel had chosen a site that was meaningful not just for him but for many residents of the present and future city. The King memorial reminded him, he had said, of a debt that was owed to the leaders of the civil rights movement—those who fought and "died believing in their hearts that we would have better opportunities." How then could the current generation destroy itself, not appreciating or taking advantage of the rights and opportunities those freedom fighters gave their very lives to establish? As Pastor Samuel had put it, "How can we just sit by idly when this kind of battle is going on in our community?"

The vigil was meant to be a solitary action, but Pastor Samuel was nonetheless joined by several parishioners from Liberty Street as well as a number of visitors who came to lend support, to pray and be prayed for, or to simply converse with others in the small crowd that eventually assembled. He was grateful for the company, but it took extra work to maintain the vigil's solemn focus. In the midst of the fellowship, therefore, he led prayers, engaged in quiet study, and kept his fast. He did this because he believed that a larger process was at work—the formation of the beloved community he envisioned. All of this was evident in one of the prayers that Pastor Samuel offered shortly after I arrived.

Called together at the base of the memorial, we stood in a circle holding hands. Two Latino men, day laborers observing the scene while waiting for work in the parking lot across the street, ran over when they saw the prayer circle form, which opened up to accommodate them. Pastor Samuel began to pray, his voice steady, his words interspersed with interjections of praise from those around him. "I want to thank you all again, those of you who have put up with this and been out here. You didn't have to be here but you were," he said. "And we came out here . . . well, *I* came out here to seek God's face in relation to what needs to be done but also to intercede for those who are suffering and grieving for losing their loved ones. And we certainly want to remember them. I don't believe that our being here has been in vain, and I believe that the Lord is gonna use this time to do even greater things in this community and, I believe, in this country. So, let's pray."

Father, we thank you once again for this blessed experience of focusing on you Lord, moving away from our attention on the problems and looking for the problem solved. Lord we lift up right now every mother and every father who had to bury a child in this city due to violence. Those siblings Lord who bear the pain right now [*yes Lord Jesus*] of a brother or a sister who will no longer be there. Even those small children [*in the name of Jesus Christ*] who had to see mother or father buried because of violence in this city [*yes Lord*].

Oh Lord we thank you because we know that you are able to bring a change upon our communities and a change upon our hearts [*yes Lord*]. Right now, Lord we pray that you would comfort those who are grieving [*yes Lord Jesus*] but bring about a state Lord that it won't have to be others that have to go down that path [*yes Lord, in the name of Jesus Christ*]. We pray Lord that 2009 would be a year, which you would work in a way that everybody would notice nobody but you Father.

We pray Father that you would touch the hearts of our young men, our young ladies, that they would realize the value of first of all their own lives [*yes Father God*], then the value of others' lives [*yes Lord Jesus*]. We pray that you would help us as a community to come together [*thank you Jesus*] with a sense of compassion and concern for one another Lord. We pray that whatever we do, we do it in a way that you are glorified.

Lord, lift up our city leaders [*yes Lord*], that there might not be a spirit of competition, that they might complement one another working in a way that would make this the best city that it can possibly be [*yes, yes*]. Now Lord we thank you for sustaining us through these days. I thank you for each and every one of your children who gave of themselves during this time. We bless you, in Jesus Christ's name we pray, Amen [*Amen, thank you Jesus, thank you very much, thank you my sister, thank you my brother*].

As the circle broke apart, the two men who had joined the group ran back across the street to wait again for work. "*Vaya con Dios!* Go with God!" Pastor Samuel called after them, and they waved. "I have to start practicing up on my Spanish," he told me.

I'm going to be preaching in Panama in about two weeks, I've been doing that for about two years. It's something that I don't do well . . . but they love it and like to make fun of how I mispronounce the words . . . We have Spanish services at the church now. I came out here after the storm and started seeing all those guys lined up over there [*pointing across the street*]. Well we got them involved, but it was hard.

A light rain had begun to fall, and a blustery wind had picked up. "How was it out here last night?" I asked. "Was it cold?" Pastor Samuel smiled broadly and shook his head, "I felt guilty . . . they actually brought a cot out here for me and set it up and the fire was going. I had two blankets, and I felt guilty. I thought, oh my goodness." "You actually slept?" I asked.

Oh, I slept. I slept. I wanted to sleep because I wanted my mind to be fresh this morning so I could study, but I've gotten very little studying done. Well. I'll just stay with it because this is a precursor to I believe something very huge in this city—something that has to happen. If we are going to survive as a people, it has to happen. It's just a matter of getting people who are not directly affected through violence or even economically to be concerned about people who are.

We were still standing at the foot of the monument, and the pastor paused for a second, looking out at the others gathered around the perimeter of the site, now facing traffic with signs commanding peace. "I just have to say also that these people motivate me too," he added. "Let me tell you, none of them have to be here. I mean, I made it easy for them not to be here." I interrupted; "Yes, I heard you on the news, and you were almost telling people to stay away." "Yes, I was not asking people to come" he replied, "And I'll tell you why."

It was because *I* felt the need to come here, and I was trying to strike a balance between getting the exposure, challenging the public about what we need to do, but at the same time being able to truly give time to prayer and fasting at *this* place . . . and it's hard sometimes, because I was out here one time before, and a lot of pastors came out here with me, and it turned into like a fellowship, you know everybody was like, "Hey I'm glad you're out here, I'm glad you're out here." And sometimes we would lose sight of *why* we were out here. So I said that to my congregation, but some of them came anyway, and they even spent the night out here with me. And I'm glad they did.

I spent several hours on the neutral ground that afternoon speaking with participants. Most were African American men, elders at Liberty Street, but there were also a few women, such as Danielle, who hand-lettered and then held a sign that read, "I am a mother hurting because of violence." I would come to know her better through the related support group for women she organized, a subject I explore in more detail in the final section of this book. There were also a few participants from other faiths, congregations, and neighborhoods as well as some additional visitors who, like me, had dropped by unannounced but were nonetheless welcomed into the group. The conversations that ensued revealed the diversity of our experiences but also the shared concern that had brought us together on an otherwise cold and wet holiday.

I had stood next to William in the circle; his interjections of praise had further uplifted the prayer Pastor Samuel had led. Afterward, he warmly grasped my hand while we introduced, and we found a moment later in the day to chat. A member of Liberty Street since 1979, William was originally from New Iberia, a small town southeast of Lafayette. He came to New Orleans for work, as did his younger brother Vince, described by William as a kind person but unfortunately "into drugs." "He used drugs, but he was very kind, he worked, you know? Very kind, very warm, very loving, very caring . . . he would give you his heart," he said, his eyes misting over. Vince was murdered in 1997, killed by an acquaintance in a minor dispute that had escalated to deadly consequence. As William recounted,

the guy who killed him, he knew my brother—the night before my brother had even fixed a meal for him and his family! But evidently my brother owed him twenty-five dollars, and the next day came, and they got in an argument. I don't know how the argument went, but it was over twenty-five dollars. And the guy came back and shot him—*over twenty-five dollars.* They arrested the guy because they had a witness, but the witness didn't show up at the hearing, so they had to release him. And I can hear my mother's voice saying right now, just as clear as the day, "Vengeance is mine, said the Lord.[5] Put it in God's hands and let him handle it." I can hear her saying that so clearly.

We talked for a few more minutes, and William shared with me the sense of comfort he felt when he participated in demonstrations like the vigil—able to share his story but also honoring the commitment he had made long ago to do something about the problem of violence. As he excused himself to join the other participants positioned along the edge of the road, I noticed a young man sitting off to the side on a bench beneath the trees. He was apart from the group and seemed lost in thought, but when he looked my way and said hello, I approached and introduced myself. He was indeed present for the vigil, had already spent one night on the neutral ground, and was prepared to stay for the duration. This was not something he had planned to do, but he had seen Pastor Samuel on television the day before, and he felt spiritually called to be there. Keith was one of the youngest participants I encountered at the vigil that day, twenty-one years old and a student at a local university. After the prayer circle, he had found a quiet place to sit and reflect. "I'm out here, I guess, because of the murder rate," he told me.

But even past that, because I think that young men need to see other young men actually caring. It's one thing for Pastor Samuel to do it. It's one thing for older people to do it, but it's a whole other ballpark when you have people your age. When you have people somewhere in your [age] bracket it's like, "Come on dog, it's out of hand."

Keith believed that he could be a role model for other young African American men like himself, and what he modeled was caring—a state of genuine concern about the conditions of violence and a belief that one's actions could inspire others. This belief was itself inspired by Keith's own religious awakening. It was one thing to serve as a role model, but one had to see and understand oneself in that capacity. What was the source of his spiritual calling? What had moved him to come to the neutral ground and join Pastor Samuel? I asked.

Truthfully? I went and found God. I know that sounds a little weird, but the Bible says seek and ye shall find, and I sought. I was raised in the church all my life and it wasn't . . . I mean I had my own issues personally about the validity of church and the Bible and all this and the other. And that's another reason why it's so important that I'm out here and able to talk to people. There is so much material out there, how do you know what to choose? Some people are in it for that dollar or that feel good, that temporary high . . . and I can't say that I'm still not one of those people. But I believe in God, and I found God out of all of that, and I know Pastor Samuel is being led by God. That's the only way he could stay out here. That's the only way I could stay out here.

Fasting was also central to Keith's religious awakening, a form of self-discipline against the odds that he also tried to cultivate and model for others. As he described it,

Fasting disciplines your mind . . . it brings you closer to God, and you do get hungry, and you do feel that urge that you need something. That's the time you rely on God fully. When I feel that hunger and I think, "Oh, I'm losing it," that's the time I go sit by myself, and I just pray, and I ask God to take it away . . . A lot of young men, even in the church think, "Oh, I can't help it, that's the way it's supposed to be." But that's not how this works.

As the afternoon wore on, the conversations became more familiar as those who didn't know each other previously became better acquainted. A small group of people formed around the fire pit, still smoldering with coals from the night before. There I met Mrs. Martin, a retired school teacher and now an occasional substitute, who was engrossed in conversation with Patrick, an assistant pastor at the church. The two bonded over their shared experience of the public school system—Mrs. Martin had pulled her own son out to send him to an all-boys Catholic school, and Patrick's mother had done the same with him. The boys had both "made it," at least in their mothers' eyes. In fact, Mrs. Martin's son had just completed medical school. Still, she worried about those who were left behind with few options on a school-to-prison pipeline that was well established in Louisiana. She recalled a recent encounter that occurred while she was subbing at a local elementary school.

I went into a class not long ago, and these were fourth graders . . . and these kids had told me that they had run the [previous] teacher off! I said, "Well I'm here, and my name is Mrs. Martin, and let me tell you—you NOT gonna run ME off, *okay?*" And so, I told them, "I want each one of you to stand up and tell me five positive things about yourself and your family." Well, everybody was saying, "my daddy in jail and he did this and that, and my mama did such and such . . ." and I thought, mmm hmm, this explains it all. We got a long way to go and a short time to get there.

"Yeah," Patrick agreed quietly, and then they each stood there, lost in their respective memories and continued fears of a system that devalued and underserved Black youth. When the conversation picked up again, it was with a more hopeful tone. "There are so many things that we can improve on," Patrick added. Mrs. Martin nodded her head, "Yes, indeed, and this [vigil] is a wonderful thing to do—calling attention to the problem." More silence. The rain and the wind had died down, but it was still cloudy. "I'm glad it's warming up," Patrick said, and everyone said they were too.

Such fellowship continued throughout the afternoon between Mrs. Martin, Patrick, Keith, William, Danielle, Pastor Samuel, and many others. However, the vigil was also about reaching out to members of the broader public, and participants did their best to engage with those passing by. And so they continued to stand along the edge of the neutral ground facing traffic and holding signs, proclaiming their identity and intent. Some drivers ignored them, keeping their eyes forward when stopped by the light. But many honked their horns in support, waved, or rolled down their windows to offer words of encouragement and thanks. A few individuals even pulled over to come onto the neutral ground itself. The size and makeup of the vigil thus shifted as the afternoon wore on.

One woman arrived with an unmistakable sense of urgency to meet and talk with Pastor Samuel. She, too, had seen him on television and wanted to share her concerns about "domestic violence too, not just street violence!" They spoke for some time, and then Pastor Samuel directed her to emergency resources and shelter. A homeless man, unaware of the fast, approached the pastor and asked if he had anything to eat. "No," Pastor Samuel replied, "But if you would like something to eat then go down this way." He pointed across the street, directing the man to the church for a free meal. The man protested and became agitated, certain that he wouldn't be served because he didn't have any identification. Pastor Samuel was reassuring but firm: "If you don't want help, then go. But if you want help, I can give it to you. I didn't ask you for any ID." He showed him the way to the church again, "four blocks up, take a right," and the man walked away in that direction.

There were more visitors with different agendas—a man with some ideas for stopping the violence in his neighborhood, more day laborers from across the street who came for prayer and went again, a man unknown to anyone, who pulled up in a car alongside the neutral ground and handed Pastor Samuel a check for $1,000, and the mayor of New Orleans himself, Ray Nagin, who dropped by unannounced to meet with Pastor Samuel and give his support. William described the nature and impact of these interactions:

Different individuals come, other ministers, city officials, people of all denominations, people of all races. They come by and talk with the pastor and meet with us. They'll pray by themselves, they'll walk around and pray with others. They come just to be among us, just to be with us, you know? And by the end of the day you find a sort of peacefulness with yourself in the cool of the evening and you can reflect upon who you talked with, who you met, the things that people said, what they have shared with your family.

While such congregation was certainly a show of unity around an issue of broad concern, participants understood these interactions more deeply as the necessary grounding for change. Guided by their faith in God, committed

143

to the cultivation of relatedness, claiming and reconfiguring place, and asserting the value of all God's children, the vigil was an important step in the creation of a beloved community. As one participant commented, with his own unmistakable enthusiasm about Obama's historic election,

When you get people talking about something then what's the next thing? They are gonna get to doing something about it! And that's the joy and that's the hope . . . that people not only talk about it, they start doing something about it. And if enough of us get to doing something about it, then we can turn this thing around, with the help and the grace of God. We can make it, we can make it. *Yes we can!*"

While this vigil gained significance from its location at a civil rights memorial, similar kinds of events were held at sites that were much less lofty. For example, Pastor Samuel led processions to specific crime sites and places of death, and the vigils that took place there were difficult but no less moving and transformative. As one parishioner, Phil, remarked, "It [death] just becomes so real. It's very much this way of seeing what happened. I remember being up in Holly Grove, and there was a man who was shot, and we were out there the very next day. There was a trail of blood along this abandoned road all the way down the street. It went on and on." He hesitated for a moment, in the middle of this description, and I asked him how he managed to stay present at a place of such tragic suffering. "I try to put all of that in prayer," he replied,

I just think about it through prayer, and I hope the best for that person, even while thinking about the act that happened. We go into places, and we go almost immediately into silence and prayer, so it's about digging deep and coming face to face with what happened. It cuts through a lot of the apathy and you get a sense of who that person was and what happened.

As much as the experience brought forth the reality of death, it also emphasized the humanity of those involved, victims and perpetrators alike. As Phil explained,

We typically distance ourselves from this kind of thing—we'll say, "Oh this person was just a drug dealer." But it's horrendous to allow this to happen just because someone has a problem with their pain and they deal with it in that way. So, our work cuts through that, and we start to see and remember these people as human beings.

I later asked Pastor Samuel why it was important, in his view, to visit these sites. His response revealed, once again, a desire to shift from a distanced stance to a more engaged and interrelated response. The objective was

first of all, to establish the value of that life and the tragedy of what happened right there. But also, to maybe . . . I try to talk to the neighbors . . . because I need to have my finger on the pulse of what is our response to it. How does that affect the community? Is that event in that community something that is going to provoke us to want to care more about one another or to do something, to step forward? And everywhere I go, I mean, people are genuinely concerned but not necessarily concerned enough to move beyond concern.

These questions were raised with horrific force just a few days after the New Year's Eve vigil when a man killed his two-year-old son following a dispute he had had with the boy's mother regarding child support. He disposed of the body in a local park, just half a mile from Liberty Street. In the midst of a community that was once again reeling from disbelief, outrage, and deep sorrow, Pastor Samuel prepared for the funeral, which was to be held at the church that weekend. He shared with me the devastating impact of this death on the child's family and community. However, he simultaneously wondered whether people were affected *enough* to step forward and become more directly involved in finding a solution. Here was an innocent child whose value and worth should be unquestioned. How could one look the other way? The tragedy, therefore, was also an opportunity in that it forced a choice—toward apathy and distance or toward care and community. As Pastor Samuel explained,

with this child that was recently killed . . . that [tragedy] has moved many people beyond just the shaking of the head and saying how terrible it is, to want to at least look for choices . . . because before, in most cases, we distance ourselves emotionally. Because it's painful already to consider death, and nobody wants to always be thinking about something bad . . . so we distance ourselves emotionally by classifying that person as somebody who was in that lifestyle [drug trafficking and its associated violence]. Or that they did something that brought it on them, maybe they killed somebody else.

But with the child that was killed . . . there's no way that you can distance yourself . . . Now you have choices. Either your emotion is going to go toward hate for the person who did it, or toward love and compassion, or at least sympathy, for the mother and other family members.

Such reasoning sheds light on the operation of value, revealing for example how determinations of worth in an "imperialist white-supremacist capitalist patriarchy" (hooks 2004, 17–18) are dramatically different for children and different still for children who are white than for Black children and especially Black boys. In New Orleans, in addition to these configurations of race, age, and gender, what also seemed to determine value was the assessment of criminality, with presumptions of guilt or innocence closely correlated with levels of response. The Black boy who was killed was certainly too young to have been involved in any kind of criminal activity (though perhaps an expectation for it, if not now then later, was nonetheless at work); he was instead wholly dependent on adults for his circumstances and well-being. The question of his value, at least by this measure, should have been inarguable. Unlike the death of an adult with a suspected or known history of criminal activity, one had no justified reason not to mourn the child's passing. This was indeed a moment of choice that revealed value's true determination while indicating at least the possibility of transformation in an otherwise established space of death.[6]

Pastor Samuel reached out to the family of the young victim and, with their permission, led a candlelight walk and prayer vigil the night before the funeral. A small crowd of about one hundred people followed a brass band that passed by the child's house and through his neighborhood. The procession ended in the park where the body had been found, with Pastor Samuel leading prayers alongside other clergy, community leaders, neighbors, friends, and family members. He mourned for the child, yet he also shared his firm belief that despite this horrific reality, God was working in powerful ways. It would be very difficult after such an event, he argued, for one to remain passive about the state of the city and the world. One simply *had* to care, one simply *had* to act, and this would lead directly to the world they all envisioned.

He did wonder, however, about how to sustain care beyond this event, and so he vowed to look for ways to better define a corresponding movement. Scanning the crowd for the boy's mother and addressing her directly, he stated finally, "We love you. We care about you, and we're going to stand by you, beyond the cemetery. We want to help you be what God wants you to be. We're gonna stand by you when the flowers are all gone and the candles go out. . . . We want you to know that we're gonna still be with you and this entire family." The next morning, when delivering the eulogy at the child's funeral, he put the same sentiment in more general terms. With a promise to continue the fight against violence, he proposed that rather than only fighting *against* something that he, and those who would follow him, could choose to fight *for* something and *for* somebody. As a community they would begin by "forgiving one another . . . loving one another . . . caring for one another, and . . . helping one another." In doing these things, he concluded, "God will be glorified."

Yes We Care!

In March of 2009, shortly after returning from Obama's inauguration in Washington, DC, Pastor Samuel launched a new ministry, "Yes We Care!" It kicked off with a rally in Louis Armstrong Park that was attended by thousands of people. As I describe in chapter 3, the objectives of the ministry were clear—to bring the Black community together, to publicly acknowledge the problem of violence, to personally commit to nonviolence in thought and action, to affirm human value, and to thereby uplift and transform the Black community. As the official literature for the event stated, the focus was on "RESTORING pride, REAFFIRMING the value of life, and RECLAIMING detached and disenfranchised children, families, and neighbors within the African American community."

African American religious organizing is often historicized according to its key moments, from the Afro-Baptist cosmos developed by enslaved Africans to the religious intellectualism that sought a new abolition after the abandonment of Reconstruction to the rise of the black social gospel and the religious activism that guided the civil rights movement of the 1950s and 1960s. Clergy and parishioners at Liberty Street extended this trajectory in response to the continuing but distinct conditions of the day. The moment that brought the Yes We Care! ministry seemed critical, in the midst of disaster recovery and on the heels of a watershed moment in Black and American politics. What happened next would determine the future of New Orleans. Pastor Samuel had said as much, at the New Year's Eve vigil just two months earlier. That event, as important as it was, was still "a precursor to . . . something very huge in this city, something that has to happen," he declared. "If we are going to survive as a people, it has to happen." The rally thus brought the people together, identifying the agents of change, the ones who were now connected and committed to the work ahead, the ones who would continue the search for, and find, love in the Crescent City.

PART THREE

Raising Dead Sons

Risen (photo by author)

Seeing

"You want me to close it out?" asked Sister Shirley. "Yeah," said
Danielle, grateful for the help. The support-group session that
evening had been long and full, marking the first-year death
anniversary of Rayshaun, Odette's son-in-law. But it was time
now for the ceremony that would bring the event to an end,
a prayer followed by a balloon release, to signify Rayshaun
"being absent from the body and present with the Lord." "Alright?" Danielle gave the signal when everyone seemed settled. The women bowed their heads, and Sister Shirley prayed.

Lord, we just thank you, Lord God. We thank you for the words that
went forth, God. God, we know that when your Word go forward it shall
not come back but it shall *accomplish* what it was set forth to do! And
God, we just thank you for being in the midst of us, for comforting us,
for giving us *strength*, Lord God. Oh God, if we had a thousand tongues
we couldn't thank you enough, but we say as humbly as we know how,
thank you God. Thank you, Lord God. We thank you for Rayshaun's life
tonight, Lord God. We thank you for his memory, Lord God. We know
we will *never* forget him, Lord God, because he will always live in our
hearts. All of our loved ones, Lord God. And God, we thank you for the
dead who are right now in *your* hands, Lord God, and *you* have the last
say, God, and so for this we give you glory, we give you honor, we give
you praise, God. For being our awesome God. For being an ever-present
help in a time of need. And now, Lord God, we just give you glory, give
you praise, and give you honor. In Jesus's precious holy name. Amen.

A resounding "Amen!" came from the group, especially
from Odette and the other family members who were present,

including Rayshaun's two boys, aged three and four, who sat restlessly on their grandmother's lap, one on each knee. Danielle went to the CD player to turn on some music and then returned to the table with the cake and other refreshments. The boys' faces lit up with anticipation and they were so excited that Danielle suggested they go ahead and have the cake first. She lit the candles. "Everybody say, 'We love you Rayshaun!'" And they all did, the boys blowing out the candles in honor of their father and the women applauding, rejoicing in their obvious delight, despite the occasion. Plates of food were passed around.

Usually these were somber affairs, intended to give the grieving mother or grandmother some support on holidays, birth and death anniversaries, and other difficult days. But the party for Rayshaun had a different feel. In part this was because Tia, Rayshaun's wife and the boys' mother, was not there. She had wanted to come, but it was apparent, at the last minute, that it would be too much, too soon, for her to bear. So Tia rested, under the care of another family member, and her mother and the boys had gone ahead. Too young to comprehend fully the circumstances around their father's untimely passing, the boys were instead enthralled by the cake, the balloons, and all other evidence of a party. The women, in turn, were enthralled with the boys. To see them healthy, happy, and for the moment out of harm's way, was indeed something to celebrate. As the women remembered Rayshaun, therefore, they held onto his children, passing them from knee to knee, serving them more cake than they probably should have had.

Things were so much in swing that Danielle nearly forgot about the balloon release, the final ritual to honor Rayshaun, signifying not his death but his ascendance to heaven. She jumped up, saying, "Oh, one more thing, what we would like to do! We've got to go out and release the balloons . . . we're going to go all the way out." The others already knew, and they gathered themselves to head out of the building, down the stairs, and into the parking lot. The boys became even more excited and began running around, singing and dancing. "What color you want?" the older one, Dwayne, asked his brother. "I want the blue one!" the younger brother David answered. When it was handed to him, he paraded proudly out the door, looking just once over his shoulder to make sure that someone, anyone, was following. Sister Shirley was right behind him. "You got to get a balloon?" he asked her. "Mmm hmm," she said. "We're going to let them go up in the sky." "Way up in the sky!" David said, pointing. "C'mon!"

Outside they stood together, waiting for the others who, by David's calculations, were far too slow to arrive. Danielle in particular was delayed—as a woman, unknown to any of them, had unexpectedly dropped by looking for information about services and other resources at Liberty Street. The main church building was closed, but Danielle took a few moments to speak with her. The others in the parking lot, especially the boys with their balloons at the ready, became increasingly impatient. The women took turns helping them. "Hold it now. Don't let it go," one of them told David, to which he promptly replied, "Let it go y'all?" Another one jumped in, trying again, "No, not yet! Don't let it go!" Dwayne helped too, as best he could, by singing and dancing around his brother, twisting his body every which way, "Don't let it go!" "Don't let it go!"

Suddenly, there was a white balloon in the air, floating up toward the sky. "Uh-oh," said David, frozen. "Ohhh, look at that!" said Dwayne, and he turned incredulously to his brother, "You *did* that man?" But Odette was quick to speak up, claiming responsibility, "Oh, sorry! That was one out of my hand!" They watched as it rose higher. David was mesmerized. He had forgotten the specifics but he knew that the balloon was supposed to honor *somebody*. "Who that one for?" he asked. "Who that one was for?" "For Rayshaun," his grandmother answered.

The release of that one balloon, though premature, had a clear impact on the group. Everyone stood, transfixed, watching it climb. The sun had not yet set, so it was visible as far as the eye could see and trace. "Wow. It's going so high," someone else said. But David, still holding tightly to his blue balloon, had lost sight. His voice dropped and became small and concerned. "I can't see it . . . ," was all he said. Dwayne still could, and he confirmed this with his grandmother, "You can see it Ma, huh?" "I sure can," she replied. But David was lost. "I don't see it Ma, I can't see it Ma." The women, their attention focused upward, were slow to respond. Dwayne tried. "It's *right there* David! Look up! Right there, way up in the sky. See it?" David kept repeating, his voice even smaller, "I don't see it Ma, I can't see it Ma," "It's *right there*!" Dwayne turned to the others, in frustration. "He can't see it. He can't see it."

While clearly this exchange was about a boy and a balloon not seen in the sky, David's difficulty hinted also at a deeper and shared desire to see and *relate*—to maintain a tangible connection to who we are and who and what we love. His small voice was a sad realization of not being able, at least not yet, to see and be part of an interconnected world beyond the current reality of loss and letting go. The possibility was certainly there, but there was no one who could really help him to transcend the limits. "I can't see it Ma," he said again, more to himself than anyone. "Well, what you want me to do?" his grandmother responded finally.

There came another chance, thankfully, when Danielle arrived outside. "Y'all ready? I'm sorry," she said, apologizing for the delay. "OK, where are my balloons? Y'all ready to release them? Oh good! Let's go. OK, One, two. C'mon c'mon!" Everyone held their balloons out and up, ready to let go. Danielle started the count over. "One, two . . . on the count of five . . . three, four, five! *Release* them! *Alright!*" They all let go, except for David, who had forgotten about his own balloon while watching the others float away. His grandmother, who had picked him up, gently pried open his hand, while the others gave encouragement: "It's going to your daddy! Look! *In the clouds!* There they go!"

Then they all stood there for what seemed like a very long time, watching the balloons drift up and away. They tracked them with their eyes and words as they moved forward, stayed together, or were pulled apart. "I see three, four, five . . . *way out* there!" someone said. "Look at them two keeping up, and that one by itself." "Now look at that one, the one that was by itself was behind there and now it's in the lead. You see that?" "Look at that blue one at the top." "OK now they done all scattered out." Danielle, caught up in the excitement but intentionally overdramatic, threw her hands into the air proclaiming, "I see Jesus! I see Jesus!" They all fell out laughing.

The balloons gradually faded from view. If one looked away, they were harder to find when one looked back. "I only see four now," Danielle said. "There's still five," someone reassured her. "I see! I see!" said Dwayne. "Well we going to watch until we can't watch them no more." There was silence, and then another flurry of comments, "The minute you take your eyes off of them, they gone," Odette said. She knew. "That white one just disappeared," Sister Shirley added. "Look. Didn't that one disappear?" "Oh, it sure did," said Danielle. "You can see the two blue now, that's all I see." But Dwayne found the white one again, "I see the white, right there!" he said with excitement. "Oh yeah, I see it, now." "I'm looking at that blue one at the bottom." Danielle, again. "My eyes is on *that* one. Awesome, huh?" The light was fading as the sun made its way to the horizon. When there was nothing left to see, "They gone now," the women said their goodbyes, until the next time. "C'mon y'all." Odette took the boys by the hand, pausing first to give Danielle a hug. "Thank you," she said. "You're welcome, my love."

FIVE

Black Mothers at the Center of Death and Transformation

Ain't no life. My loved one is gone. Ain't no more life. But we must go through, because this is when God want us to stand, when things seem like we can't make it. And this is where He is glorified. And it's hard, but if we trust Him, He'll give us the strength . . . I've been there. But now I have peace. **DANIELLE**

I arrived at the party for Danté and Marcus just before 6:00 p.m. Danielle, who had organized everything, greeted me at the door and ushered me into the main hall where a few guests, all women, were waiting. I introduced myself and took a seat along the far edge of the room. The place was simply but thoughtfully decorated with a red-checked cloth on the center table anchored by a colorful bunch of balloons tied together and weighted down. A smaller table over to the side held refreshments, including a sheet cake with candles and blue frosting, which spelled out "In Loving Memories." A hand-lettered birthday card and a program from Danté's funeral, with his photograph on the front, were placed nearby. Gospel music from one of the local radio stations played softly.

Danielle was rushing around, making coffee, and getting things ready. She placed a clipboard with a sign-in sheet on the table along with photocopies of a prayer she planned to share. She seemed anxious, wringing her hands and looking at the clock. I overheard her say that she had been trying to contact Miss Vivian, Danté's grandmother, all day just to check in and to make sure that she would be coming. She had not been able to reach her and she was concerned. Marcus's mother, Mrs. Adams, was already there, accompanied by her daughter. A few additional guests arrived, and they greeted and hugged each other before settling quietly into chairs around the room.

At a quarter past six Danielle decided to start even though there was still no word from Miss Vivian. She offered first a prayer, giving thanks for those who were able to come and expressing hope that the group would still be able to give Miss Vivian "the support that we intend to give her." Continuing with broad affirmation of the gathering and its purpose, she added, "and we want to say thank you Lord, as we are here to lift up the mother who have lost her child to violence. . . . So, we pray that you are going to guide us at this time. In Jesus, Lord, we pray."

Danielle looked up, making eye contact with each of the guests. "I want to once again thank everyone for coming out," she said. "We're going to start out by introducing ourselves."

As everybody know, I'm Danielle. I'm the founder of the Mothers Group. We meet here every week talking to mothers who have lost children to violence, giving them the courage to deal with their pain and helping them to see a way out. Today, as you can see with the cake, we are here to celebrate Danté's birthday. Even though his grandmother is not here. But that doesn't stop us from celebrating his birthday. We are also here to celebrate the first year [death anniversary] of Marcus, which is the son of Mrs. Adams, and I'm happy to see her daughter here with us, to give her mother that support.

Mrs. Adams, who was seated at the far end of the table, turned to her daughter and smiled. Her daughter was holding a baby in her lap, Mrs. Adams's new grandson, and his squirms and sounds lightened the mood for just a moment. But Danielle was still preoccupied, Miss Vivian on her mind. "And I just want you all to know," she continued, her voice breaking, "that I'm glad to be of service."

Every day that I pray . . . that's what I ask God to do, to help me to be of better service today than I was yesterday. I don't do everything right all the time. And if I made the errors somewhere I want to make it up, because I'm all about trying to *help* somebody, not to take them down. Because I know what it's like. When you are dealing with the pain of losing your child.

Danielle's knowledge and corresponding concern had everything to do with the violent death of her own son Rock. While her mourning was now supported by a deep religious faith, she nonetheless worked day by day to arrive at a level of acceptance regarding his passing that was necessary for her own well-being as well as the support she hoped to provide for others. It was an ongoing process to say the least, and on this occasion, she worried that she had somehow let Miss Vivian down.

She was interrupted by the door opening. Miss Vivian had finally arrived, accompanied by three other women. Danielle jumped up, with an "Oh, hi!" and "Thank you Jesus! Come on in and get your spots." She went around shuffling chairs so Miss Vivian, her two nieces, and a family friend could all sit together. "We had just finished praying," Danielle told them.

And we were just getting ready to introduce ourselves and I had started off. I'm glad that we sent up a special prayer for you Miss Vivian because I was just sharing with the group that I hoped that you were OK because I know it's a very critical time for you today, you know, as Danté's birthday. And you know at any moment when you want to do something and all of a sudden it hits you and you lose your composure and next thing you know it's a different story. So, I just thank God you were able to make it.

Miss Vivian apologized for her lateness and thanked everyone for being there, "especially my nieces, and their friend." "I thank God for them," she added quietly, as the women who surrounded her gently but firmly placed their hands on her arms and back, steadying themselves for the stories of life and death they were about to share.

Events like this, marking the birthdays and death anniversaries of the deceased, were an important part of the Mothers Group, founded by Danielle in 2005, shortly after Rock was murdered. The group was affiliated with and supported by Liberty Street Baptist Church, where Danielle had long been a member, and it extended from the church's larger ministry against violence. While the women who gathered each week came from different neighborhoods and congregations, they were united in their Christian faith and by their shared experience of the violence that persisted in New Orleans's poor Black communities. Each of them had lost a child, grandchild, or other close relative.

The women came together first and foremost for support, knowing that birthdays, anniversaries, holidays, and other significant occasions were extraordinarily difficult days for surviving family members, far too easily spent in grief and solitude. The group thus functioned as a critical safety net. Danielle was acutely aware of the need, based on her own experience but also indicated by her great concern for Miss Vivian's whereabouts as the hour grew late. Indeed, Miss Vivian appeared quite fragile when she arrived despite being buffered on either side by family members and friends.

The women also gathered, however, to honor their lost loved ones, claiming them as significant and valued persons—members of families and communities on earth and now in heaven. The relatedness they cultivated thus countered larger processes of social and physical death, and it moved them all, slowly, from the devastation to the sacred development of the Crescent City.

I was privileged to be a guest at these meetings over a period of six months from January to June of 2009. I observed and documented weekly support-group sessions as well as special events. I also interviewed participants outside of the group setting to learn more about their individual histories, and I followed them into different arenas where they shared their stories, for example, at church vigils, revivals, community forums, and rallies. Through all of this, I maintained a somewhat distanced stance. In some ways, this was intentional—I situated myself along the margins to minimize my intrusion. In other ways it was unavoidable, given the nature of the group and my own life circumstances. While I was certainly not a stranger to the reality of violence in Black communities, I was not mourning in the same immediate fashion. These differences made me appreciate even more the ways in which the women so graciously allowed me to witness their work.

In this chapter I examine the formation and purpose of the Mothers Group at Liberty Street. I focus on Danielle, the founder of the group, as it was through her narrative and "testimony" that much of the information about the group and its work was shared. Danielle's testimony makes clear the persistent conditions of violence and death found disproportionately within this and other Black communities. However, it also makes clear the transformative work that simultaneously occurs. For example, as we learn about Danielle's life, and Rock's life and death, we learn not only about the violent severing of social bonds but about the work of their restoration. Black women were frequently at the center of this process, and Danielle's narrative also reveals her own vision of a beloved community, as practices of relatedness extended beyond the standard boundaries of place, position, or realm of human existence. In this way, the women countered the devaluing or dismissal of "God's children" as they developed specific practices to "raise" the dead.

Brought Up and Returned

Born in New Orleans, Danielle was raised primarily by her grandmother, who made sure she was brought up in the church. "I got baptized at Liberty Street when I was nine years old," Danielle recalled in a testimony she began at our very first meeting. "I sang in the choir and came to Sunday school, vocational Bible school . . . I did that till I was like fourteen." It was in her teenage years, shortly after her father was released from prison, that Danielle's life took a turn. She began to spend time with her father and his extended family in the Melpomene housing project, where she was lured, like so many others, into the false freedoms that are often promised to Black youth with few alternatives. She was pregnant at age fifteen and dropped out of school. She had another baby not long after. But it was her involvement with drugs, as a dealer and then a user, that brought her, finally, to the edge of danger and death.

Addicted to crack cocaine by the age of twenty-six, Danielle found herself at a point of no return. "I had hit rock bottom where I was just doing anything for money, neglecting my kids," she confessed. "I almost lost my life." Never far from the community of her early childhood, however, she remained in sight of the church. And the church kept its sight on Danielle, still recognizing her, despite her condition, as one of its own. She recalled with deep emotion the ministry and care she received.

Pastor Samuel used to see me in the streets. And I used to wave at him, cry out to him and he used to tell me to come on to the Lord's house . . . And then I came. I came to church and cried out many, many times after relapsing every three or four months. A lot of people thought that I was just playing, but I was really just under the spell of a demon, and then one day Jesus set me free. And that happened through prayers, through other people praying for me. And today I am twenty-one years free from the bondage of drugs, *in the name of Jesus!*

Such outreach was performed in word and deed, with the church providing Danielle and her children with critical resources and services. She would not forget the nonjudgmental way in which it had all been delivered. "That why I love my pastor today," she declared. "He's a man that don't look down on people. And a person like me, like I was then, many ministers don't even accept them into their congregation cause they feel they are coming in there with a whole lot of bull crap. But Pastor Samuel, he used to pray for me. And he would welcome me any time."

To provide this kind of critical support was central to Liberty Street's mission, as it was and remains for many Black churches, especially in impoverished communities (Sexton et al. 2006, 3; Taylor and Chatters 1988, 193). As Jeffrey Levin, a public health scholar who focuses on the role of the Black Church in community medicine, argues, the church often becomes the primary social institution in the Black community—"it has had to attend to the total needs of its members. . . . The Black minister has been teacher, preacher, funeral director, and, recently, agent of health change" (Levin 1984, 478). Danielle gave further example of this care in her own recovery:

This same building we're in right now? I remember I went to the church and I told him [Pastor Samuel] I didn't have anywhere to stay, and this [building] was a house, and he put me and my children in this house. Gave us money for food. He never once said, "Get her out of here until she really make up her mind that she want to do right." He never done that. And there were others that prayed, but just him being the leader, man of God . . . you know? Like I said, there's a lot of ministers [who would have] told their deacons, "When that girl come here next Sunday, don't let her come in disturbing the congregation." And I used to come bare feet, dirty, drugged out, and they had people that gave me, showed me love . . .

The support made a critical difference, returning Danielle to God. "I came to know that I tried everything else," she finished. "And I knew the only hope for me was to come back to the church." It is important to note, however, that while Danielle's recovery was undoubtedly made possible by the services and resources she received, it resulted more fundamentally from the salvation she experienced, an experience that still anchored her religious conviction. While Pastor Samuel and the members of Liberty Street had taken her in, it was Jesus who had set her free.

Centering the (Religious) Experience and Knowledge of Black Women

Danielle had just begun to share her testimony, but it already revealed a deep knowledge, based on an experience of life and death in the contemporary American city. This was, however, the knowledge of a poor Black woman, and while its significance seemed clear from the perspective of those who were privileged, as I was, to listen and learn, it was otherwise devalued by the world. As I discuss in the introduction to this book, the suppression of Black women's knowledge "makes it easier for dominant groups to rule . . . [and] has been critical in maintaining social inequalities" in the United States and across the African diaspora (Collins 2000a, 3). This suppression takes multiple forms, and while Black women continue to resist, their concerns are still subordinated to the agendas of white male elites, white feminists, and a Black intellectualism with a "prominent masculinist bias" (7). A corrective centering is thus required (Collins 2000b, 44).

This work has already begun, as existing scholarship makes clear. Extending from the legacies of several African American women forebears (including Zora Neale Hurston, Katherine Dunham, Caroline Bond Day, and Johnnetta Betsch Cole) and beginning in the 1960s, the corrective centering of Black women was fueled by the formation of several related disciplines, including women's studies, Black studies, and urban studies (Mullings 1997, 2; see also Bolles 2001, 30–32). Despite institutional and other roadblocks (Mullings 1997, 2), an intersectional approach emerged by the 1980s that understood that Black women's experiences "were shaped not just by race, but by gender, social class, and sexuality" (Collins 2000a, 18).[1] Anthropological research on Black women in the United States has thus focused on a number of important themes, including the nature and impact of violence and Black women's methods of survival (Stack 1974; Waterston 1999; D.-A. Davis 2006), activism around key issues such as affordable and safe housing (Gregory 1998; Isoke 2013; Cox 2015), and Black women's health, with a focus on disease, access to health care, and practices of health recovery and resilience (Fraser 1998; Waterston 1999; Mullings and Wali 2001; Mattingly 2014).

However, Danielle's testimony suggests a closer alignment between research that attends to the social and political groundings of Black women's lives and research that explores the religious and other transcendent dimensions of their simultaneous strivings for healing, justice, and peace. This kind of alignment, I argue, would produce an inquiry that is cognizant of the realities of Black urban life but attuned to the fundamental interventions (of personhood, relatedness, value) necessary for change. Black women's religious experience and knowledge, therefore, must also come to the forefront.[2]

Within existing scholarship on African American Christian women, several historical studies make visible the contributions of women to the Black Church (Collier-Thomas 1997, 2010) and to the Black Baptist church in particular (Higginbotham 1993). Higginbotham, for example, examines the work of Black Baptist women from the late nineteenth century through the early twentieth century. Following the everyday actions and interactions of church laity rather than clergy, Higginbotham traces the women's movement that emerged alongside the National Baptist Convention. This movement became a base of power within a male-dominated institution, a space where Black women could address social problems and provide services as they forged a new identity. As Higginbotham (1993, 186) states, "a national constituency of black women asserted agency in the construction and representation of themselves as new subjectivities—as Americans as well as blacks and women." Such studies, as Judith Casselberry (2017, 4) summarizes, demonstrate how women used faith and the institution of the church as "springboards to social, civic, and political associations, sometimes under the auspices of the church, [and] sometimes in distinct faith-inspired organizations for Black advancement."

Ethnographic research has brought more direct attention to religious experience (Frederick 2003; Abrums 2010; Butler 2007; Crumbley 2012; Abrams 2014; Casselberry 2017). Marla Frederick examines the spiritual lives of twentieth-century Black Baptist women in the rural South, finding that women anchored their spirituality in a range of practices and expressions. These included gratitude (the ability to turn experiences of struggle into prayers of thanksgiving for God's benevolence and intervention), empathy (the expression of compassion for others, particularly the ability to feel another's pain of loss or misfortune), and resistance in the form of righteous discontent (e.g., through the creation of alternative Black public spheres that address and resolve community concerns) (Frederick 2003, 65, 94).

More recently, Casselberry's ethnographic study of the religious labor of twenty-first-century Black women at a male-headed Pentecostal church in New York City points out a broader entanglement of religious experience, Black subjectivity, personhood, and the development of religious authority. The women in Casselberry's (2017) study develop an "unmediated relationship with Jesus" (171), which grounds their formation as "authentic religious subjects" (172) and guides the related authority they develop despite the gendered church hierarchy in which they remain. Casselberry's primary intent, however, is to understand "the circumstances of producing a *holy Black female personhood* within faith communities" (2017, 5, emphasis added) and how this identification then translates to "righteous living within the church community, in [women's] professional lives, and homes" (Casselberry 2013, 73). As Casselberry (2017, 171) writes, "[women] develop strategies and create negotiated spaces, ultimately formulating a politics of righteousness. Thus, they are able to (re-)produce women-driven patriarchies, emboldened by the knowledge that, like Jesus, they 'have the power to submit.'" Through particular registers of labor ("organizational, emotional, intimate, and aesthetic"; 44), and "navigating webs of spiritual, social, and organizational relationships," these women direct their efforts "toward personally growing in Christ and growing the church—both the institution and the Kingdom" (172).

The centering of Black women's religious experience develops also through the aims of womanist theology. As Cheryl A. Kirk-Duggan (2014, 267) explains, "womanist theology emerged as a corrective discipline during the 1980s, concerned about the plight of black women in the United States, of global African diaspora women, ultimately the wholeness of all persons across gender, race, class, age, and ability."[3] Distinct from Black theology (which privileged the perspectives of Black male theologians) and feminist theology (which privileged the lives of white women), womanist theology, in the words of J. Kameron Carter (2014, 180), accounts "for how black women have been forced to exist in their bodies in ways that differ from both white women and black men and *how they have constructed faith responses to negotiate and renegotiate the terms of their existence*" (emphasis added). The theology has five core elements: it "works against oppression, for liberation; is vernacular of everyday realities; is non ideological, abhorring rigid lines of demarcation toward decentralization; is communitarian, where collective well-being is the goal of social change; and is spiritualized: it acknowledges a spiritual/transcendental realm where humanity, creation, and matter interconnect" (Kirk-Duggan 2014, 268).[4]

Danielle's own faith response, a renegotiation of existence about which she continued to testify, revealed a similar emphasis on the cultivation of personhood as well as a sense of spiritual and moral authority that developed despite the continued hierarchies of church and society. Much of this was based on her growing awareness and capacity, as a holy Black female and authentic religious subject, to mediate the space of death and transformation. The restorative practices that she and the other women subsequently developed, therefore, included the cultivation of one's personhood through relatedness with the living and the dead as well as the repositioning of the deceased as valued somebodies in both earthly and eternal realms. To center this work is to shed light on the histories, realities, and possibilities of African American women's religious life and labor beyond traditional frameworks and apart from more visible proceedings.

Organizing Support

Shortly after Rock's death, in the spring of 2005, Pastor Samuel approached Danielle to ask whether she would speak with the news media about the impact of violent crime. He had been inspired by Danielle's strength in the face of her devastating loss, noticing how she had been able to "stand" with God's help "in the midst of it all." However, when the television crew arrived to interview her, it was on a day when Danielle did not feel strong at all. "They caught me at a time when I was down and out," she told me, continuing her testimony. "I was going through a grieving process [about] my son, and I almost did not let them in because I just felt that they wanted me to do their work."

In that moment, however, Danielle's sorrow somehow became the inspiration for her service. She thought about the other women who were also suffering from the impact of violence and how she might use her own experience and knowledge to be of support. "I had a different mindset after I thought about it," she said.

I thought, this could be an opportunity to reach another mother, so I'm going to go ahead on and let them [the media] in. And when they came I asked them if they had any other mothers that they had talked to . . . and the lady said "Yes, but none of them want to come forward and say anything, they are afraid to talk."

Danielle had faith, however, that the women would talk to *her* and to each other, and this gave her the idea for the support group. As she explained,

I called up a couple of people that I knew and asked them would they be interested in coming to a mothers group and they said, "Yes, we want to come." And I asked Pastor Samuel about it, and he said, "That would be good, if that's what you want to do." He said, "It's needed . . . with all the crime we got going on . . . and there is nothing like a mother's pain."

Danielle recruited group members in a variety of ways. She talked to people she knew, and they in turn helped spread the word, armed with informational flyers and a number to call with questions. Her most effective method, however, was more personal and direct. Upon hearing about a murder, Danielle would simply go to the neighborhood where it happened and ask for the victim's family: "I finds out where it happened, and we go in that area and we just ask anyone, 'Do you know where that young man lived that got killed?' Something like that, and they say, 'Oh yeah, he lived right over there,' because they know. And then I'll just introduce myself and just go and share with the mother." At what seemed like the appropriate time, she would invite the mother or the grandmother to come to the support group. I asked whether the women she encountered were receptive to her overtures. "Oh yes," she replied.

There was a murder a couple of weeks ago . . . and that grandmother called me up yesterday and we talked for almost an hour. She's never been to group, but she's got questions. And you know that fourteen-year-old child who got shot the other day? I spoke with his mother twice today. I've never seen her in person, but I will see her tonight when I go over there.

The group met weekly, first at the church and then later in the community development building across the street, which had more room and was open in the evening when people could attend. Danielle explained the change of venue:

When we were across the street [at the church] we had only one hour, because you know they had to turn the alarm on and clean up. And it was too short. So, I told Pastor that we need two hours, and we do. And he said, "Well, when things get settled across the street, I'm gonna let you in that building, and you'll be able to have group how long you want.' And I said, "OK, Pastor."

She smiled as she recounted this exchange, pleased that she had got what she wanted while making it seem as if she had never asked. "And now we're here on Thursdays and I have this little office, and that just makes me feel so good to be able to do certain things you know, and have the group," she finished. "But we still try to close out by 8:00."

During the time that I attended group sessions, the women who gathered were all African American and Christian (predominantly Baptist). Besides Danielle, only two others were members of Liberty Street; the rest came from congregations across the city. Nearly all of them had lost a child, a son or a grandson, within the last five years. This may have been due to Danielle's recruiting strategies as well as the acute need for support in the first few years of grief. The meetings functioned best, however, when women with longer experiences of grief were also present. Sister Shirley, for example, who lost her son in 1995, was a regular attendee and a strong source of support for newer members, sharing her own spiritual journey toward acceptance and a sense of "total peace" that others hoped to one day experience. Apart from a core group of about four or five women, including Danielle and Sister Shirley, the other attendees came and went. As Danielle noted, "They were coming faithfully for a while [when the group first began] but it has slowed down. But I still keep in contact with everybody, and if they feel the need to come they do. We just let people know that we're here."

The group received support from Liberty Street in the form of meeting and office space as well as some financial support for supplies. As founder, Danielle handled the administrative affairs and served as the group's main contact person and facilitator. She often worried, however, about her ability to sustain the group, especially given the limits she perceived of her skills and her reliance on sporadic volunteers. Danielle hoped to secure nonprofit status so she could apply for operational and program support. As she explained, "I want to apply for grants, but for some reason I can't find the right person to help me . . . so, I just go with it. But I know eventually God is gonna have someone to help me . . . because [there are] other things that we want to do."

A Women's Group

Danielle's organization of the support group sheds additional light on the reach and impact of Black women's religious labor, both within and outside of the church. In particular it makes clear the challenges that are inherent in such work as women navigate the complex terrain of the church as institution. However, it also demonstrates the ways in which they create space for their development as religious subjects and for their contribution to the church and broader community. While the division of labor in the Black Baptist church has historically been determined according to a male-dominated hierarchy (Higginbotham 1993, 3),[5] women nonetheless find the sites and methods they require for their worship and work.

While specific gender roles were not explicitly prescribed at Liberty Street, it was clear that men and women were perceived to be different, with different capacities and responsibilities. These differences came forward especially in the church's antiviolence ministries, where male clergy and parishioners assumed most of the visible and public roles. They did so with an intent, however, that seemed less about claiming power and more about the responsibility that many men felt to take a stand against violence, which meant also taking a stand against the larger forces that continued to see these same men as the cause of violence to begin with. They found strength and solidarity, therefore, in declarations of "Black Men Standing *Together*" (emphasis in original), which appeared on the T-shirts they wore ("ENOUGH" on the front and "Black Men Standing *Together*" on the back) as they placed themselves on the front lines of marches, rallies, and other events. Their claim to authority within the church, therefore, intersected with the authority they sought more broadly as the leaders and protectors rather than the destroyers of the Black community.

The women of the church were supportive of these claims. They, too, wore T-shirts to these events, theirs emblazoned with "Black Women Standing *Behind* Strong Black Men" (emphasis in original). With such statements, women appeared to be accepting of existing structures of authority and committed to the mostly behind-the-scenes labor they still provided for the growth and success of the church. As Higginbotham argues, in reference to Black Baptists in the late nineteenth and early twentieth centuries, while Black religious women most certainly became the leaders of many causes—including the fight against lynching and campaigns for voting rights, employment, and educational opportunities—more often than not their work was located in everyday action through the provision of social services (Higginbotham 1993, 2) and not in the frontline battles where men typically took the lead. Casselberry (2017, 171–172) reminds us, however, that everyday actions can still challenge gender hierarchies and lead to authority in subtle yet effective ways.

These dynamics were certainly at play in 2005 when Danielle founded the Mothers Group. While the group was clearly her idea, it could not form without the blessing and support of the male leadership of the church. Indeed, it was Pastor Samuel who had encouraged Danielle to speak with the media in the first place, and it was to him that Danielle went for permission and resources to get the group off the ground. Her ability to navigate both internal and external relationships was not insignificant. It was Danielle who spoke with the media and the pastor, and it was she who then reached out to women in the community.

This initiative came not from a desire for authority but from an understanding of violence and the depth of pain that was experienced in its aftermath as well as a belief that her efforts could make a difference. However, it led to authority all the same. For the premise of the support group was also tied to the belief that there was something distinct about a *mother's* pain following the death of a child. As Danielle explained, "You know, a mother is different from a father when she lose her child. I'm not saying the father don't care but there is a unique love there that a mother have *natural* that only a mother have, you know, and a grandmother, I would say." I asked if any men had inquired about the group, and Danielle told me that a few had, one of them declaring, "*Mothers* hurting? Well, fathers hurting too!" Danielle, however, was clear about her mission: "I really want to keep it mothers and grandmothers right now. Dealing with the men, you know, it's alright too. But *I've* been made to deal with the mothers and the grandmothers."

Her statement demonstrated the continued development and assertion of women's capacities in specific dimensions of religious and social practice even if claims to authority were not overtly made. Based on the experience of violence through the death of a son or grandson, the women at Liberty Street developed a distinct knowledge—with God and Christ at the center—of social and spiritual relatedness, its severing, and its potential

CHAPTER FIVE

restoration. As Danielle said, "The pain, the pain is so severe to see. I went to so many funerals, and it's like I ask God to just, you know, it's like he prepare me, he preparing me to be there . . . my chest get tight. Then I go to thinking about her [the other grieving mother] pain. I be feeling sorry for *her*. And I really believe that my pain is not essential as it was before. It's all about *her* pain now, because God is healing *me* to deal with *her* pain."

Raising the Dead

The pain that Danielle spoke of, with authority, was as complex as it was acute. It was rooted in oppression and a resulting vulnerability that had accumulated over generations and it was experienced most frequently in the wake of death, be it sudden death or the denial of personhood that preceded and followed. To address this pain, therefore, required not only practices of mourning, or mutual support, but the *restoration* of kinship through the assertion of relatedness and worth. In this way, the women "raised" their dead sons and grandsons.

As I describe in the introduction to this book, the context of vulnerability and violence at the urban margins is productively understood as a "space of death," a space conceptualized as a condition of endemic terror connected to the painful world history of conquest and colonization (Taussig 1987, 5). However, it is by coming close to death, understanding firsthand its social and physical entanglements, that "a more vivid sense of life" becomes possible (7). This way of living and thinking through terror is transformative; thus, the space of death is "important in the creation of meaning and consciousness," allowing for "illumination" as much as it brings about "extinction" (4). Sharon Patricia Holland (2000, 4) draws on Taussig to constitute the United States as a continued space of death and to consider the illumination that occurs at the intersection of death and Black subjectivity. In her focus on the creative and cultural innovations of Black, indigenous, and queer writers, artists, and critics, Holland sheds light on an essential process—that of "raising the dead" (4). This is primarily a figurative and intellectual endeavor focused on uncovering silences and "transforming inarticulate places into conversational territories" (3–4). And it allows the dead to speak, "providing them with the agency of physical bodies in order to tell the story of a death-in-life" (4). However, given the extent to which "black subjects share the space the dead inhabit" (6), a consideration of "raising the dead" as lived experience is also warranted. As Holland asserts, "Perhaps the most revolutionary intervention into conversations at the margins of race, gender, and sexuality is to let the dead—those already denied a sustainable subjectivity—speak from the place that is familiar to them" (4).

For Danielle and the other women in the Mothers Group, raising the dead occurred in a variety of ways. Gathered together, the women opened their meetings with prayer. As they introduced themselves, they shared testimonies recounting their own movements through grief and toward acceptance and peace. They affirmed their relationship with God and their belief in His power not only for their continued recovery but for the recovery of their families, communities, and the city at large. With this foundation, they named and honored the dead, identifying the relationships that were meaningful to them and asserting the value of lost loved ones regardless of social status and history. These practices extended to special events, such as the marking of birthdays and death anniversaries. In addition to providing support for grieving women on difficult days, such events gave a recurrent structure to the raising of the dead, which challenged death's presumed finality. Beyond the church setting, the women engaged in outreach and advocacy work. They supported each other in more public dealings with law enforcement personnel and the criminal justice system. They accompanied each other to court, made phones calls, distributed flyers around the neighborhood asking witnesses to come forward, and provided assistance with basic needs such as food, medical care, and shelter. They also organized retreats, which served as opportunities to get away for an occasional weekend, as Danielle described it, to "release that stress."

To illustrate, I continue the description of the support-group session, which began this chapter, marking Danté's birthday and the death anniversary of Marcus. With Danielle, Miss Vivian (Danté's grandmother), and Mrs. Adams (Marcus' mother), now settled around the center table, the women were invited to introduce themselves and share their testimonies, providing as much detail as they desired about their circumstances, their journeys of faith and recovery, and the lives and deaths of their loved ones. When Miss Vivian's turn arrived, she took a moment to compose herself, and then she spoke, her voice low and unsteady, her words filling up the room. "I lost my only grandson, Danté, on February twenty-fifth. He was sixteen years old," she began.

And when I lost him I just lost *everything*. He was in my home for Carnival, he had visited me from Texas, and he came down. Me and my nieces and all my family, we took him to the parades. He was so happy. And this was after I had begged him not to come. I said, "please don't come, they killing people out there and it's dangerous!" He said, "Mom, I want to come and see the parades. I haven't seen the parades since before Hurricane Katrina." So, his other grandma bought him a ticket, and I said OK.

We went out the weekend, Mardi Gras Day. We had a good time. And he was on the phone, with his little cell, he loved to talk to the girls, he had so many little girls. And so, he left out my home like Monday night about ten after ten. And I told him, I said, "You know it's too late to go anywhere." He said, "Mom I'll be *right back*, you always think it's something to happen to me but I'll be *fine*." So, he walked out the door and I never saw him again. He was a little mad, he shoved me, well he didn't shove me he kind of nudged me to the side, you know, because I'm always so protective of him and stuff. He left, and I have never seen him again.

The women around the table nodded their heads in recognition; all of them had been protective of their own children and grandchildren, trying their best to keep them safe but free in a world they knew was neither. Miss Vivian's voice slowed as she continued, remembering the moment she found out that her grandson had been killed.

They didn't even find his body until 7:00 the next morning. And I kept calling him all night on his cell phone. And by me living alone, I didn't have nobody to go with me to walk the streets looking for him . . . I said well maybe he done slip out to meet his friend at the basketball goal, until that next morning when everybody knocking on my door and calling me and stuff . . . when I looked, he was, well all I could see was the crime tape out there. And everybody come running to me and I was just, you know, I was just in another . . .

Her voice trailed off, and the women beside her tightened their grip on her back and arms. Some of them had heard her testimony before and they knew where it was leading—to the remembrance of a previous death, in a cycle of violence with which they were all too familiar.

And I couldn't believe it had happened to me again. Because I lost my only child, too, which my only child was his father, and I lost him, he was carjacked. He testified; he was a witness in a murder trial. He was gunned down ten hours after, carjacked, after he testified. And the only grandchild I had was Danté. My life will never be the same. I want justice. I want to go to court and I want to find out who did this . . . because he was a good kid, you know? And he didn't deserve to die like this. They shot him in his back. You know it's hard, how things are, I have all my family and so many others that support me. But sometimes I don't know if I can walk.

The air was heavy in the now silent room, but the others quickly voiced their support. Danielle did her best to comfort, saying quietly, "Yeah. I feel your pain and we all do here, you know. But I want you to know Miss Vivian, you're not alone. We are here for you anytime we can be. And we are praying and we know that it's going to take time and anything that we can do to support and help you with this we will." Miss Vivian nodded, grateful. An elderly woman sitting next to her, another grandmother whose grandson had also been murdered, leaned in close to confirm, "Yes, indeed," she said, simply.

The introductions passed next to Mrs. Adams, who was there to mark the one-year death anniversary of her son Marcus. While Mrs. Adams was a regular attendee at the group sessions, the testimony she gave on this anniversary was more detailed, set in the context of her own family's cycle of violence, with life punctuated by the violent deaths of not one but two sons.

I lost my son Xavier in 2000 . . . that was my first son that got killed . . . it was the worst thing that ever happened to me. And I just, I wanted to die, because I really didn't want to, you know, see my child leave before me. But I had to. God had told me, "I didn't take them all, I only took one. I left you some more." And I thank God for the rest of my children. And then in 2008, I lost my second son, Marcus . . . I was just numb to that one right there. You know? It was just devastating to me. But nevertheless, I know that God is good . . . he gives them [children] to us for a while. And I'm not even worried about them because I know they are up there [in heaven] having a joyful time.

She smiled then, tacking back and forth between sorrow to joy in a way that was characteristic of many of the women's testimonies.

And I just thank God because God is keeping me and He uplifts me. And I miss them, I miss my happy children . . . And you know it's hard when they birthday come, my birthday come, mother's day come, father's day come. It's very hard. You know, it's very hard when the holidays come when your family members is gone. I think we do more suffering around that time. But I know that God has everything in hand, and I thank God that he is taking care of me and the rest of them.

In the middle of Mrs. Adams's testimony, the doorbell rang. Danielle excused herself and went to the front of the building, returning with two women. The meeting paused as everyone shifted to open up space at the table. After Mrs. Adams finished speaking, Danielle welcomed the newcomers and invited them to introduce themselves. The elder woman spoke first, "OK, I'm Odette," she said. "I've been hearing about this, but I never came." "We're glad to have you," Danielle responded. Odette continued, "And . . . um, I feel the pain for people. I just lost my son-in-law. That's what really brought me here." She put her arm gently around the shoulders of the daughter beside her. "Her husband," she said. "Oh, I'm sorry," Danielle said, the other women nodded their heads in sympathy. Odette continued,

I also lost my son and then last year I lost my grandson. That's his baby. And I lost an adopted son. I just lost and lost. But God is good and through it all I really have learned, because when it first happened . . . it's so devastating . . . but I've learned to lean and depend on God, and I realized by me fighting his will [it] made me suffer longer. When I realized to accept his will then I could . . . *lay down with it*. I talked to my daughter even though she's young but she's had a terrible blow, [and] I've been trying to tell her things to make it easier for her.

As far as I'm concerned, death bring you closer to Jesus than anything I know. Because He the only one who can help you. [*Amen!*] People look at me just saying, "How are you . . . you're a strong woman, you done lost all your children and you're strong?" Well baby, it is not me. It's not me. He got something *good* for me. He didn't put me here for nothing and left me here!

With this, the room erupted in spontaneous praise, the other women clapping their hands and shouting out "Yes *ma'am!*" "Amen!" "That's *right!*" Encouraged, though not really one to be deterred, Odette continued with the details of her family's most recent loss. "So, I don't know if you all heard about it," she said, "but that was my son-in-law who got killed in his place of business, in a bar." Danielle had indeed heard of the murder and turned quickly to Odette's daughter, "Oh that was your husband?" she asked. She nodded. "I'm so *sorry*," Danielle said. Odette's daughter was not ready to speak, so Odette responded on her behalf, taking care to situate her son-in-law in close family relation, apart from the associations that were so quickly made about homicide victims and criminal activity. "Yeah, and we were very, very close me and him. He was like [placing her hand on her heart] . . . and that did it for me, too, because like he didn't live *that* life. People liked him." Danielle jumped in, "I heard he *was* a very nice person." Odette nodded, continuing,

He was a good father and husband. I wouldn't lie to you, you know? Everybody liked him. . . . And he . . . I have two grandchildren . . . that he had been dressing since they were babies. Putting they clothes on, putting the two chairs in the car, taking them to school. And he did that until the day he died. . . . That's a big void in my daughter and the boys' lives, and it hurt me to see that, but the Lord gonna make her strong. And we gonna get through it. So, we heard about this [group]. . . . I'm gonna try to make this a regular thing.

Danielle responded, energized by Odette's enthusiasm for the group and what she believed it would provide. "Well good," she said. "We would be very, very happy to have you."

Odette's daughter had not yet spoken, and Danielle kept glancing in her direction, keen to offer help to a young mother so obviously in pain. Her tone shifted slightly as she continued to describe the group and its purpose, which was a subtle way of gently urging the young woman not to lose faith and promising, as much as she could, that knowledge and strength would come *through* the experience of death and mourning with time and by the power of God.

We know that the only person can do the healing is the good Lord Jesus Christ, but . . . we want to make this a safe environment where we can come if we have to cry. If we want to mourn, if we want to just laugh and have a good time, we can do it here. And keep the memories alive. And some may say, well how can I? How can I do this when my loved one has been murdered? But God will give you the strength to give you the joy that you need to get where you need to be . . . God can bring you through anything, anything that you are going through, okay?

Apprenticed to (Black) Death

Practices of Black death and dying, such as those illustrated at Liberty Street, remain understudied within existing inquiries in the humanities and social sciences. While the anthropology of death is well established, the focus of research has arguably been narrow. As Antonius Robben summarizes, despite the contributions of early studies—for example, of death as social event or rite of passage (Frazer [1890] 1940; Hertz [1907] 1960; Van Gennep [1909] 1960)—the inquiry lay relatively dormant until the 1970s (Robben 2004, 2). Even after its revival, primarily through ethnographic research, its aims and findings remained unclear. Johannes Fabian, writing in the early 1970s, identifies no major groundbreaking work, concluding that "the anthropologist's contribution toward understanding death in modern society can only be made in a roundabout way" (Fabian 1972, 544), that is, through the aims and findings of other disciplines, such as psychology. Palgi and Abramovitch (1984, 386, 413) reach a similar conclusion a decade later, finding little consensus within existing scholarship regarding the seminal questions that should concern the anthropologist's study of death and calling for more comparative cross-cultural research. While Robben answers this call, using "the trajectory from dying to afterlife" as an organizing principle and categorizing relevant research into six main areas—conceptualizations of death, death and dying, uncommon death, grief and mourning, mortuary rituals, and remembrance and regeneration (Robben 2004, 2)—the result is a current but still hesitant inquiry, its theoretical and comparative potential not fully realized and certainly not expanded to the contemporary Black context (12).

Veena Das and Clara Han, editors of a volume on living and dying in the contemporary world, put forward a more integrative conceptualization, productively situating the inquiry within the simultaneous perils and possibilities of the everyday among ordinary people but in an increasingly interconnected world (2015, 1). This opens space in particular for research on the circumstances, beliefs, and practices of historically marginalized populations in part by understanding the relationship between life and death as close and constitutive rather than opposed or in finite terms of beginning and end. As Robert Desjarlais (2016, 242) states, in scholarship that both grounds and extends this perspective,

Death is often taken to be the polar opposite of life. Yet it can also be said that the words "life" and "death" mark situations more complicated than that binary arrangement alone. The ever-changing flow of life and death, presence and absence, includes varying intensities and thresholds of existence, the circling of memories plush with life, moments at once actual and virtual, ghosts as real as people and people as vacant as ghosts. The end of one set of bonds leads to new strands of connection.

These new strands of connection were certainly key for the women at Liberty Street, whose rituals and practices, at support-group gatherings and in other settings, focused on the identification, cultivation, and *restoration* of the bonds that formed and sustained a valued human existence. As Das and Han (2015, 623) suggest, "death is present within life," and "dying is not simply something that happens to individuals but calls forth a response from all those affected by this process as much as it does from the dying person." What comes into view, therefore, are the ways in which people become "apprenticed to death," meaning "that for both the dying person and the caregivers and survivors, the issue is of coming to death not so much in general but with the particular—a sense of an ending here and now in relation to a concrete other as body, as person, as future memory" (624).

Desjarlais examines this process ethnographically among Yolmo Buddhists in Nepal, exploring the work that the dying perform to prepare for death and to leave things right for the living as well as the work that the living do on behalf of the dying and the deceased (2015, 648; see also Das and Han 2015, 624). As Desjarlais argues, Yolmo Buddhists are concerned with dying "a good death," and they thus "undertak[e] a quiet apprenticeship on the matter" through a number of preparations involving the dying person and their supporting family members and friends (2015, 651). What emerges is an essential relationship that engages the living and the dead "in delicate technologies of cessation and transformation" (Desjarlais 2016, 9). Their practices, such as cremation or the burning of effigies to deliver consciousness from the body, are understood as "a kind of co-poiesis . . . a collaborative fashioning and unfashioning of self and other, as well as . . . a poiesis-on-behalf-of another." Thus, "The call for the living to labor on behalf of the deceased makes such efforts a matter of care, responsibility, and honor, implying an ethics of mourning" (15).

The kinds of apprenticeships that emerge at Liberty Street, however, are distinct, as they relate not just to death but to *Black* death in its normative and frequently violent repetition. The untimely nature of death for Blacks in the United States and across the Americas is an unconscionable reality, in many ways part and parcel of the Black experience. Karla F. C. Holloway (2002, 3) describes this as a "cultural haunting" or a "re-memory" traced through "the residue of riots, executions, suicides, and targeted medical neglect." One must certainly begin this tracing with slavery and its lingering effects, what Saidiya Hartman (2007, 6) refers to as the "afterlife of slavery," before moving, as Tonya Armstrong (2010, 83) does, through the extended trauma of Jim Crow, the violent opposition to civil rights, disease, social neglect, violence, and systems of criminalization and incarceration to arrive at the peril that persists "in the collective African-American consciousness." Christina Sharpe (2016, 15) connects this to an understanding of Black being—where living "in the wake" of slavery or of terror more broadly in past and present time—is "the ground of our everyday Black existence . . . in that in much of what passes for public discourse *about* terror we, Black people, become the *carriers* of terror, terror's embodiment, and not the primary objects of terror's multiple enactments; the ground of terror's possibility globally."

To be apprenticed to Black death is thus something else, its preparations and practices emerging through what Sharpe (2016, 17–18) calls "wake work," the development of new ways of being and dwelling, through modes "of inhabiting *and* rupturing this episteme with our known lived and un/imaginable lives" (emphasis in original). As Sharpe asks and then answers, "What does it mean to defend the dead? To tend to the Black dead and dying: to tend to the Black person, to Black people, always living in the push toward our death? It means work. It is work: hard emotional, physical, and intellectual work that demands vigilant attendance to the needs of the dying, to ease their way, and also to the needs of the living" (10). These questions lead to others, particularly concerning the ways that we might understand both the "orthography of the wake" (20) and wake work in the everyday. What were the particular dimensions of this work for the women at Liberty Street? What were the beliefs and practices of mourning, remembrance, and continued relatedness that directed an apprenticeship such as theirs?

To explore these questions, I am further guided by an emerging theoretical and ethnographic inquiry that focuses on Black women, the maternal, and the raising of the dead at the critical juncture of violence, sorrow, and death. The forward motion of this inquiry is best encapsulated in a special issue of the journal *Transforming Anthropology* titled "Sorrow-As-Artifact: Radical Black Mothering in Times of Terror" and guest edited by Christen A. Smith. In a note by the journal's editorial team, the aims of the issue are stated: the articles "shed light on the continued need for transformative writing and research to address the myriad forms of racism, sexism, homophobia, transphobia, as well as the diverse structural inequalities—the transnational and diasporic hegemonies—that constrict our movement, maim our communities, and infect us with sorrow" (Ralph et al. 2016, 3). Smith (2016a, 31) makes clear the reach of these conditions across the Black diaspora, describing a collective "slow death caused by sequelae . . . the gendered, reverberating, deadly effects of state terror that infect the affective communities of the dead." "Nowhere are these effects more acutely visible," Smith (2016b, 31) argues, "than in the experiences of Black mothers who have lost their children to state violence."

Black women's sorrow is thus an important "artifact," one that sheds light on the development, dimensions, and possible dismantling of a larger social condition. As Smith (2016b, 6) states,

To think of sorrow as artifact is to consider the way that sorrow, as grief, as mourning, as longing, as suffering—is the residue, that is, the trace left behind *in the wake* of tragedy. . . . To think of sorrow as artifact within the context of a discussion of Black mothering is to consider sorrow as something more than just an emotion of sentience; it is the aftermath of our social moment. Sorrow as artifact thus provides clues into what it means to mother as Black women in times of terror. (emphasis added)

This framing broadens our view of state violence and its impact, but it also calls for research that better recognizes Black women's responses as they individually and collectively guide the way to safety and social and political change (Smith 2016a, 38). Such progress hinges, as Smith further argues, on the recognition that Black women's responses emerge from a fundamental desire for hope and human dignity, "not just to live but for our children to live as well." It is this desire that emboldens women to resist oppression, to choose the terms by which they respond, and to "affront the necropolitical power of the state by harnessing death in the service of life," to the extent that they are able. This is what constitutes Smith's notion of "radical Black mothering" at the juncture of life, death, self, and other—"at once terrifying . . . potentially liberating . . . [and] by definition, poetic" (44).[6]

In my examination of these practices at Liberty Street, I again bring religious experience to the forefront to understand not only the terrifying and potentially liberating juncture of radical Black mothering but how women mediate that juncture, particularly in ways that extend beyond expected means and realms of engagement. While there is not a great deal of ethnographic research on these processes, I draw on two recent examples. In an essay written for the same special issue of *Transforming Anthropology*, Rhaisa Kameela Williams examines the suicide of her paternal grandmother, who took her own life just two weeks after the murder of her daughter, Williams's aunt. The suicide resulted from the grandmother's stated desire to travel to the afterworld in order to save her daughter from the pains of purgatory, given the sins she had committed in life (2016, 23). Williams considers both the reactionary and revolutionary dimensions of such an act, her analysis troubling our expectations for Black maternal grief by rethinking especially our reliance on narratives of survival and sacrifice (29). What is also compelling, however, is the extension of the maternal across standard boundaries of life and death, spanning material and immaterial realms of being and belonging in the here and the hereafter. Grief in this instance, as a response to terror, forces us to consider women's capacity to understand and mediate such expansive geographies.[7]

LeRhonda S. Manigault-Bryant's (2014, 2) ethnographic study of "talking to the dead" is another important guide. Set among Gullah and Geechee women—the African American inhabitants of the barrier islands and coastal lowlands of Georgia and South Carolina—and working at the intersection of religious studies, gender studies, history, and anthropology, Manigault-Bryant investigates a central question: "How do Gullah/Geechee women negotiate traditional practices associated with their cultural identity in the midst of significant historical and generational change?" The most immediate answer, Manigault-Bryant maintains, is that they talk to the dead.

To understand this engagement, one must first understand the open-ended rather than restricted notion of death that Gullah and Geechee women maintain. As Manigault-Bryant writes, the women in her study interpret the dead not "as inactive or silent but as consistently present." Talking to the dead thus occurs in multiple ways. It begins with an initial "sensing or feeling a deceased person's presence." One then "listens to what the deceased has to say or tells the deceased about one's concerns, needs, or hopes" (Manigault-Bryant 2014, 105). This exchange is frequently silent, based on a sense of connectivity to one's family and community that extends the past through the present and guides women forward in their daily lives and future aspirations.[8]

This connectivity sustains women as they navigate daily life, supporting them as they make vital choices and decisions: "Talking to the dead greatly informs how they negotiate changes in their own lives and within their communities as it helps determine their actions and reactions while simultaneously gesturing to the histories and past experiences that inform their present" (Manigault-Bryant 2014, 18). In this way, the practice is both grounded and generative—critical to cultural survival, especially given the contemporary context of "commodification, commercialization, urbanization, and modernization" in which the lives of Gullah/Geechee women now unfold (201).

What emerges is a deep spiritual connection that surpasses formal religious and social structures (Manigault-Bryant 2014, 18). Talking to the dead thus carries women past the perceived limits of their position or capacity, demonstrating the ways in which African American women inhabit but move beyond the spaces that have been historically defined for them. As Manigualt-Bryant states, the women "structured their own religious, social, and cultural networks; created their own spaces; and articulated their religion and spirituality in the terms that best suited their experiences and social locations" (202).

The implications of thinking about Black women in this way, less bereft by Black death and more apprenticed to its transformation through the raising of the dead, are both powerful and provocative. The framing allows mothers and grandmothers in New Orleans to step forward as the vital agents of change in ways that acknowledge their suffering and still affirm their insight and influence. Such a view was already expressed by the women themselves—one local clergywoman went so far as to compare the actions and interactions of grieving mothers to the care and mourning performed by the Blessed Mother at the foot of the cross. Referencing Michelangelo's sculpture the *Pietà*, Joan recalled the following:

I saw a picture, I think it was about two weeks ago. I was browsing the internet, and it showed the *Pietà*, Jesus in his mother's arms after he was taken down from the cross. And to me that says a lot about many of the mothers here in New Orleans. They are holding their dead sons, just as the Virgin is holding Jesus's dead body, you know, full of anguish and sorrow, and probably terror . . . that violence comes so close, so close to our homes, so close to us.

This capacity to "hold" the dead at the juncture of death and social and spiritual transformation—is important to consider. However, its assertion is also a risky enterprise, as Black women's facility in this regard has long been denied. In *American Pietàs: Visions of Race, Death, and the Maternal*, Ruby C. Tapia explains the context for this denial through an exploration of contemporary representations of the now iconic *Pietà*, especially its racialized and gendered renderings. Tapia's interest concerns "how and toward what end the racial project of the nation imbues some maternal bodies with resurrecting power and leaves others for (the) dead" (Tapia 2011, 24). "It is in the spaces between these different maternities," she argues, "that U.S. citizen-subjects are born and reborn" (24). Placing Black women and their deceased sons and grandsons at the foot of the cross, as Joan did, did more than affirm their relatedness in grief; it situated them as valued members of the divine family, on earth and in God's eternal kingdom. As Tapia argues, such positioning requires us to watch for and work against the dominance of sanctified "ideologies of patriotism and white supremacy that continue to support racialized, global technologies of memory, death, and ghosting" (21).

With this charge, and despite the risk, the women at Liberty Street continued to raise the dead. They maintained religious beliefs that countered the devaluing of Black lives; they created, accessed, and shared essential resources; and they developed specific practices of relatedness that extended beyond the standard boundaries of human existence. Their ultimate objective, which remained closely aligned with the mission of the church, was to lay the foundation for a beloved community based on the recognition and cultivation of a sacred Black humanity and the restoration of Black personhood, value, and connectivity that requires.

SIX

Restorative Kinship: Birthdays and Death Anniversaries for Children of God

I sing because I'm happy,
I sing because I'm free,
for His eye is on the sparrow,
and I know He watches me.   MARTIN AND GABRIEL (1905)

Sister Anne leaned forward to offer some final words of encouragement. It was near the end of the support-group session for the mothers and grandmothers who mourned the dead, and this evening they had gathered to mark the one-year death anniversary of Brian, Monica's son. They had also gathered to honor Monica herself, and they showered her with praise for how far she had come through what had been an extraordinarily difficult year. They were all quite relieved to be at this juncture, for there had been periods of grave concern about Monica's health over the last year, with friends and family genuinely afraid that she "wasn't going to make it." But there she was, sitting at the far end of the table, listening, and doing her best to keep it together.

Danielle had made special arrangements for the session to take place, explaining to Monica that, "We don't usually have group on Tuesday . . . but we put this day aside just for you, to be here in fellowship and support you." Sister Anne called the occasion a "milestone," worthy of celebration.

Nonetheless, she offered some suggestions to ensure Monica's continued well-being as the meeting came to a close. She urged her to call, anytime, if she needed anything. "Nothing you want to do or suggest to us is going to sound ridiculous," she told her.

As an example of something that might on the surface "sound ridiculous," Sister Anne shared a story about her cousin, who was also a grieving mother, having lost her own son just a few months before. "My cousin was about to break down at work one day and she told her coworkers 'I've got to go, I've got to go!'"

And so, she left. She went out to the cemetery, sat by her son's grave—she said she just cried her eyes out. In the midst of it she said a bird came and landed on the tombstone and began to sing. And she stopped crying, and was just looking at the bird. And so, the bird just sang and sang and sang. She said she just stared at the bird. And then the bird flew away.

Monica and the other women were quiet. "My, my," one woman remarked. "Wow, that's awesome," another added. Sister Anne went on, "Then my cousin got a phone call and went back to work. When she got there, everybody said, 'You back?' And all she said was, 'Yea. A bird sang to me.'" At this, the entire group laughed, but it was with a collective sense of reverence, not ridicule, at what had transpired. "My, my," the same woman remarked again, shaking her head in wonder.

Such contemplation of a bird singing in the cemetery might seem out of place when set against the backdrop of vulnerability, violence, and death in Black New Orleans. However, it was these very conditions that brought the women together in sorrow and support at Liberty Street Baptist Church in Central City. As I detail in the introduction to this book, such communities are still perceived, in both scholarly and popular analysis, as bounded and restrictive—places where Black people live and likely die. Especially given the high incidence of homicide in these locations, death seems an expected condition for Black urban dwelling. Reverence and wonder do not.

One might expect that residents' responses to death would be similarly scripted. Indeed, in many Black Protestant communities, surviving family members turn to the church. The bereaved request funerals, where they are joined by clergy, family members, and friends. After the services, they process to the cemeteries where the deceased are buried, and forever after mothers like Monica work hard to mourn the young men whose value the world has long denied. Thus, they speak to media outlets and grieve on camera; share testimony at public vigils and other events;

perform rituals; guard funeral programs, photographs, and other materials; and gather in support groups like the one at Liberty Street.

As I discuss in chapter 5, scholars have characterized the violent and untimely reality of death for Blacks in the United States and across the Americas as all too familiar, in many ways part and parcel of the Black experience. Death becomes a "cultural haunting" or a "residue" (Holloway 2002, 3), a lingering trauma that extends from slavery to the continued "peril" that resides "in the collective African-American consciousness" (T. D. Armstrong 2010, 83; see also Hartman 2007, 6, and Sharpe 2016, 15). We know, however, that death is neither constitutive of nor confined to the Black experience. Characterizations of Black death, therefore, also direct our attention to the structural, physical, and symbolic aspects of violence, so that we may situate the deaths of young Black men in New Orleans as stemming from multiple causes despite statistics that insist on the prevalence of drug trafficking and associated "black-on-black crime."

The grief that the women at Liberty Street felt in the aftermath of death was thus coupled with anger in direct response to violence and its disproportionate impact on Black families and communities. More fundamentally, it was tied to the sobering realization that underlying violence's forms were persistently negative determinations of Black social value. This fueled a deep sense of injustice with multiple origins, in response to the structures of oppression, the perpetrators and victims of violence caught up in cycles of killing and retaliation, and law enforcement and criminal justice personnel who seemed unable, more often than not, to ensure safety or bring about justice. While the frequency of death might confirm a cultural haunting, its causes were certainly no mystery.

To better illustrate how this condition of death might be expanded through a consideration of reverence, I return to the support-group session that marked the birthday of Danté, Miss Vivian's deceased grandson, and the death anniversary of Marcus, Mrs. Adams's son. Danielle had welcomed the attendees, including newcomers Odette and her daughter, who were reeling from the recent murder of Odette's son-in-law, her daughter's husband. Odette had just given a rousing testimony, confirming the joy she found in the Lord in the midst of the violence she encountered on earth. Her daughter, however, remained silent until Danielle turned gently in her direction. "Would you like to share who you are?" she asked. "I'm Tia," was all she could manage. "You say you're the wife, huh?" Danielle asked, and Tia nodded quietly, shaking with grief. "I am so sorry for your loss Tia, and we're very happy to have you with us. You're a young mother? How many kids?" "Two," came the reply. "Two kids. And how old is the oldest?" "Four."

"Four. I know it can be very hard for you right, because it's only been a month huh?" "Yeah." "And I can assure you, you're going to have some very hard times missing him and mourning him, but God will give you the strength that you need." Tia broke down and began to sob, burying her face in her hands. "He will give you the strength honey," Danielle's voice broke, too, and she began to cry along with others in the room.

Danielle got up from the table to get some tissues, then still standing she continued, "You just have to trust and depend on Him, and any questions that you have to ask the Lord, you can ask Him." Her demeanor began to shift, the anger rising in her posture and tone.

We wonder why, why bad things happen to good people? And I've learned that it happens because we have some bad people out here. They don't mind killing! They don't think about our children! They just want to kill, kill, kill! And the spirit that is going around—and we got to know it's a spirit because the Bible tells us that we wrestle not against flesh and blood, you know, but against principalities. And it's an *evil* spirit . . . but guess what? God sits high and He looks low . . . [and] He has the power to stop this killing. But I truly believe, like I always share, that it's going to take us to come together.

As she spoke the other women voiced their support: "That's right!" "Amen!" And they joined in when Danielle quoted from Scripture: "not against flesh and blood, but against principalities" (Ephesians 6:12), and "He looks low" (Psalm 138:6).[1] Angry though it was, this was still a religious response based on a firm recognition of the Bible as "the authority and standard for all issues of faith and life," as the church covenant declared. But Liberty Street was also well known for its outreach and activism, and this was also evident in Danielle's now emboldened narrative, which took a social and political turn.

Let them see our tears, let them see our innocent kids how they have left these children fatherless and motherless. It's not fair to the children! The community, society got to do something to stop the killing. Something *have* to be done. And if they don't hear our voices, nothing is going to be done. I say this here in a mighty way. If we had violence like this here in the white community, much more would have been done. Because you know why? *They* gonna step out and *they* gonna get more attention. And we want them to know that our children's life was valuable! Our husband, sons', lives was valuable! And guess what? We don't want this no more.

She composed herself with a declaration of faith, essential ground for a problem with no easy solution. "So, we have to continue just to pray and trust God to heal the land. He can heal the land," she said. Returning her attention to Tia, whose suffering had fanned this fire, she finished, "I just want to encourage you, my sister, to be strong." Tia listened closely and seemed to settle a bit into the space and support. However, she was still not ready to speak, so the invitation to testify was passed to another. These statements reflected the various stages of the work at hand, from painful struggles through grief and anger to a sense of acceptance and peace. After everyone who wanted to had shared, the refreshments were brought out, and people lingered around the table, talking in small groups. Those who knew Danté and Marcus provided additional details about their lives—their hopes and desires, the obstacles they faced, their popularity and potential. Photographs were passed around.

In time, a cake was brought over and placed in front of Miss Vivian, who blew out the candles with tears in her eyes as everyone sang "Happy Birthday" to Danté. While the refreshments were shared, Danielle walked around orchestrating people into small groups to take photographs, which would later be distributed. When it came time to close, she quieted the room and thanked everyone for coming, recognizing in particular the guests of honor for their courage and offering a prayer for their continued healing. Then, taking the bunch of balloons from the center of the table, she directed Miss Vivian, Mrs. Adams, and the others outside. There, in the middle of the parking lot, the women released the balloons in memory of their children and grandchildren. It was a tradition that closed all birth and death anniversary gatherings, symbolizing the ascension and final resting place of their loved ones. As everyone made their way across the parking lot to waiting cars, there were hugs and promises of support until the next occasion.

This sense of continuation, rather than closure, makes clear the broader aims of support-group sessions. While it was important to provide a space for mothers to process difficult emotions, the larger project had to do with the assertion of relatedness and value. Thus, as the women mourned their lost loved ones, they also *claimed* them, as children, and as children of God above all, in life, death, and in the eternal life they now experienced.

The story with which this chapter begins, of a grieving mother and a singing bird, is thus refined. Expanding beyond characterizations of Black women as perpetually haunted or incapacitated by death, it brings into view an interrelated awareness of human being in the crescent city. Was the singing bird the voice of God? Was it the voice of the deceased? Was it simply a confirmation of connectivity, between self, other, and the world beyond? The women came to no firm conclusions, but they continued to find themselves, with reverence, at similar intersections of death and transformation. This chapter explores their work.

A Matter of Life and Death

Each member of the support group had the opportunity, if she desired, to mark the birthday and death anniversary of their deceased loved one. Held in lieu of the regular weekly sessions, these events followed roughly the same format. However, the mother or the grandmother marking the occasion became the guest of honor, and she frequently invited family members and close friends to attend for extra support. Decorations and refreshments were more elaborate—for birthdays a cake, with inscription and candles, was always featured and served.

It was Danielle who came up with the idea, although the practice was already familiar within the Black community and not uncommon in others, especially when parents and caregivers mourned the death of a child (Klass 1997, 163; Howarth 2000, 132). Its significance, however, has not been adequately explored. For the women at Liberty Street, the main purpose was clear—to provide support and safe passage through a difficult, even dangerous emotional time. Grief was unpredictable on significant days such as birthdays, death anniversaries, and holidays. Emotions could intensify without warning, and they were harder to manage when women were isolated and already suffering, like many were, from a range of other conditions. The possibility of further harm was great and could take many forms, from disease to injury to violent and destructive behavior.

As a recovering addict, Danielle understood the risks all too well. She recalled, for example, the fragile state in which she had recently found herself on her own deceased son's birthday. The situation had been, quite literally, a matter of life and death. As she explained,

I didn't know anything about grief, how it can bring a toll on your body. How it can even cause you to go back to alcohol and drugs, you know? And that is true, because during my son's birthday in November, and you know birthdays and holidays can be *very, very* difficult. And I was just sitting up thinking about my son . . . and I said, "Is my child really dead?" You know the denial always set in first, and I started getting emotional. And a voice came to me and said (and God is my witness), "You might as well go get high, he ain't coming back." And I did like *that* [*snapping her fingers*], just like that. So, I know that was the work of the enemy . . . You see Satan thought he had me, but I got away.

Even though Danielle did not fall victim to the "work of the enemy," she feared that others might not be able to get away. The support group, therefore, was an essential resource.

Birthdays and death anniversaries were also important occasions for the women to honor the mother or grandmother, shoring her up for the days and nights ahead. They praised her for being there, for doing what she could to take care of herself, and for "making it" thus far. They encouraged her to stay strong, to call on the others whenever she needed, and to lean and depend on God. Nothing they could say or ask for, as Sister Anne had assured Monica, would sound ridiculous. "I think that's one of the reasons that we're here this evening," she continued, addressing Monica directly. "You made it a year. And that's worth honoring you for. You made it an entire year, you know? Tough as it's been . . . And the good thing about it, you know who is keeping you strong. And that is the good Lord." Thus, while "making it" was a big deal on its own, worthy of recognition, it also affirmed the faith the women had in God. It was "the enemy" who threatened or caused harm, but it was "the good Lord" who ultimately kept them safe and strong.

"If You Don't Know Him, You Got to Get to Know Him"

While it was important for the women to gather together, what was needed, and what they worked to cultivate, was a close relationship with God. This was the bedrock on which a holy Black female personhood was formed. Danielle organized and led the group sessions, but she did so with the understanding that it was God who *led* her to the task. Thus, she "leaned on Him" in turn, believing in His power to guide her, to heal her, and to help her to support others.

Those who already claimed a level of acceptance and peace regarding the loss of their loved one made sure to identify God and His power as the source. This declaration was regularly made by one longtime member of the group, Sister Shirley. Without fail, she arrived with her bible, which she described as an "old friend." It was a well-worn edition—one could see how each page was marked up, the text underlined, and notes, reminders, even phone numbers, written in the margins. She used it like a daily planner, her every thought and action guided by the Word of God. On occasion, another group member would notice the book and comment; Sister Shirley didn't seem to mind, telling everyone that she knew it was well worn but she was reluctant to replace it—she didn't want to lose all of that "good information."

What Sister Shirley's bible revealed was her close and intimate relationship with God, which extended through every aspect of her life. While there were a few women in the group who claimed a similarly integrated experience, it was largely one to which the others aspired. It was proof that new life was possible, if one would simply place their faith, their life, in God's hands. This was an especially important concept for newcomers to understand, the mothers and grandmothers of the recently deceased who were struggling and in need of immediate support. The senior women of the group thus made sure to emphasize the process in their testimonies, giving long descriptions of their own journeys and the peace they had ultimately found. At one session, for example, Sister Shirley described the moment she came to terms: "Yes, I was angry with God," she began. "But being sanctified and filled with the Holy Ghost I knew I had no right to be angry with God. So, I did it sneakily."

I said, "God? *You* said you wouldn't give me no more than I can bear!" And He came right back at me [and said], "And I am not a man *that I should lie.*"[2] So I had to work this out, I had to go "Well okay, if He's not lying . . . [then] this gotta be something I can bear." But I didn't *want* to. That was the thing that was standing between acceptance and denial. The fact that I didn't want to. But there was nothing else I could do. And so, when I accepted it, right at that moment . . . I got total peace. Total peace.

"But only God can give you that, only God," she quickly added, looking around at the others. "No pain pills, no medicine, nothing else, no drugs, only God. You know?"

The reference to drugs was not offhand within a community where rates of disease and substance abuse were high, particularly in the extended wake of Hurricane Katrina. Again, the senior women feared especially for the newly bereaved—they knew how acute the pain could be and what one might do to find relief. An equally powerful force was thus required that would save rather than destroy. As another woman testified, "losing a child is the worst thing that can ever happen to a mother. It's tremendous . . . and a lot of times the enemy uses this to take us farther away from God. But you got to draw *closer* to God, and if you don't know Him you got to get to know Him because that's the only way you can deal with anything like this."

In the Black Baptist tradition, drawing closer to God was tied to one's salvation, an essential step on a long and difficult Christian journey. Some women in the group described this as a sense of being cared for and "kept" on the right path and out of harm's way. Danielle, for example, citing her own health and history, made it clear that her relationship with God was the primary reason why she had not relapsed in over twenty years. As she said, "God won't allow that to happen to me because I believe that He's showing people. He's showing *me* that He has the power to keep me . . . He's proven His word to me that He's a keeper for those that want to be kept." This was not, however, solely about one's own keeping; it directed and supported those who would then care for others. God could give you peace, but He also made you strong so that you could reach out and support others in need.

Restorative Kinship

On more than one occasion, Danielle described the pain that she and the other women in the support group felt as *kin pain*, the term rolling off her tongue with authority as if it were an official diagnosis with cause and symptom. "This is what this support group is about," she said. "We do whatever we can to help that mother to get through that kin pain, because a mother will never get over losing her child, and especially when he has been murdered, you know?" Kin pain resulted from the impact of violence and the suddenness of death. It was debilitating and interminable, critically important to manage and preferably in the company of others who understood and could offer strategies and support. This was the core of Danielle's mission, as she explained, "to reach out to other mothers that is dealing with their kin pain, helping them to walk through their crisis," because "no one knows what another person is feeling and how they're dealing with something unless they're actually walking in their shoes."

In scholarly analyses of African American death and dying, the role of religion is front and center. This focus on faith makes sense and follows from both historical and ethnographic evidence, with religion providing "the theological, scriptural, sacramental, liturgical, pastoral, and spiritual tools to transcend the disappointing, sometimes bitter realities of African-American life, particularly at the end of life" (T. D. Armstrong 2010, 85; see also H. L. Perry 1993; Holloway 2002; Rosenblatt and Wallace 2005). In light of Danielle's reference to kin pain, however, what seems less well explored are the distinctly social practices that also accompany death and dying that may or may not intersect with religious ideologies, structures, and practices. The women at Liberty Street alert us in particular to expanded forms of kinship that address the loss of connectivity that violence in Black communities by design or default achieves. Both social and spiritual forms of relatedness were thus essential for the management of "kin pain," including the supportive relationships that women formed with each other but also the relationships they worked to sustain with the deceased, now in heaven. To develop the inquiry on death and dying in this way seems essential given the ruptures that continue with such force in Black communities. Efforts to repair, to engage in practices that affirm and sustain Black life, are thus worthy of additional study.

The religious work of women at Liberty Street suggests a kind of *restorative* kinship, one that asserts the value of those who have been lost by restoring their position within the family and community, in this world and the next. The idea derives from existing theories of kinship, especially theory that connects kinship practices to social survival and transformation. For women in poor Black neighborhoods, Patricia Hill Collins's (1994, 47) notion of "motherwork" remains an essential starting point. As Collins argues, the struggle to provide for one's children is at the center of social action for Black mothers, indeed for all mothers within marginalized and vulnerable communities. Describing this work as "reproductive labor" or "motherwork," Collins (2000a, 201) argues that it is a fundamental and necessary grounding to larger movements of social sustainability. Motherwork might thus be considered a critical form of empowerment, and it operates with particular intensity at the intersection of social death, physical death, and the struggle for Black survival (Collins 1994, 57). While motherwork is often overshadowed by more traditional and visible forms of labor, especially work that directly confronts state power (Collins 2000a, 202), it is no less significant. In fact, motherwork brings about change in part because of its ability to subtly undermine structures of domination through everyday actions and interactions. What results is the crafting of "Black female spheres of influence" within which change can originate and from which it can extend (2000a, 204).

The women at Liberty Street demonstrated a broad range of mothering activities. When Danielle's son Rock was alive, for example, she did everything she could to keep him safe. While she had many conflicting feelings about her identity as a mother, she held firm to what she *had* been able to provide: She found housing and food, she never brought her drug use home, and she saw to it that her son had been baptized and educated. Another group member, Cheryl, had a son who had been shot but had survived, although he remained vulnerable—in her words, "involved in some things." She wanted desperately for him to "turn," to find Jesus and be saved, and she did her best in the meantime to provide care and support. This involved moving out of her house, which was next door to her son's house, and asking her son's good friend to move in instead. The idea was to surround her son with positive influences, "so he can see what it's like to get up and go to work in the morning." Mothering activities also extended beyond the immediate family, as the women fulfilled their roles as grandparents, aunties, and "othermothers" (Collins 1994, 55). They would intervene if they saw a child being treated badly—breaking up fights, telling drug dealers to move away from the area, chiding young people when they acted out, and even taking children in when others could not properly care for them.

What was most remarkable, however, was the way that mothering activities extended to the *deceased*, as the women addressed their kin pain by claiming and caring for their children and grandchildren long after their deaths. The marking of birth and death anniversaries provided an important structure for this, testing the perceived limits of human existence and giving women the space to assert continuous connectivity and thus value in the face of its denial or destruction. Particularly where social and physical death seemed to overlap in nonnegotiable conclusion, these boundless practices of motherwork formed the foundation of restorative kinship in the Crescent City.

The Meaning of (Black) Birthdays and Death Anniversaries

It is common, across cultures, to mark the key moments and transitions of human life and death. The celebration of birthdays, for example, has a distinctly Western and Christian origin, from the Twelfth Night festivities of the Middle Ages, which may have inspired modern practices, to the more familiar assessments of belonging and status that define the contemporary self (Chudacoff 1989, 127). Birthdays play an important role in the working and reworking of subjectivity, for example, by identifying a person as related and valued within a larger family and social network.

Such rituals undoubtedly have special significance for African Americans and the members of other historically marginalized communities whose subjectivity is worked in particular ways, especially in the face of uncertainty and given the closeness of violence and death. The topic is undertheorized; however, a few important examples exist, particularly where birthdays and death anniversaries are concerned. John L. Jackson, in his ethnography *Harlemworld: Doing Race and Class in Contemporary Black America* (2001), includes a chapter titled "Birthdays, Basketball, and Breaking Bread: Negotiating with Class in Contemporary Black America." It opens with the story of a young African American man named Paul who holds two separate birthday parties for himself—one in the afternoon at his mother's apartment in Bedford-Stuyvesant, attended by family members and childhood friends, and the other one later in the evening at a friend's upscale brownstone in Harlem, attended by Paul's professional colleagues and a newer and more diverse set of friends and acquaintances. As Jackson argues, the two parties were key to Paul's negotiation of race and class, allowing him to express yet keep separate the seemingly incongruous aspects of his identity.

The marking of the birth or death anniversaries of the *deceased* is even less well studied. However, Cheryl Mattingly (2014) includes a useful and very poignant example in her ethnography of moral transformation among African American families struggling for a "good life" in California. Mattingly describes a funeral that is also a birthday celebration— one last "going away party" for a little girl named Belinda who had died from cancer just a few days shy of her sixth birthday (2014, 142). Belinda's mother Andrena organizes the event, and as invited children run and play in the grass around the tombstones, she shares a view of life and death as continuous. In reference to Belinda, Andrena declares that "she's still havin' her birthday. Her life is going on in heaven forever" (145). Mattingly frames this party/funeral as an event that "played upon and resisted the usual convention of space and time . . . it remade a blank impersonal space, or even a mournful space, into an underworld child's playground, one where children (above the ground) could safely play with their dead" (147). The research thus reveals the literal and symbolic collapsing that such practices allow as the usual demarcations for the beginnings and ends of life blur, allowing relatedness to extend across social, physical, and metaphysical realms.

Restorative kinship practices at Liberty Street, especially the repeated marking of birthdays and death anniversaries, provided an important scaffolding for these same processes as the place of the deceased in earthly and now eternal realms was confirmed. This is the renegotiation of subjectivity in the space of death, where the *deceased* Black subject, as Biehl, Good, and Kleinman (2007, 14) might theorize, is "at once a product and agent of history; the site of experience, memory, storytelling and aesthetic judgment; an agent of knowing as much as of action; and the conflicted site for moral acts and gestures amid impossibly immoral societies and institutions." For it was with righteous discontent that Danielle had spoken out about the disproportionate impact of violence in her community, declaring, "Our children's life was valuable. Our husband, sons', lives was valuable. And guess what? We don't want this no more!" And it was with resolve that the women continued to mark the births and deaths of lost loved ones, healing their kin pain as they reconfigured the boundaries of space and time.

Continuing Bonds

In existing social and psychological analyses of death and mourning, research on *continuing bonds* is also useful for the more practical examination of restorative kinship I now propose. *Continuing bonds*, a term introduced by Klass, Silverman, and Nickman (1996), refers to the bonds that mourners maintain with the deceased. The broader inquiry from which the term derives, however, challenges traditional theories of mourning, namely Freud's assertions in "Mourning and Melancholia" ([1917] 1953), that the success of mourning—that is the degree of one's recovery from it—depends on the mourner's ability to disengage, severing bonds with the deceased and thus freeing the mourner to make new attachments (Klass, Silverman, and Nickman 1996, 3). In a reexamination of the bereavement process, however, researchers found that rather than severing these connections, mourners continued relationships with lost loved ones in a variety of ways (xviii). Death was not the end of relatedness; rather, it led to "a new set of relationships with new dimensions and possibilities" (xix).[3]

Such practices are already well established within African American communities and have been identified by scholars in psychology, social work, and related fields as common characteristics of both individual and collective responses to death despite the heterogeneity of the Black experience (H. L. Perry 1993, 53; Barrett and Heller 2002, 794). Particularly for those who claim a strong identity and heritage in the Black Protestant church (Barrett and Heller 2002, 794), continuing bonds are developed through the prominence of a church funeral after death, the gathering of the family and community during mourning, a belief in the afterlife, and the consideration of death as a transition rather than a final stopping point (H. L. Perry 1993, 63–64; Barrett and Heller 2002, 794–97).

Two practices seem especially relevant for thinking about the continuing bonds that the women at Liberty Street sustained. The first concerns the gathering, activation, and building of family and community. As Hosea Perry (1993, 58–59) states, "No matter how much the customs among mourners have changed, either through the influences of the white culture or as a result of the increased urbanization and education of blacks, the pervasive quality of black mourning customs is their use as a builder of community." The second is the inclusion of the deceased person within this community, an inclusion made possible by a firm belief in the afterlife, a view of death as a transition, and an expanded notion of what "family" and "community" mean. Psychologist Ronald K. Barrett confirms, in an interview conducted by Karen Heller on African American mourning practices, a holistic and continuous view of birth and death: "In the European/Western view, you are born and eventually you die," Barrett states; "In the traditional black cultural experience, you are born, you die, and then you continue to exist in other realms" (Barrett and Heller 2002, 796).

These views come into stark relief in New Orleans, where residents already exhibit a "peculiar fascination" with the dead (Osbey 2015, 25), setting the stage for expansive and multidimensional understandings of human being. Residents routinely test and transcend the boundaries, for example through embodied and creative expression. The jazz funeral is arguably the best-known and most visible practice even though its form has changed, shifting in response to the persistence of violence. Jazz funerals thus increasingly belong to the young, who take to the streets to honor those who have passed too soon while also claiming a right to the city in which they live and die (Osbey 1996, 101; Regis 2001, 762; Sakakeeny 2013, 131). As I reference in the introduction to this book, such practices are part of a much larger local repertoire of memorialization and continuation (Regis 2001, 764), the study of which should expand to include the relational responses to death developed by Black women.

Within the support group, the continuing bonds that women developed were sustained first by the belief that their deceased sons and grandsons were with God in heaven. This gave the women great comfort in part because it went against other determinations made by the world at large, which placed young Black men not in heaven but in jail, in hell, or somewhere in between. They were dismissed—abandoned, criminalized, incarcerated, murdered, and then killed again by the implication, tacit or not, that they got what they deserved. The women at Liberty Street certainly did not accept this view, for they understood repentance and salvation as the pathway to freedom and peace for all God's children. Rock, Brian, Corey, Danté, and Marcus were definitely part of this calculus no matter what they had been doing before or at the time of their deaths. As Danielle stated about Rock, "I really believe that he is at peace . . . because he accepted Christ, in spite of his shortcomings . . . He knew God and was pardoned for his sin." Rock's relatedness, therefore, was not in question; he was "up there" in heaven, "absent in the body but present with the Lord."

Such affirmation was not a denial of the troubled life Rock had led. In fact, the women encouraged each other to honor and share both the good and the bad memories they had of the deceased. "Don't hesitate to include the painful stuff," Sister Anne had told Monica on the occasion of Brian's one-year death anniversary, reading aloud from a self-help book on grief. She encouraged her to testify about the whole of their relationship. "You know, the times when he made you just scream," Sister Anne said, "as well as all those other times when you could've just kissed him all over." At this, Monica and the other women smiled, knowing how fine the line between the two could be. "But relationships are like that," Sister Anne continued. "They're good and they're bad. They're happy and sad."

The confirmation of eternal dwelling, however, was just the first step. For it was through these relations, in heaven and on earth, that the work of the Lord proceeded. This belief was framed in several ways, but it referred most frequently to the work the women continued to perform to fulfill the religious and social mission of the church and the connection they felt with their deceased loved ones, who watched them from heaven with pride. Danielle spoke about this with certainty, describing how Rock looked down on her from heaven with pride for all the organizing work she was doing: "He telling me, 'Look at my mama,'" she said. "And I mean, I got joy in this here. . . . It's not a time I leave group that I don't look up and say . . . 'My son.' And in my spirit, I can hear him say, 'Mama, do the work of the Lord.' You know?" The encouragement meant a lot; it enabled the women to persist in their efforts, knowing that while their work was challenging, the effort was being praised from on high. The women spoke also of the work they believed the deceased were doing in heaven. As Mrs. Adams shared with the group on the anniversary of Marcus' death, laughing and crying all at once, "I think about my son up there with the Lord. He's up there doing the work. And I'm doing the work down here . . . So, I . . . you know . . . I cry. When I think about him I cry, I cry . . . And I thank God that we will see him and God one day."

This belief, of one day being more directly united with one's loved ones, through death and in the coming of Christ, was a crucial backdrop for restorative kinship. Death was not an end, it was simply a change in form and location—a shift in relatedness, not the end of relatedness all together. As one woman expressed it,

this is not the end. You gonna see him again. Because . . . we don't sorrow like those who have no hope. Hallelujah! We don't sorrow like those who have no hope.[4] Of course, we are going to hurt. It's a pain . . . an unbearable pain, and we feel it. But we don't *linger* there, and we don't *stay* there. Because He [God] let me know that there is life after death . . . We shall meet again.

Until that day, however, the women also sustained their connection with the deceased by remembering them as they were—imagining, for example, what each person would be doing if he were still alive. It was thus *between* heaven and earth that continuing bonds fully extended. This view was often reflected in the women's testimonies. On the occasion of Danté's birthday, for example, Miss Vivian was sure that Danté was present with the Lord. But when Danielle asked her, "If Danté was here, what would he be saying and doing, at age seventeen?" she didn't hesitate to respond: "Well, I know *I* would be cooking a lot of food," she said, as everybody laughed.

He loved to eat. All day all night, you know? Then he'd be on the phone with all the girls because he was a ladies man. He had a number of girls. And none of them knew about each other. So, he'd probably be walking with his cell phone, playing basketball, he'd be eating, sleeping, in the computer room . . . I know where he'd be for his birthday.

The same question was put to Mrs. Adams on the one-year anniversary of Marcus' death: "What do you think Marcus would be doing, if he was here today?" Danielle asked. Mrs. Adams gave it some thought. "Well first of all he loved to throw a fabulous party. One year, I remember . . . he throw a birthday party with a horse and buggy. Have you ever seen someone driving up in a horse and buggy? It was just ridiculous. But after it was over he said, 'I got to do better! I'm really having it [the party] *big* next year.'" Mrs. Adams paused in the middle of saying this, because of course the party never happened—there had been a funeral instead. However, rather than let grief overtake her, she switched the location of the party, telling the others that she knew that Marcus was now "up there" in heaven, "having a joyful time" and "not going through nothing." "Once they go home [to heaven] I don't think they want to turn around and come back!" she finished.

"Every Time I Talk to Somebody I Bring Him Up"

The assertion of relatedness, its extension between heaven and earth, happened also through testimony, the narratives of violence, loss, mourning, and faith that the women regularly shared. Testimony was central to the work of raising the dead in three main ways. First and foremost, to testify was to affirm one's spiritual journey by describing what one had been through and where one was now. Over the course of a long and difficult Christian journey, testimony conveyed one's identity, struggle, and capacity. This sense of self was so fundamental that testimonies were often delivered as introductions. At each support-group meeting, just after the opening prayer, the women gave their names and then they went on, sometimes for several minutes, sharing the details of their lives, the lives and deaths of their sons and grandsons, the nature of their pain and mourning, and the process of their recovery. Second, and in the context of lingering sorrow, testimony was an important defense, central to each woman's ability to stay physically and spiritually sound. It reminded her of how far she had come, or had been brought, and it directed her forward as the work continued. To hear the testimonies of others was also an indispensable source of encouragement, especially for those who had just begun their journeys or were suffering on any difficult day. Finally, in testimonies women honored their children and grandchildren by continuing to tell their stories long after their deaths and the sanctioned period of mourning, if mourning had been sanctioned at all.

Testimony was critically important for Danielle. She made this clear at our very first interview when I asked how the support group had started and she launched into the story of her life, her son's death, and the work that followed. In the middle of it, the phone rang. She excused herself to answer it and when she hung up I apologized for taking up so much of her time. She dismissed this with a wave of her hand, saying "No. That's quite OK. I enjoy doing this. This is my testimony." I asked her to explain the term, and she said, simply, "My testimony is where God brought me from." But the point was not just about what her testimony *was*; it was also about what it *was doing*—in this case keeping Danielle alive. Acknowledging her long battle against drug addiction, she continued, "I really believe the reason why I haven't relapsed in these twenty-one years is because I keep sharing my testimony. I truly believe that's my weapon . . . and the day I stop telling what God did for me . . . there's a possibility I could relapse. And I mean that from the bottom of my soul."

What further grounded testimony beyond the affirmation of faith and recovery was its focus on the people, living and dead, with whom one was connected. Introductions of self were thus simultaneous introductions of one's valued relations, especially the children and grandchildren they mourned. Mrs. Adams, for example, spoke about her two deceased sons in the testimony she gave at Marcus's death anniversary. "I call them my most happy children," she had said. "My two sons that loved to smile, that loved to joke, that always kept the family together." She went on for some time, describing family gatherings and other events—identifying and placing the dead within a broad relational story.

The role of narrative in the expression of human experience is an important focus of anthropological inquiry. Elinor Ochs and Lisa Capps, for example, rely on a phenomenological perspective to understand the links between experience, narrative, and the knowing of self. As Ochs and Capps (1996, 20–21) argue,

Personal narrative simultaneously is born out of experience and gives shape to experience. In this sense, narrative and self are inseparable. Self is here broadly understood to be an unfolding reflective awareness of being in the world, including a sense of one's past and future. We come to know ourselves as we use narrative to apprehend experiences and navigate relationships with others.

The relationship between narrative and self becomes particularly important when experience unfolds through violence and terror in the space of death that Taussig conceptualizes (1984, 467). However, narrative remains underexamined as a vehicle for the simultaneous illumination of meaning and consciousness that Taussig maintains the space of death allows (1987, 4). As Taussig (1984, 494) writes,

While much attention is given to "ideology" in the social sciences, virtually none as far as I know is given to the fact that people delineate their world, including its large as well as its micro-scale politics, in stories and story-like creations. . . . Surely it is in the coils of rumor, gossip, story, and chit-chat where ideology and ideas become emotionally powerful and enter into active social circulation and meaningful existence.

While the narratives of terror that Taussig traces in the Andean jungle, with their interplay of fiction and reality, become "high-powered tool[s] for domination and a principal medium of political practice" (492), narratives might also operate as tools of liberation. As Taussig (1987, 4) writes at the end of his description of the space of death, "Sometimes a person goes through it and returns to us, to tell the tale."[5]

These ideas help to broaden the scope of Black women's authority, here as storytellers in similar conditions of violence and terror, and to consider what testimony means and offers in the space of death and transformation. As Ochs and Capps suggest, as a form of narrative, testimony works to develop and articulate knowledge of the self while also articulating the self in relation to others, including in this case the deceased. Furthermore, and following Taussig, it is with the closeness of death that this integrated knowledge becomes transmissible. However, testimony for the women at Liberty Street was not just about telling the tale of death and recovery; it was about the mediation of Black subjectivity and relationality, about seeing and affirming the connections that lead through death—among the living, between the living and the dead, on earth, and in God's eternal kingdom. Such processes are essential, as Holland (2000, 3–4) argues, for the "raising of the dead," where the writer, the artist, and in this case the grieving mother or grandmother "ventures into conversations at the boundaries between worlds" (5).

The role of testimony here thus retains a fundamentally religious purpose, as the women at Liberty Street saw their stories as part of a larger story—God's story. As Anne Streaty Wimberly (1994, 3) explains, in research on religious education and storytelling,

What clearly emerges in conversations with African Americans is the . . . quest for the soul's story to be shared and for a larger story—God's Story—to inform and transform that story. Persons are in pursuit of liberation and hope-building . . . or a way of being and acting in life that grants them a sense of positive relatedness to God, self, others, and all things.

Testimony, in this sense, brings divine wisdom to the production of knowledge about self and other, with liberation founded on a deep sense of spiritual connection essential for the development of a beloved community.[6]

The women at Liberty Street were thus resolved to share their stories and would continue to do so as long as they were able, not just for themselves but for the relational and spiritual integration that placed their stories, and the stories of lost loved ones, before God and the world. Sister Anne, for example, encouraged Monica to continue to talk about Brian. "You have to honor your loved one's story," she said. "So, I don't know if you think people are going to get tired of hearing it. But you need to continue to tell us: 'Now my son used to do this, and he used to like it this way,' and you need to continue to say that because . . . that's going to help you get past it on the difficult days." At another session, an elderly woman named Mrs. Wright shared her testimony, which included many details of her deceased grandson's life and death, and told the group that she was determined to *keep* sharing his story. "I just been going on and on and on and praying and praying . . . and I miss him to the highs. I really do," she said. "Every time I talk to somebody I bring him up. They say, 'Mama stop saying that stuff!' But I say *never* stop saying it." The women around the table agreed. "Never," said Sister Shirley. "No, never," agreed Danielle.

Taking this to heart, the women routinely shared their testimonies outside of the support group and before diverse audiences. Danielle gave an example of a recent event at another church at which she had given a special address and the impact it had on her as well as on those who listened. After sharing her testimony, she had felt weak and despondent. "I started crying," she recalled. "I was like, you know, missing my baby." She stepped off the podium and over to the side to compose herself when she was approached by a woman who had been in the audience. As Danielle recounted, "She said, 'Miss? You just don't know how much you help me.' She said, 'My son was murdered too.'" They chatted, and Danielle told the woman about the support group, inviting her to come. She promised that she would.

The women also reached out, with special concern, to the children of the community, to help them through grief and to deter them from getting involved in criminal activity. Testimony played an important role; as Danielle explained, "We're planning to go out into the community, in some of the schools, camps, and let the kids know that we don't want you to kill one another. Tell them, 'My grandson was murdered, my son was murdered. If you see someone, one of your friends with a gun, tell your mama.' You know, things like that." This work was closely aligned with ministries at Liberty Street, including a recent Youth Revival, which was attended by several hundred people. Between the preaching and the prayers, a few of the mothers and grandmothers shared their stories, pleading with the young people in the audience to take heed. As Danielle recalled, "We shared with some of those kids who we were worried [about] and hopefully we had a chance to put something on they minds . . . there's hope that some child will say, 'Mama, you know I wouldn't want you to feel that [grief]. I don't want to see you up there [testifying about the death of a child].' So that was our purpose."

Joy and Struggle

In witnessing this work, it was difficult not to be moved. The challenges were great, but the support group was well organized, and the women were committed to the programs, activities, and practices they had developed. Danielle, especially, embodied a certain resolve. She had a way with people and with words, apparent to all as she led group meetings, shared testimony, and reached out to those in need. In her navigation of daily life, "in group" or out in the world, she seemed to walk with God at one hand and her son at the other. It was a sense of being kept while also keeping, of mediating the space between.

In one of our meetings, I shared with Danielle how inspired I was by what I had observed, including the great strides she herself seemed to be making in her personal and professional work. My words slowed, however, when I saw her face deflate. I stopped talking, and Danielle confided, "I can't seem to get it there though. I'm struggling." Her remarks caught me off guard, although I really should have known better, aware as I tried to be of the assumptions we make about what progress is supposed to look like and given what I knew about the depth of kin pain. Danielle continued, "I mean like, you know, I feel like I'm just going through the motions. That's what I feel." Her eyes welled up with tears.

I looked around for some tissues. We had just finished discussing her plans for the support group and the joy she found in doing the work, so her switch to sadness and stagnation seemed abrupt. As I would come to understand, however, the joy and struggle of religious work existed side by side—it was naive to expect one to preside over the other. On the one hand, Danielle wholeheartedly believed in the power of God to keep her. On the other, her feeling of "going through the motions" was real; it confirmed that the conditions of violence remained—a daily if not lifelong challenge to the quest for peace, love, and community to which she remained so clearly committed.

"I'm sorry . . . here, take a tissue," I said, handing her the box from her own desk. Danielle took a breath, "Yeah, you know what? It's gonna be alright," she said. "I have been told that ministry work can get you to feel that way sometimes. But I enjoy what I'm doing. It's just that . . . I have a lot of regrets. For example, not getting my education, that beats me up a lot now." She described the frustration of wanting to "walk right" but feeling held back by a lack of resources and opportunities. This remained so, despite the major steps she was taking forward, including studying for her GED and completing a training program in substance abuse counseling. As she spoke, she returned to her faith as a place of both gratitude and stability: "Well I think I'm fine. I think I just . . . I'm grateful to be used by Him because if He wouldn't use me, who would? Besides the devil, you understand?" I offered her some additional words of encouragement, which she seemed to no longer need. "Yeah, yeah. He makes a way, He makes a way for me. I mean I be like, okay, every month I pay my rent late [laughter]. But then I look, and I have a roof over my head, you know? So, God is good . . . It's gonna be alright."

The other women moved through joy and struggle in similar fashion, although individual situations and needs were distinct. Many of them experienced financial hardship; others had no transportation and relied on family members to get around. Some had medical issues, which prevented them from getting out and doing things, even coming to the support-group sessions. All of them dealt with the impact of continuing violence in their communities, and they continued to mourn for their own children and grandchildren while witnessing the daily deaths of others.

While many women found the support group to be a reliable safe haven from all of this, others found it difficult to detach from the struggles that made the group necessary in the first place. For example, one woman, who had been coming to the group for a while, suddenly stopped and had not returned. Danielle saw her again in church one Sunday and inquired.

I said, "Hi, why haven't you been coming back to group?" And she said, "No particular reason." And I said, "OK . . . well if there is anything you want to talk about, you know, you can come." Then it got back to me . . . we had a meeting and she up and said . . . "I want to tell you why I didn't come back to the group. Because a friend told me that *her* [another group member] nephew had something to do with *my* son's death." I said . . . well, maybe I need to do one-on-one [sessions], and on Fridays I'm here if anyone need to meet with me, you know, outside of the group.

Danielle continued, lamenting the cycle of violence and retaliation that surrounded them. "So many of our children today are killing one another, the moms are going to meet face-to-face . . . Just be careful not to let anger build up in your heart toward it, because then you have a problem."

The women were therefore thinking about expanding their efforts so that they could also support the mothers and grandmothers of the *perpetrators* of violence. The prospect was complicated and controversial in a community of mourners still searching for justice and in a close-knit network in which the victims and the perpetrators were likely connected. However, it also felt necessary, given this very same fact: the victim and the perpetrator could be from the same community, and they could even be the same person, depending on the context, situation, and timing. Either all of these children were valuable, Danielle maintained, or none of them were. "We have questions, we have children, we all mothers," she said. "Everybody is grieving for what they lost."

While this approach was certainly in line with the teachings of the church, it was not an easy thing to accomplish in practice. Danielle shared a conversation she recently had with another woman at the church who was clearly in the throes of grief and anger. As Danielle recalled, "I had a mother say that she wants this person who killed her child to be *crucified*. She don't want him to go to hell but she want him to be crucified. And you understand her frustration. That's her child! She don't want God to have mercy on him [the killer]. Well what if the shoe was on the other foot? We always have to consider those things." Speaking, as always, with her personal experience in mind, Danielle thought out loud about what that would mean. "The person who killed my son? What if my son would've killed *him*?" she asked. "I'd be asking everybody in this city to pray for my child! You know? He killed six people! He's vexed with a demon! Help him! Who is it? *My son*! Oh, he killed your son too? I'm *sorry*! I'm *sorry* my son killed your son!" "It goes both ways," she finished.

Even though joy and struggle existed side by side, the women remained oriented, in line with the church's teachings, toward the coming of a new day. This was something that Danielle practiced intentionally in regard to her own loss and mourning. As she told me,

> I never hated the person who killed my son, that's how free I was about it. I got angry about it, but I have prayed for that young man, and when I seen him on TV, I just looked at him and said, "Lord have mercy on him." Because if he was *my* child . . . I would want someone to have mercy on *him*. See that's the way we have to be.

The ultimate direction and support for this way of being, she stressed, should come from the church. "We got to get it together in church house. We got to stop the animosity, the back biting, and all of that . . . and then we'll see a difference on our side."

It was a tall order, one that required a fundamental belief in the interrelatedness of all human beings—an interrelatedness that included those who were devalued by society as well as those who devalued. This in turn depended on a belief in forgiveness above vengeance—a belief that was especially hard to reconcile alongside the thirst for justice, so strong in communities long besieged. Finally, the work required stamina, with faith sustaining the women between group sessions, in joy as well as in the darkest moments of doubt or despair. While achieving such a state of being on both an individual and collective level was the ultimate goal, the process was uncertain at best.

One final element at work in the relationship between joy and struggle was laughter. While laughter was an indication of emotional uplift, it was more specifically about the "joy of the Lord," reflecting a close integration with God's love, which helped to direct everyday experience and movement. Mrs. Adams was a living example. Because of her poor health she came to group sporadically, and when she did she always began her testimony by giving a report on her various ailments. She had a number of health concerns, some of them serious, yet while she made it clear that she was struggling, she simultaneously could not be bothered. In one breath, she gave details of her episodes and pains, and in the next she declared that she was nonetheless making it, by the grace of God. "I'm sick, my health is not that good," she said. "But I just keep on going on because I know that God is good."

The other women encouraged Mrs. Adams to speak as long as she wanted to, in part because they knew how difficult it was for her to get around and make it to various things. However, they also encouraged her because they understood, from their own experiences, what she was going through. "Yeah, that's right," said Danielle, and Mrs. Adams went on: "I've had two heart attacks and I'm a diabetic and deteriorating hips. All kinds of things wrong with me and every time I look around I've got something else wrong with me. But . . . God is good. He got me here for a reason." Mrs. Adams was smiling as she said all this, in awe of not her own stamina but the love and support she felt from a God in whom she so firmly believed.

She shared the details of a recent trip to the doctor. "The doctor, he says to me, 'Do you know how bad your heart is?'" she began. "I say, 'Cain't be that bad.'" At this, Sister Shirley began to chuckle, and the others joined in. Mrs. Adams continued. "I lost two children," she deadpanned, "and I didn't die after going through the first one, I didn't die going through the second one. So, the heart ain't that bad," she concluded, having dismissed the doctor with a shake of the head. "Cain't be that bad." Sister Shirley, who could no longer contain herself, shouted out, "Yeah, that's *right*! Cain't be that bad, that's what I'm talking about! That's what I'm talking about!" When the laughter around the room had settled, Mrs. Adams told the others how important it was for her to be grateful and even happy for what she *did* have, despite the struggle. "But you know sometimes God has to remind us of things, you know, because we get in our little pity party and He have to say 'Hey! Wake up!' Okay now, you know? So, I thank God . . . I thank God that I'm rooted in Him."

After all of this, Danielle was moved to say, "I just want to let you know Mrs. Adams, as we sit here and as we see you speak, that I can just see the joy of the Lord all over you." "*Amen!*" Sister Shirley emphatically agreed, as Danielle continued,

Because for you to come out like you do, barely can make it physically and after having two kids being murdered and still have the joy of the Lord. You know, His word got to be real! And we thank God, like we say, that we know that it's Him that's keeping us. And to have the support group like this here, I just, my heart just opened up, because I mean you know it's like we have our moments where we gonna lay up, we gonna cry . . . you know it's a season for everything. So, I just wanna compliment you on how you is just hanging in there and just counting it all joy, knowing that. And I'm just very grateful to even have you to come forward and be a part of the support group.

To experience this kind of joy was an essential objective for the women at Liberty Street, and they reminisced on this occasion about the laughter they had shared over the years. Sister Shirley remembered a newcomer who was joyfully caught off guard: "she said that she hadn't laughed like that in I don't know how long . . . She said, 'I had a tremendous burden lifted off me just from sitting here laughing like this.'" Sister Shirley took a moment to consider how this could be, deciding that getting together and sharing with each other meant moving past the pain to enter into community.

Because when we all get together and tell our stories . . . sometimes we go *past* our stories . . . we go *past* our pain . . . and we just joke around, and we tell about some things that made us laugh. And then you start laughing and then you realize in yourself, yes, I can laugh again because as long as you alone and thinking about it and holding it to yourself, then you think . . . oh woe is me, it ain't gonna get no better . . . all this and all that. You know? But when you get away from that and come into group like this where we can open and freely talk about our lost loved ones . . . we can share some things about them that'll make us laugh when we get home.

The joy was at times so intense that it seemed out of place to those outside of the group. As Danielle remarked, "You'll have some people wonder . . . 'Well how can you, what's all this laughing about? What's going on? Why you so happy?' . . . You know? But we have a different way of just releasing because we have to . . . no need to hold on to it . . . because we got to. We have work to be done."

On Singing and Being Sung To

I began this chapter with a story about a grieving mother who encountered a singing bird in the cemetery. Sister Anne had shared the story while trying to assure Monica, on the death anniversary of Monica's son Brian, that she could count on their support for whatever she needed. Nothing she could ask of them would seem ridiculous. She shared the story of the singing bird as proof—Sister Anne's cousin had gone to the cemetery in despair, a bird alighted on a tombstone and sang to her, she stopped and listened, and then she got up and went back to work. The story had filled the room with a collective sense of reverence. "My, my," one woman had said, shaking her head in wonder.

This expression of reverence was not just a response to the space and process of mourning, it also reflected an understanding of death that went beyond its presumed limits, especially the expectations and characterizations of Black death with which these women were all too familiar. Regardless of how the story was interpreted—as the voice of God, the deceased, or simply the song of a bird—what seemed most important, most relevant to their progress, was the experience of relatedness, of *singing* and *being sung to*. The interaction was a confirmation that one could be present and part of the world in multiple dimensions. It thus provided comfort, but it also informed their broader building of community through an awareness of the shifts that must occur for the transformation they envisioned.

The presence of Black women at the center of these encounters is both corrective and constructive. It is a centering that challenges assumptions about Black women's limits and capacities, while also directing our attention to their work as essential agents, mediators, and guides. What results, as Aimee Cox (2015, 8) writes, is the development of "collective strategies for living fuller, self-defined lives without the threats of extinction" that remain so common for Black people. Such strategies are exceedingly important to understand, as we assert a sacred humanity in an increasingly precarious world. At the same time, we must continue to examine how such violence develops in the first place, focusing especially on why and how it has developed with such unrelenting force for those of African descent. We thus continue to identify the collective strategies that *negatively* determine Black humanity, as we search for and find the productive pathways that the juxtaposition of struggle and joy reveals.

At the support-group gathering, after each woman had shared her testimony, Danielle brought out the refreshments and placed them on the table. Lightening the mood, she announced, "We have a salad and we're going to thank Cheryl because she brought us a cake here that I really think you guys are going to enjoy." She turned the cake around this way and that so that everyone could read its dedication to "Sanctified Women" scrolled in frosting on the top. "That's a special cake," someone said, and everybody laughed. Before they would bless the food and eat, Danielle had one final song to share, a popular gospel tune titled "I Need You to Survive." She passed around a sheet with the lyrics and music, written by David Frazier, but it was a song that most of the women already knew, and it highlighted the connections they worked so tirelessly to sustain, the social and spiritual value they affirmed, and the necessity of all of this not just for Black survival but for the future of humankind. "It goes like this," Danielle began to sing, but there was no need for an introduction. The others were with her from the very first note.

The sound they produced was clear and strong. It rose up from the table to fill the room with an anthem that, with eyes closed, was a harmonious blend of individual voices. The lyrics were first about the need for one another, the interdependency on which religious work was based. But the song was also an invitation. It asked the listener "you" to stand with "me," in agreement and fully recognized as members of God's Holy Family. This required an assertion of value, and the lyrics confirmed the worth of each person. But need was not solely about interdependency; these valued persons were the orchestrators of a shared future: "You are important to me" they sang to each other and to those they remembered, "I need you to survive." The song was also a recognition of God's will, an acknowledgement that it was by His grace that all these things were possible. This did not absolve the women of responsibility, thus they promised to pray and to love—to do no harm, in thought, word, or deed. They repeated these affirmations again and again, the melody ascending and then returning in loops that went on as long as necessary, mirroring the highs and lows of life and death through which the women were continuously moved and set free. "Amen!" exclaimed Danielle when the song came comfortably to an end. "Glory!" shouted another woman. "Hallelujah" praised a third.

The Crescent City Illuminated

Mirror Lake (photo by author)

He could never be dead until she herself had finished feeling and thinking. The kiss of his memory made pictures of love and light against the wall. Here was peace. She pulled in her horizon like a great fish-net. Pulled it in from around the waist of the world and draped it over her shoulder. So much of life in its meshes! She called in her soul to come and see.

ZORA NEALE HURSTON (1937, 286).

My fieldwork in New Orleans came to a close in the summer of 2009. At the time, clergy and parishioners at Liberty Street were expanding their work, developing ministries and programs that reached beyond the confines of one church and community. Their purpose remained the same: to uphold the church covenant and to promote the African American religious ideal in which they believed, a vision of a sacred, interrelated, and beloved community. The women in the support group, for example, continued to develop connections, sharing testimony and working with various community organizations on issues of poverty, violence, and public safety. While relatively small in scale, these expansions were positive signs of growth as ministries became movements across the city. Still inspired by Obama's recent election, with the Yes We Care! ministry well underway, church members carried on their work with a sense of enthusiasm and possibility. While the violence had not subsided, the ministry and its participants were nonetheless sustained by a continued resolve to live within and work to transform the Crescent City.

Despite the two years I spent in New Orleans for fieldwork, leaving felt abrupt. Not only did it seem like certain projects relevant to my research were just beginning, I was also finally settling into personal and professional relationships. These included the deepening connections I was experiencing with family members, extended family, and friends as well as the relationships that were developing through the sites and interactions that structured my work. My entrée into certain settings had been difficult to orchestrate, and I worried that the direct access to local knowledge that I enjoyed would end. I was also concerned about the impression my relatively short stay would leave while simultaneously wondering whether my presence had been noticed enough to miss. I considered extending my time, but this proved impossible. My funding had expired, and the next source of support required residency in another state. So I said my goodbyes. The women in the support group saw me off with a prayer: "Dear Lord, please give Rebecca the strength to finish her thesis, or whatever it is she is doing," Danielle had said, head bowed, to a few chuckles in the room. And then I left, with my own sense of resolve and obligation to complete my work from afar, though the outcome remained uncertain.

In the months and years that followed, the distance I felt from New Orleans became strangely productive. I remembered with much nostalgia my childhood and early impressions of the city in the 1970s and 1980s, immersed as I was in family and social life. All of this was now contextualized by a more nuanced understanding of the processes by which places converge, conditions of vulnerability and violence develop, and experiences of Black life and death unfold. Not only could I better situate my own experiences and the experiences of those I had come to know, I could see a way forward, which began with survival and recovery in still devalued communities but was now directed beyond—the possibilities of a sacred Black humanity anchored by a broader call for social and moral awakening.

It is this trajectory that I hope the book has revealed. I began with the history of southeast Louisiana and the development of the urban delta in order to understand the development, decline, and recovery of the *Black* urban delta. Rather than adhering to the expectations for life and death in the "ghetto" or "inner city," I framed New Orleans as a "crescent city" on the cusp of change, with processes of forced settlement, oppression, and violence at one hand and with movements of freedom, equality, justice, and peace at the other. I remain most interested in the space between, with the crescent city still a relevant conceptualization not just for understanding particular moments of change, be they shifts in one direction or the other, but for seeing the city as a dynamic process. This framing permits us to rethink urban recovery and development, recognizing the challenges while envisioning the next phase. It also allows us to better identify the agents of change, those who already inhabit and mediate the space of death and transformation, and follow as best we can the pathways they establish.

The pathways I followed through a diverse religious landscape led me to Liberty Street in Central City. The site made clear the evolution and impact of violence, but it also revealed the centrality of African

American religion in the peaceful recovery of place and people. My historical tracing led from the Afro-Baptist cosmos to the rise of the black social gospel and to lingering yet reinvigorated notions of human value, somebodiness, and relatedness in response to the shifting parameters of violence and death. The religious ideal that has emerged is thus as old as it is new; still, it serves as a blueprint for the building of a beloved community in the current moment with attention to the relational dismantling of dominant value systems such progress requires.

What clergy and parishioners developed in particular was a framework for human being that transcended the boundaries that otherwise determine the course of life and death in the "ghetto." They did this through a range of beliefs and practices, bringing "they" and "somebody" together on the battlefield for the Lord and affirming the religious and moral principles that would guide their collective work. Centering the experiences and knowledge of Black women revealed the internal and external dimensions of these tenets; their practices formed the basis of the restorative kinship I proposed. By marking the birthdays and death anniversaries of the deceased, the women sustained connectivity, "raising" the dead despite the negative determinations of the world. None of this was easy. Participants walked a long and difficult Christian journey through many challenges, trusting and relying on the Word of God. They believed they would someday arrive—perhaps over generations, but certainly in judgement—at a glorified place of peace, as struggle turned finally to eternal joy.

After the Rain

I did my best to keep track of how this work was proceeding, paying attention to local concerns and outcomes while seeing their reflection in national events and movements. For example, the Yes We Care! ministry continued, but despite the inclusion of a cease-fire agreement, it seemed to have little impact on the rate of homicide. While organizers and participants remained committed to its objectives, the difficulty of the broader task, the work of care and value, was apparent. Rather than a reduction, statistics from the NOPD showed an increase in the homicide rate in the years just after my departure, rising by nearly 14 percent between 2010 and 2011.

In many ways, this was not surprising—the violence had multiple causes, which were especially difficult to address in the extended wake of Hurricane Katrina. Rates of poverty, for example, were not drastically improved, but the distribution had shifted, particularly following the demolition and decentralization of low-income housing (Berube and Homes 2015). It is important to stress, however, that the efficacy of anti-violence ministries should not be wholly measured in relation to the rate of violent crime. While a primary objective was certainly to stop the killing, this work was influential in other ways. The continuing violence only confirmed the need for the ministry to expand, perhaps through greater interventions that would ground more conventional methods instead of merely occurring alongside them.

Religious work thus proceeded at a relatively patient pace even when responses to oppression and violence coalesced on the national stage. In 2012, Trayvon Martin, an unarmed Black seventeen-year-old boy walking home in his father's subdivision in Florida, was killed by George Zimmerman, an armed white and Hispanic man who was a neighborhood watch captain in the same subdivision. In a trial closely watched by people around the country, Zimmerman was found not guilty of murder or manslaughter—a decision which outraged many people and led to protest, certainly on behalf of Martin and his family but also in response to the still routine killing of young Black men. Obama's remarks, following the verdict, were significant for their affirmation of this tragic state. In an unprecedented presidential yet personal account of racism and its impact, Obama declared that Trayvon could have been his own son and that he, in his youth, could have been Trayvon. He then called for a conversation on race, one that he believed would most productively occur in familiar settings—such as the family, the workplace, or the church. To have a Black president at the helm during such moments, for they would continue, was uncertain but inspiring. As Ta-Nehisi Coates (2017, 50) writes in an article for the *Atlantic*, Obama stood "against the specter of black pathology, against the narrow images of welfare moms and deadbeat dads." His time in the White House would subsequently "showcase a healthy and successful black family" (50), a portrait that was sustained by the possibility, not probability, it confirmed for others.

In late June 2013, in the middle of jury deliberations for the Zimmerman trial, the beloved pastor at Liberty Street, Pastor Samuel, passed away. He died at his home in New Orleans, surrounded by family but finally succumbing to a terminal illness against which he had quietly battled. The leadership of the church shifted to one of the assistant pastors who continued the mission and ministry, doing more than his best to guide the congregation with the same level of passion and charisma. These transitions took place within a national conversation on violence and Black social value that was gaining momentum. Just a few weeks after Samuel's death and just after the acquittal of George Zimmerman,

Alicia Garza posted the "love letter" to Black people on Facebook to launch the Black Lives Matter movement.

The conversation in New Orleans continued under a new city administration. Mitch Landrieu, the former lieutenant governor of Louisiana, was elected mayor of New Orleans in 2010 and was reelected to a second term in 2014. That same year, the former mayor, Ray Nagin, was tried and convicted on twenty-one counts of wire fraud, bribery, and money laundering and sentenced to ten years in federal prison. Nagin had once called for Black love in a speech at the Yes We Care! rally, though in light of his offenses, many were astonished that he had had the nerve to do so. Landrieu, however, had a different approach, based on the assertion that Black lives should matter all the time—that is, not just as a declaration to counter police brutality but on the statistically identified terrain of "black-on-black crime," where killing seemed to occur with equal disregard. While Landrieu certainly spoke about the structural causes of violence, he also referred to violence as a "quick-trigger" cultural or personal problem and argued that it should be addressed through a wide range of interventions focused on saving young Black men in large part by providing them with the resources to save themselves. "If I knock you off a chair, that's on me," he had said during an interview with a journalist from the *Atlantic.* "If you're still on the ground a week later, that's on you" (Goldberg 2015). None of this sufficiently acknowledged the inequalities that perpetuated poverty and joblessness, the lure of drug trafficking, the impact of lax gun laws, or the negative determinations of human value and their impact, be they externally or internally founded. However, it did confirm that the assertion of social and spiritual relatedness, in the broader development of a beloved community, remained an urgent project.

The relationships of care that anchored my own life dramatically shifted when my father died in the spring of 2014. While his passing was sudden, it seemed like the end of a slow decline over a period of nearly ten years. After Hurricane Katrina, and the flood and fire that had destroyed their home, my father and stepmother had moved to an apartment on the Northshore. They decided not to rebuild, and my father immersed himself in his work in a process of recovery that was aided by routine. Despite this and the support of family and friends, the loss of place and possession proved more than his heart could bear. "New Orleans kind of grows on you," he had said in an interview conducted by his neighbor the year before the storm. "This city has all the problems of a major city . . . sometimes worse, because you know how it is down here—the distance between the haves and the have-nots is a matter of a few blocks. But . . . I don't have any plans of moving anyplace else."[1]

We waited until after Mardi Gras to have the funeral. When it was over, we processed in cars to the cemetery in Biloxi, where he was laid to rest among those who also gave their lives to care and service.

Monuments and Manifestations

As time went on, I felt further distanced from the city, increasingly out of touch with the people I knew and struggling through the work of reflecting on research that felt like it had happened so long ago. When the book finally came together, during an extended sabbatical leave from 2016 through most of 2017, the context in which my data was produced seemed again unexplainable without consideration of its extension through a newer and more dire set of social and political circumstances. While I had started fieldwork on the heels of Obama's election, I was finishing the manuscript in the first tumultuous years of the Trump presidency. While in many ways this brought a sense of urgency to my work, in other ways the destructive force it confirmed was immobilizing. What would the change in administration mean, especially for those whose value the world had already denied?

Trump's presidential campaign had been alarming enough, his nativist and violent language targeting the most vulnerable and provoking, as Henry Giroux puts it, "society's darkest impulses" (2017, 891). This in turn galvanized a range of extremist and racist groups, including the alt-right, white nationalists, anti-Semitic groups, "and other breeding grounds for a new authoritarianism" (891). As frightening as all of this remains, it is important to recognize that Trump's election and the simultaneous surge of white supremacy were the product of a much longer legacy of authoritarianism that included "the election of Ronald Reagan in 1980 . . . the Third Way politics of the Democratic Party, and . . . the anti-democratic policies of the Bush-Cheney and Obama administrations" (889). As Giroux makes clear, on the way to Trump, "democracy was sold to the bankers and big corporations propelled by the emergence of a savage neoliberalism, a ruthless concentration of power by the financial elites, and an aggressive ideological and cultural war aimed at undoing the social contract and the democratic, political and personal freedoms gained in the New Deal and culminating in the civil rights and educational struggles of the 1960s" (889).

The number of reported hate crimes soared in the first few months after the election, with white supremacists and others emboldened by Trump's caustic campaign rhetoric, his irreverence, his impulsive proclivity to incite and attack, and his more than dubious allegiances. The Southern Poverty Law Center reported over one thousand hate crimes in a ten-week period, an astounding number compared to the fifty or so incidents typically reported in that length of time (DeVega 2017). The impact of this was devastating, to say the least, but what it confirmed was fully disheartening—that the dehumanization of black and brown people continued and now with brazen support (even in a hesitancy to disavow) from the highest levels of government. This brought new pain to a heavily scarred injury, especially for those who believed the country had progressed and for young people who came of age in the supposedly postracial Obama era. However, it did signal to clergy and parishioners at Liberty Street that their work was on track; they had been calling for a social and moral recovery that would counter such forces for many decades.

I was also finishing the manuscript in the extended wake of a specific and horrific hate crime that happened on June 19, 2015 in Charleston, South Carolina, the day after Trump announced his bid for the White House. Dylann Roof, a white supremacist, murdered nine Black parishioners at the Emanuel AME Church. Arguably a product of the same forces that permitted a Trump presidency and emboldened hate (Bouie 2016), photographs of Roof surfaced on social media, which showed him standing alongside a Confederate flag, a symbol of white supremacy that unthinkably still flew on the grounds of the South Carolina State House. Following a period of heated debate and violent demonstration, both for and against the display, the flag was removed from the capitol in July. But a nationwide debate had already begun, regarding the presence of similar markers in other places with several key battlegrounds emerging, including New Orleans. In December 2015, an ordinance to remove four Confederate and Reconstruction era monuments was approved by the New Orleans City Council and signed by Mayor Landrieu. Because of death threats from opposing groups, the monuments came down under the cover of night, the workers protected by armed guards.

In the spring of 2017, after the last monument had been removed, Landrieu gave a public speech to explain the action, which took the form of a message from New Orleans to the nation. He began, notably, by describing "The soul of our *beloved* City" as being "deeply rooted in a history that has evolved over thousands of years; rooted in a diverse people who have been here together every step of the way—for both good and for ill" (Landrieu 2017, emphasis added). He used this opening to point out a particular "historical malfeasance, a lie by omission," represented by the prominence of monuments and other markers that "purposefully celebrate a fictional, sanitized Confederacy; ignoring the death, ignoring the enslavement, and the terror that it actually stood for." Landrieu had known that removing the monuments would be controversial, but he stood firm with the assertion that the action was "not about taking something away from someone else." It was not about politics or blame or retaliation. It was about "showing the whole world that we as a city and as a people are able to acknowledge, understand, reconcile and most importantly, choose a better future for ourselves making straight what has been crooked and making right what was wrong."

It was clear, however, that the removal of the monuments would not by itself bring about this correction. The task, therefore, was not simply to do away with the markers of white supremacy; it was to replace them with new markers—of unity, relatedness, value, equality—that would inspire progress through continued social and political intervention. As Landrieu stated, "This is not just about statues, this is about our attitudes and behavior as well. If we take these statues down and don't change to become a more open and inclusive society this would have all been in vain." Such change required, however, a commitment to work together. "Here is the essential truth," Landrieu continued. "We are better together than we are apart. Indivisibility is our essence. Isn't this the gift that the people of New Orleans have given to the world?" He did not acknowledge the many obstacles that invariably stand in the way of unity, finishing instead with a lofty view of equality and opportunity: "In our blessed land we all come to the table of democracy as equals. We have to reaffirm our commitment to a future where each citizen is guaranteed the uniquely American gifts of life, liberty and the pursuit of happiness." In working toward this vision, in speech and in followed action, the goal was to make New Orleans "a beautiful manifestation of what is possible and what we as a people can become." This was not a far-off vision; the matter was of immediate and urgent concern: "We can't wait any longer," Landrieu said. "We need to change. And we need to change now."

In many ways, the speech was bold and moving, and it was generally well received, shared around the city and the nation. It was especially relevant for those in cities where similar battles were underway, where demands to remove the markers were gaining momentum despite the increasingly violent opposition of alt-right and other white-supremacist groups. In other ways, however, the speech seemed hollow and short on specifics. Was this a defining moment for the city as much as Landrieu claimed? It had been over a decade since Hurricane Katrina, and it seemed logical, in some sense, to position New Orleanians as leaders on matters of resilience and rebirth. However, the city still had a ton of problems, poverty and urban violence chief among them, which made this declaration feel more like a pitch than a plan. While many residents rallied around the mayor, many of them also struggled and suffered as before. To what extent did this or any other notion of indivisibility, freedom, equality, and happiness extend to those families and communities? What places and practices, what actions and interactions, were in place for its development? What frameworks and movements did it connect to, including those developed at Black churches and at other religious, moral, and social institutions, and what might those movements collectively accomplish? Clergy and parishioners at Liberty Street, for example, already knew a thing or two about monuments. Since the late 1980s they had claimed the one to Martin Luther King Jr. on the neutral ground of South Claiborne Avenue as a platform for many of these same ideas.

Movements, Awakenings, and Connective Politics

Landrieu made no direct mention of the history and continued work of local religious organizations. This was especially curious given the fact that religious activism had essentially made the moment possible—this was a legacy with deep roots in the Black Church from which the call for unity and change in the beloved city, particularly in the face of white supremacy, must surely extend. The speech may have been tempered, however, by a concern that a focus on religion, and African American religion at that, would divide rather than repair. One only had to recall Mayor Nagin's assertion after Katrina that New Orleans was and would remain a "chocolate," that is, African American city, an assertion that had not been well received. Whatever the reason, the omission was perhaps not that curious after all given the fact that Black social and religious movements are rarely given center stage when calls for change require collective buy in, particularly when Black people are still seen, in many circles, as the source of the problem rather than the solution.

What all of this points out is the need to connect the dots between the significant moments of an important but not yet unified movement. In doing so, we might identify the various points of origin as well as the threads that weave across time and context—sorting through the ideas we can collectively embrace, eliminating what harms or divides, and following the pathways that emerge toward a beloved, just, and sustainable world. While this task has particular urgency given ongoing conditions of precarity, the endeavor is also driven forward by the need to understand, comparatively, the process itself. How do such movements emerge? What supports or impedes their development? This is already a well-established inquiry in anthropology and attendant fields, for example as the study of revitalization and religious movements confirms (Wallace and Steen 1970; McLoughlin 1978; Fabian 1979; Stark 1996; Harkin 2004). However, the ideas are not well aligned, nor do they extend sufficiently beyond familiar themes and settings.

In this, the centering of Black experience and knowledge remains an important project not just for what it provides for Black communities but for the ways in which it might inform the strivings of all people. When clergy and parishioners at Liberty Street defined the terms of relatedness for a beloved community, for example, they aligned with King's ([1967] 2010, 141) call for a "radical restructuring of the architecture of American society." As George Lipsitz (2011, 17) reminds us, such restructuring would "transform both Blacks and whites (and everyone else) into new kinds of humans, into people capable of creating new racial and spatial relations." King's followers would then aspire to become "those creative dissenters who will call our beloved nation to a higher destiny, to a new plateau of compassion, to a more noble expression of humaneness" (King [1967] 2010, 142).

Such work asks us to also consider how processes of awakening connect to and influence more familiar projects of social and political change—a consideration with great urgency given the high stakes of the current moment. Henry Giroux (2017, 902), for example, identifies a "war culture" with a "white supremacist, ultra-nationalist underside," and he calls for "a new language for politics" that "must be historical, relational, ethical and as comprehensive as it is radical." Rather than positioning this new politics as unconnected from preceding frameworks, it is important to follow the threads that extend from leaders such as King to more contemporary teachers. Giroux, for example, identifies several Black women intellectuals and activists, such as Angela Davis, whose view of "connective politics" (903) frames the call for progressives to build links to other struggles for justice; Michelle Alexander ([2010] 2012, 903), who offers "a totalizing view of oppression [that] allows us to see the underlying ideological and structural forces of the new forms of domination at work in the United States"; and the Black feminists who founded the Black Lives Matter movement, which extends beyond single policy issues through coalition and platform building (903).

As I discuss in the introduction to this book, some scholars nonetheless maintain that traditional methods of social and political change, as connective as they may be, are not enough. Without a moral or spiritual awakening, Alexander asserts, "we will remain forever trapped in political games fueled by fear, greed and the hunger for power."[2] Alexander is careful not to suggest that traditional methods be abandoned; however, she maintains that "none of it—not even working for some form of political revolution—will ever be enough on its own" (2012). In this sense, awakening becomes a necessary process—achieved not just by declaration or grand gesture but by productively anchoring the fight for freedom and equality within the systems and institutions that structure modern life.

Giroux does not place the same importance on awakening. Instead, he argues that the work of resistance in the Trump era requires a destruction of the "economic, political, educational and social conditions that produced [Trump]" lest the nation further descend into authoritarianism (Giroux 2017, 904). He also describes the work of resistance as having a pedagogical challenge—a challenge that seems enormously important for both the new language for politics Giroux points to and the awakening that Alexander argues must accompany it. Education thus becomes a central process, through the identification of problems and in the development and sharing of the messages and methods of change. I note finally the places where such work might proceed. In New Orleans, they included the houses that were lived in and lost; the neighborhoods and dwellings some made it back to; the schools and street corners that competed for a young person's attention; the churches and other places of worship and ceremony; the courtrooms and prisons; the places of protest and vigil; and the cemeteries and other locations for the continued raising of the dead. At these sites, and in the movements between them, the people of New Orleans might continue their transformation of the crescent city.

Love and Light

In a broad consideration of the links between religious awakenings and social reform in America, historian William G. McLoughlin (1978, 2) describes great awakenings as "folk movements," which frequently emerge in response to disjunction. These awakenings, McLoughlin writes, "are the results, not of depressions, wars, or epidemics, but of critical disjunctions in our self-understanding." They begin "when we lose faith in the legitimacy of our norms, the viability of our institutions, and the authority of our leaders in church and state," and "they eventuate in basic restructurings of our institutions and redefinitions of our social goals."

Awakenings are thus, in large part, about the restoration of faith—"faith in ourselves, our ideals, and our 'covenant with God'" even when they direct us to reinterpret or modify that covenant "in the light of new experience" (2). Such processes remain essential for the growth of a nation and its people (8).

Awakenings are widespread and diverse, with no single origin or cause. Nonetheless they can reveal a set of shared beliefs and practices even as they form with different strategies, in various locations, and through multiple stages (McLoughlin 1978, 10). To explore the common elements of the religious ideal I have examined in this book, particularly the possibilities for its development as a collective project of awakening and corresponding social reform, I return to the specific sites of congregation that came forward during my time in the Crescent City, the central conduits through which people and ideas converged and new frameworks extended.

Liberty Street certainly emerged as such a place, and this in turn opens up questions about the Black Church and its role, more broadly, in processes of social recovery and transformation. To consider the church in this way, however, poses simultaneous challenges and opportunities. The challenges in part have to do with the changing landscape of Black life, which is characterized, as Lincoln and Mamiya ([1990] 2003, 384) have noted, by "the increasing bifurcation of the black community into two main class divisions: a coping sector of middle-income working-class and middle-class black communities, and a crisis sector of poor black communities involving the working poor and the dependent poor." This produces a community whose needs are "both deeply spiritual and agonizingly physical" (397–98), and it requires the Black Church to look, be pulled, and serve, in all directions.

This challenge points to another, which has to do with the disjunctions that disable the capacity, and thus reach, of the church. As Lincoln and Mamiya ([1990] 2003, 391–92) also assert, the lack of unification in the Black Church limits its potential power as a social institution, a power that "has never been fully realized and . . . probably never will be so long as sectarianism is the norm." Ecumenical visions have at times emerged for a church that might "move with one unified spirit and singleness of purpose" (392). However, they seem hindered by the lack of an unequivocal acceptance of diversity and unattainable given the unlikely redistribution of authority and power that such a vision would require. Even if this unification could one day be supported, the broader marginalization of the Black Church would likely persist, its external reach struggling against the notion that Black religious ideals could not possibly pertain to, generate, or inspire the broad awakening on which the peaceful world now seems to depend.

The opportunity, therefore, is to gather and articulate the ideals by which the Black Church has formed while asserting its position as a productive site through which new awakenings and movements might be directed. In this way the church might also better align itself with the many other sites and movements that are emerging to form an expanded network of institutions, organizations, coalitions, and communities working toward a sustainable Black future. There are many important and potentially transformative theological and practical currents running through these sites, far greater than what I have been able to explore here. Three recent examples, which extend from, reinvigorate, or move beyond the historical forms of African American theology to which they nonetheless remain linked, are the theological thinking of love and *communitas* that Corey D. B. Walker (2013, 653) elucidates (see also Thurman 1961, 5), the African American religious naturalism that Carol Wayne White (2016, 2–3) proposes, and the "radical inclusivity" exhibited by the African American Pentecostal worshippers in Ellen Lewin's (2018, 8) ethnographic study.

Some of these ideas already weave through the space of death and transformation in New Orleans. For example, in the introduction I conceptualize love as the expressions and practices that affirm, value, strengthen, and celebrate Black people. This follows from the aims of the Black Lives Matter movement, as the "love letter" to Black people with which the movement was launched makes clear (Bailey and Leonard 2015, 69–71). My return to love here, after my time in the Crescent City, is more contextualized, stemming from the ways in which love was expressed, embodied, and enacted by the people themselves—from divine love (Black sacred cosmos) to the love of self it sanctions (somebodiness) to the love for others and the protection of the vulnerable (relatedness and value) to the sense of sacred humanity that moves us forward as a people (beloved community).

Intellectually, this fits with the love ethic that Black scholars have already proposed (West [1993] 2017, 19; hooks 1994), an ethic without which we might remain "seduced, in one way or the other, into continued allegiance to systems of domination" (hooks 1994, 243). Therefore, the love that develops in the crescent city seems also dependent on what Kristie Dotson (2013, 40) describes as forward driven "acts of inheriting." This is "radical love for black people" (38) perpetuated within, through, and beyond particular places, institutions, and structures. What is inherited and then transmitted are the fruits of cultural and theoretical production that extend from a commitment to Black thought, faith, action, and being.

Dotson, drawing on the work of singer, scholar, and social activist Bernice Johnson Reagon, thus describes the process of "throwing ourselves into the future" (Reagon 1983, 365; cited in Dotson 2013, 40). Here, we think not only about the principles and practices we find meaningful but where they come from, how they are developed and shared, and how we leave them behind *and* ahead. The process requires us to trust, accordingly, "that our ancestors have indeed thrown their theoretical production (i.e., their practice and their principles) into this century, as we, by engaging in black theoretical production and beyond, throw ourselves into future centuries" (40). In this way, all of us, together, might soldier on toward a better tomorrow.

—————

In August 2017, I took a short vacation with my young son to visit family in Charlottesville, Virginia. I was nearly finished with a first draft of this manuscript, feeling stuck, exhausted, and without conclusion. Our time in Charlottesville, I imagined, would be a welcome change of scenery. We always felt rejuvenated by the time we spent there with family we lived too far away from—stepping into a love that, at least in this instance, needs no analysis.

Charlottesville had been in the news earlier that year regarding the city's own attempts to change the narrative on race, equality, and humanity by removing the markers of white supremacy that were still prominent throughout its public and urban landscape. The news coverage, however, had focused more sensationally on the violent response, or at least the potential for it, brewing up a storm between those who supported the removal of the markers and those who were clearly opposed. In May 2017, a group of white supremacists gathered to protest the city council's decision to remove the statue of Confederate General Robert E. Lee, located in Emancipation Park (formerly Lee Park). A KKK rally then took place in July at the base of another statue, that of Confederate Lieutenant General Thomas "Stonewall" Jackson, located in Justice Park (formerly Stonewall Jackson Park). Emboldened by the attention these events received and despite the strong presence and impact of counter demonstrators at each one, the same group planned a much larger rally for August, again at Emancipation Park. The event was billed and projected, with great alarm by the Southern Poverty Law Center and many others, to be the largest hate gathering of its kind in decades in the United States.

That I remained relatively unaware of these events, their magnitude and overlap with our visit to Charlottesville, was a reflection of how overwhelmed I was with writing and other work, which made it difficult to keep track of the news, especially in an oversaturated and frequently toxic media space where agenda and effect were hard to determine. Once we arrived, however, and got wind of the local discourse, the real danger of what was about to unfold became clear. While some seemed to brush off the coming rally, purposely not giving attention to something they hoped would dissipate on its own, others took the threat quite seriously, lobbying officials at city hall to cancel the event. When the city did attempt to move the rally to a larger park where it could be better contained, rally organizers went to court to confirm their right to gather and protest at Emancipation Park, arguing that the statue of Robert E. Lee was an essential focal point. The organization of the rally thus continued, as did preparations for counterprotest, with churches, activist groups, and civil rights organizations leading the way.

The tension increased by the day. More people arrived from out of town. Planning meetings were held. News crews were dispatched. One stepped boldly or cautiously when in public, as skin color or other circumstances dictated, or retreated with relief to the spaces and places that felt familiar and safe. Trying all the while to enjoy my time with family, my brother and I scheduled a day trip out of town, which happened to fall on the same day as the scheduled rally. While this was not a direct response to the events that were unfolding, the timing was nonetheless ideal, especially for shielding the youngest members of our group from the hate and violence that everyone, increasingly, was expecting.

We left in the late morning, but not before the helicopters began to circle over the apartment at which we stayed, just four blocks from Emancipation Park. My young son froze when he looked out of the window; he had spotted a group of police offers in riot gear who were assembling equipment before deployment. They reminded him, uncomfortably, of *Star Wars*—Stormtroopers of the Imperial Army. There was no time for the full conversation I knew we would inevitably have about the state of violence in the world and its target, so I did my best to explain who they were and what was happening and to reassure him, as much as seemed reasonable, that we were safe. I was quite relieved when my brother arrived with the car to drive us away, the kids distracted by video games in the back and the adults checking news and social media on cell phones until the reception thankfully got spotty in the Shenandoah Valley. It was not until we reached Luray Caverns, one of the largest caverns in the United States, and had descended some 250 feet toward the center of the earth that the noise subsided. Usually claustrophobic, I had not the feeling of confinement but of comfort, not darkness but illumination.

On that day, Luray Caverns was celebrating its birthday, or "discovery day," when cold air rushing out of a limestone sinkhole blew out the candle of explorer Andrew Campbell 139 years before. Campbell and his thirteen-year-old nephew lowered their way down into a wondrous world, both old and new. One still had a sense of what that discovery must have felt like, as several hundred votive candles had been placed throughout the cave in celebration, gently lighting the way past formations some seven million years old to dripping wet walls of active growth. We would return to Charlottesville, of course, and wherever else our lives and work would take us, but for the moment we were stilled by the strength and beauty of the earth despite the violence we have wrought upon it. My family and I thus mourned those we have lost, as we provided some shelter for those who will inherit the principles and the tools to heal our living world. This is both the challenge and the opportunity of our present age.

Acknowledgments

This book came to life at a difficult time, its ideas formed in the wake of disaster and in the space of violence, death, and recovery. The people of New Orleans welcomed me just after Hurricane Katrina even though they were getting on with their lives and were thus not prepared or in the mood for company. I begin, therefore, by thanking my father, James Puckette Carter Sr. (1933–2014), in whose memory this book is dedicated. He and my stepmother, Carolyn Harris Carter, generously opened their doors even after their house had been destroyed and despite the fact that I could not fully explain why I had come. I believed that I was there to help and to work, but I was drawn in a deeper sense to recover some part of my past and to participate, however tangentially, in the rebuilding of the city. This determination went back to an earlier time, a love for New Orleans that was anchored in the life my father had created there—his home and the park that had surrounded it, the art he displayed from around the world, the stacks of books and papers he had written, the people who extended our family, the food and ideas and love we shared. I am grateful for the support he and my stepmother continued to provide despite all they had lost.

Research and writing are uncertain projects even in the best of circumstances. At a tarot reading by a Voodoo practitioner in the French Quarter, I pulled just two cards, both of Azaka, the Lwa who is a hardworking peasant and the patron of agriculture. "Ah, you must have Papa Zaka on your head," the woman told me, with a knowing smile. "Your *met tet*." While not determined by proper ceremony, the suggestion was fitting all the same. It confirmed the hard labor while also revealing the nature of what was really a group project, a cultivation by many hands, though the final form and what the book might nourish took years to decide. A favorite poem by Joy Harjo ([1983] 2008, 37) titled "New Orleans" reminded me of the stakes:

There are voices buried in the Mississippi
mud. There are ancestors and future children
buried beneath the currents stirred up by
pleasure boats going up and down.
There are stories here made of memory.

I am forever indebted to the people of New Orleans, whose stories anchor and guide this work. They graciously gave of themselves—allowing me to ask questions, observe, take photographs, visit their homes and places of worship, and be somewhat underfoot despite my best intentions. I continue to be inspired by the courage with which they confront the most painful situations, demonstrating to me if not to the world a level of resolve to live within and improve the conditions that surrounded them. I'm not so sure that I would have been able to communicate with as much openness and candor were our positions reversed, and I hope that I have presented their voices and visions as they themselves would.

The formative work of this project took place at the University of Michigan, Ann Arbor, where I earned my doctoral degree in the Department of Anthropology, expertly advised by Gillian Feeley-Harnik. I consider myself extremely fortunate in this regard, and Gillian's influence is hopefully evident in the integrative approach I use to consider the anthropology of death and dying, the study of American religious life, and theories and practices of kinship and relatedness. Perhaps more important, however, are the strategies Gillian continues to share with me for how to listen, think, and work—intensely and creatively—and how to persevere in uncertain or difficult times. I also thank my other committee members—Tom Fricke, Stuart Kirsch, and Paul Christopher Johnson—for their encouragement and support and for essential training in ethnographic research and writing, engaged and environmental anthropology, and theory of religion respectively. My academic growth at Michigan was also made possible by generous financial support; I am especially grateful for funding from the Center for the Ethnography of Everyday Life, the Center for the Education of Women, and the Rackham School of Graduate Studies. During this time, my life was otherwise greatly enriched by the company and care of cohort members and friends. Despite the journeys that have since taken us to distant places, I send heartfelt thanks especially to Karen Hébert and Anneeth Kaur Hundle.

My fieldwork in New Orleans was made possible by a grant from the Social Science Research Council through a fund created to support research related to Hurricane Katrina. Additional support came through part-time employment, and I am grateful for the opportunity I had to work and learn alongside new friends at the New Orleans Video Access Center, where I thank Liz Dunnebacke, and the Contemporary Arts Center of New Orleans, with thanks to Nanette Saucier. In both of these positions I was introduced to a vibrant arts community that further sustained my time in the field. Several individuals at local institutions provided additional resources, helping me to build community and do my work, including the faculty at the Department of Anthropology at Tulane University, who approved library access through visiting scholar status; Shirley Laska at the University of New Orleans, who gave office space at the Center for Hazards, Assessment, Response, and Technology; and staff at various archives who went out of their way to direct me to materials, for example, at City Archives, the Amistad Research Center, and in the internal archives of many churches and local dioceses.

I returned to my home state of Tennessee in 2009, taking up residence at Middle Tennessee State University for a predoctoral fellowship and lectureship in the Department of Sociology and Anthropology. I thank the administration, faculty, and students there for hosting me, especially as I transitioned from fieldwork to an intensive period of data analysis and writing. I moved to Brown University in 2011, arriving as a New Faculty Fellow in the Department of Anthropology, supported by a postdoctoral fellowship from the American Council of Learned Societies. I officially joined the faculty at Brown in 2013, jointly appointed in anthropology and urban studies.

It was at Brown that the content and organization of the book were really decided, in an intense period of intellectual growth that was supported, in large part, by Brown's commitment to open, cross-disciplinary, and engaged scholarship. I am grateful for the support I have received from administrators, mentors, colleagues, and especially my department and program chairs: Cathy Lutz and Dan Smith in anthropology, and Hilary Silver and Dietrich Neumann in urban studies. I have also benefited greatly from the intellectual exchange that has occurred outside of my home department, for example, in a seminar at the Center for the Study of Race and Ethnicity in America directed by Tricia Rose and in a writing group for women of color in the academy funded by the

Pembroke Center for Teaching and Research on Women. I also learned a tremendous amount from the undergraduate and graduate students with whom I have been privileged to work, and I thank especially those who assisted me with the book: Lily Gutterman, Alice Larotonda, Jordan McDonald, Anna Pierobon, and D. Rhys Wilson.

The most important factor in the book's development and final completion was time—for listening, studying, and conversing; for the testing of ideas; for the larger structure of the book to emerge; and for the writing itself. This proved, however, to be the most difficult resource to secure, given increasingly high demands for productivity in academia and with the seeming impossibility of finding balance in work and life responsibilities. I am extremely grateful, therefore, for the people who make up my small but strong local network—their friendship and support has made all the difference. The list is long, and I fear incomplete, but I thank Angela Alston, Nancy Diaz Bain, Lisa Dady, Cedric DeLeon, Joanna Doherty, Paja Faudree, Lina Fruzetti, Ricky Gresch, Sherine Hamdy, Emily Heaphy, Helaryn Hernandez, Amanda Jamieson, Melissa Kievman, Jessaca Leinaweaver, Courtney Martin, Brian Mertes, Keisha-Khan Perry, Alex Rempis, Leo Selvaggio, and Korn Suom.

An extraordinary gift of time came in the form of an extended leave, supported first by a junior sabbatical at Brown and then by a 2016–2017 fellowship at the Radcliffe Institute for Advanced Study at Harvard University. To be able to think and write in a space so supportive of people and ideas in process was an incredible experience that changed me as a scholar and quite literally made the book. I thank Dean Lizabeth Cohen and Associate Dean Judith Vichniac for the opportunity and for their leadership; I am grateful also to the fellows who were in residence with me and from whom I learned so much. I thank especially Amahl Bishara, Tomiko Brown-Nagin, and Aisha Khan for their excellent company. I also thank Solange Azor, who provided research assistance through the Radcliffe Institute Research Partnership Program.

Several individuals read early drafts of chapters and gave extremely helpful comments, especially as I worked to reduce the size of the manuscript and prepare it for submission. I thank Cecelia Cancellaro, Gillian Feeley-Harnik, and Matt Gutterl for their time and suggestions. I feel lucky to have landed, finally, with Priya Nelson, editor at Chicago, who, along with editorial associate Dylan Montanari, production editor Caterina MacLean, copyeditor Carl Steven LaRue, and indexer Jan Williams, shepherded the manuscript and this first-time author through the publishing process in an incredibly straightforward and responsive fashion. I also thank the anonymous reviewers whose suggestions greatly improved the manuscript with much-needed encouragement as the process of revision began.

The book stands finally on a foundation of love and wisdom that comes from my family—in Louisiana, in Tennessee, in Virginia, and in places beyond. I consider this a great inheritance, over generations too long to trace, but it comprises the many hands involved in the cultivation and continuation of this work. I give special thanks to my mother, Gena Hunter Carter, for her unwavering support. My mother *fed* me constantly, with advice, encouragement, laughter, love, and other essential resources. "You are *going* to finish," she would say, without so much as a hint of doubt, and it is only with her help that I have. I thank also my brother Geoff and his family, who cheered my progress and were understanding of my preoccupations and limited time. Most of all, I am forever grateful for the love I see mirrored in the eyes of my son Evan, who remains the greatest gift and the most joyful companion as life and work roll on. "You got it, mama," he continues to say and believe. These acknowledgments, therefore, extend beyond the production of this one book to what it might produce and be part of as the movements and awakenings of a better world proceed. For this possibility, for my son and for all God's children, we can all be thankful.

Notes

1. The names of participants have been changed, and
    anonymity-compromising details have been eliminated
    as much as possible. This includes changing the names of
    specific sites (such as churches) in which participants were
    located. However, I identify the region, city, and neighbor-
    hoods in which my research was based, naming public
    officials along the way, as I develop the historical and
    social-geographic context within which my ethnographic
    data develops. These decisions were difficult to sort out. I
    followed the standards for research set by the institutional
    review board at the University of Michigan, which oversaw
    my fieldwork, adopting measures to minimize risk through
    informed consent, data security, and the careful dissemina-
    tion of research findings. Despite this protocol, I remained
    nonetheless concerned about the extent to which research
    participants were actually protected. For example, ensur-
    ing privacy can be a challenge in the close-knit communi-
    ties where I worked, particularly when contextual data is
    featured so prominently in the text. However, as I became
    more aware of the vulnerable and violent conditions that
    participants faced, I became equally concerned about the
    use of pseudonyms, wondering whether they contributed,
    albeit unintentionally, to harm via processes of silencing and
    erasure. What is the impact of anonymizing participants,
    especially if they (or those that knew them) would prefer
    (them) to be named? When deciding to name, on the other
    hand, how can we know the full impact of such exposure
    for participants and for researchers over time? While in the
    end I erred on the side of caution, adhering to my approved

research plan, I am not fully satisfied with the process or the result. I hope that participants and readers alike will forgive my missteps and that debate on these issues will continue, particularly regarding the dilemmas of ethnographic transparency, verification, and accountability (Reyes 2018).

2. I use the terms *African American* and *Black* carefully according to how people identified themselves or how they were identified in census and other demographic data. I also use these terms historically in order to remain consistent with existing literature, for example. when referring to "the Black Church," "African American religion and theology," or the late nineteenth-century settlement of "African Americans" in Uptown New Orleans. When the preferred term was not clear, I use and capitalize *Black* as a primary signifier of racial identity. According to the Chicago Manual of Style (17th ed.), section 8.38, "Names of ethnic and national groups are capitalized." However, "terms such as *black* and *white*, when referring to ethnicity, are usually lowercased unless a particular author or publisher prefers otherwise." The wording hints at the complexity that underlies the deployment of racial and ethnic terms, confirming that decisions about their use are less a matter of style and more a question of politics. A debate about the capitalization of *black* has existed since at least the 1960s, when that term ascended over *Negro* (a term that had its own struggle over capitalization) as a racial and ethnic label (Kennedy 2004/2005, 78). As Martha Biondi (2003, as cited by Kennedy 2004/2005, 79) argues, the designation of *Black* with a capital *B* "reflects the self-naming and self-identification of a people whose national or ethnic origins have been obscured by a history of capture and enslavement." While one could counter that *white* should also be capitalized, even though Caucasian exists as an ethnic group, Biondi explains that " 'white' is not capitalized because historically it has been deployed as a signifier of social domination and privilege, rather than as an indicator of ethnic or national origin." My own choices for capitalization follow suit, not only to properly align my scholarly work but to support the broader processes of empowerment and liberation to which such practices ideally connect. This system, however, is far from perfect. For example, it trips over itself when terms that are not historically capitalized are concerned, such as the "black social gospel." And while the practice might align with social and political progress, I am not convinced that it gets us exactly where we want to be, particularly given the necessarily collective processes of social and moral awakening to which this book leads. Thus, while I capitalize *Black*, I think also about what this choice facilitates as well as what it might preclude, and I look forward to continued dialogue on this issue from a stylistic as well as a political standpoint.

3. https://www.facebook.com/permalink.php?story_fbid=1090233291064627&id=168304409924191.

4. http://www.datacenterresearch.org/data-resources/katrina/facts-for-impact/, http://new.dhh.louisiana.gov/assets/docs/katrina/deceasedreports/Katrina Deaths_082008.pdf.

5. In 2000, African Americans made up nearly 67 percent of the total population; by 2010 their number had dropped to 60 percent (205,747 residents of a total population size that was estimated at 343,829); http://www .datacenterresearch.org/data-resources/population-by-parish/, http://www .datacenterresearch.org/data-resources/who-lives-in-new-orleans-now/.

6. Recent and more balanced analyses of urban violence include its other factors, such as social and racial inequality, poverty, lax gun laws, and the social codes that perpetuate brutal cycles of killing and retaliation (Beckett and Sasson 2004, 43). I expand on these factors in chapter 2.

7. FBI Uniform Crime Reporting, *Crime in the United States* 2009, Table 8: Offenses Known to Law Enforcement by State and City, 2009; Table 1: Crime in the United States by Volume and Rate per 100,000 Inhabitants, 1990–2009, https://ucr.fbi.gov/crime-in-the-u.s/2009.

8. Early uses of the term appear in W. E. B. Du Bois, *The Black North in 1901: A Social Study* ([1901] 1969), George Haynes, *Conditions among Negroes in the Cities* (1913), and St. Clair Drake and Horace Cayton, *Black Metropolis: A Study of Negro Life in a Northern City* (1945) (Haynes and Hutchinson 2008, 349–50).

9. Mitchell Duneier (2016, ix) provides a useful intellectual genealogy of scholars who make this system clear, arguing that the ghetto "remains a useful concept—provided we recall its rich historical background and stop divorcing it from its past."

10. *Merriam-Webster*, s.v. "crescent (*adj.*),", accessed October 12, 2018, https:// www.merriam-webster.com/dictionary/crescent.

11. See Sharon Patricia Holland's (2000, 4, 30–31) discussion of life-in-death in her interdisciplinary exploration of death and Black subjectivity.

12. Patterson (1982, 45) argues, however, that the slave still has a prominent role, being essential for the survival of the society, and is thus necessarily incorporated, although to the minimum possible degree. Therefore, "slavery involved two contradictory principles, marginality and integration" (46). This constitutes the liminal state of social death, "the ultimate cultural outcome of the loss of natality as well as honor and power" (46).

13. As Brown argues, the concept of social death is "a theoretical abstraction that is meant not to describe the lived experiences of the enslaved so much as to reduce them to a least common denominator that could reveal the essence of slavery in an ideal-type slave, shorn of meaningful heritage" (1233).

14. My use of *transformation* as a term throughout the book refers primarily to the desired shift in consciousness and relatedness that religious work at Liberty Street sought to bring about. It was a shift that practitioners

believed occurred through religious salvation, but it was also conceptualized more broadly as a social and moral reckoning. However, I also use *transformation* to refer to a corresponding shift in the determination of value, which enabled relatedness but also grounded the disruptive political work that Cacho (2012, 31) and others consider necessary.

15. This relationship is not without controversy, as continuing debates about religious freedom in Louisiana demonstrate, with prayer in schools and same-sex marriage (legal since 2015) among the most fiercely contested issues.

16. In a special issue on "Religion and the Future of Blackness" edited by J. Kameron Carter and published in *South Atlantic Quarterly*, M. Shawn Copeland (2013) identifies a productive relationship between religion, theology, and Blackness (626), directing the process through an alternative route that "would lead theology through and into silence to humble encounter with ambiguity, perplexity, uncertainty, dispossession, and loss . . . to a richer and more complex understanding of the emergence and character of black religious consciousness" (635–36). Corey D. B. Walker (2013) elucidates a *"theological thinking* of love—expanded and limited by blackness itself," that "open[s] the conditions of possibility for living and being otherwise" (653, emphasis in original).

17. Such work is thankfully underway, from the identification of formative scholarship in anthropology and attendant fields (Bolles 2001) to the development and dissemination of Black feminist theory, especially as it informs a decolonized and Black feminist anthropology (Collins 2000a; Harrison 1997; McClaurin 2001), to the late twentieth-century urban anthropological and ethnographic studies on African American women these works subsequently inspired (Stack 1974; Mullings 1997; Waterston 1999; Mullings and Wali 2001) to recent scholarship on Black girls and women across the diaspora (Isoke 2013; K-K. Y. Perry 2014; Barnes 2015; Chatelain 2015; Cox 2015).

18. Much of this research is further developed through womanist theology, which works to recover the voices and perspectives of Black women as a necessary point of departure for the reconfiguration of Christian doctrine (Carter 2014, 181; Cannon and Pinn 2014, 3). I return to this influence in chapter 5.

19. Carsten (2007, 1) draws attention to "the subtle and complex interconnections among everyday forms of relatedness in the present, memories of the past, and the wider political contexts in which they occur." These interconnections take a variety of forms: "the myriad articulations—of temporality, memory, personal biography, family connection, and political processes," and while they are "manifested in subjective dispositions to the past," they also look forward "in the imagination of possible futures."

20. This inquiry can extend beyond religion, for example, by aligning with scholarship that focuses more broadly on the ways that Black women

creatively inhabit and transcend their otherwise bounded circumstances. Building on Black feminist theory and recognizing the visible as well as hidden forms of Black women's social, political, and spiritual agency are studies of women and girls in the United States who negotiate the terms of value and citizenship as they contend with conditions of vulnerability and violence (D.-A. Davis 2006; Boylorn 2013; Isoke 2013; Mattingly 2014; Barnes 2015; Cox 2015). Beyond the context of the United States, scholars such as Christen A. Smith (2015, 386) make clear the "diasporic realities of anti-black state violence" to reveal the life and death stakes of "radical black mothering" (C. A. Smith 2016b, 5–7), a praxis which I discuss in chapter 5. This work draws together scholars from various contexts to understand the engendering of sorrow and the pain and power of Black women around the world who, as Dana-Ain Davis (2016, 14) writes, "carry deceased children while simultaneously negotiating imagined futures."

21. I am guided here by the work of several Black women scholars who draw on personal experience to chart a course through the past and present realities of Black life and death, demonstrating the necessary merging of history, memory, ethnography, narrative, and poetry to understand Black subjectivity and futurity (Hartman 2007; Campt 2012; Trethewey 2010; Harding and Harding 2015).

CHAPTER ONE

1. The "neutral ground" refers to the wide grassy median that runs down the center of many streets in New Orleans. The term is linked to the history of Canal Street and appears in local records as early as 1862, most likely referring to Canal Street's location between two separate and somewhat hostile social and political jurisdictions—the mostly Creole French Quarter on one side of the median, and the rapidly growing American sector on the other (Chase [1949] 2007, 108–9; Laborde and Magill 2006, 26).

2. New Orleanians have defined neighborhoods in a variety of ways since the founding of the city, from colonial designations of bourg and faubourg to still-active geographic designations of upriver or downriver, Uptown or downtown, front or back-of-town. While the City identifies seventy-three "official" neighborhoods and thirteen planning districts, these do not necessarily correlate with popular identifications, which emerge from "bottom-up awareness rather than top-down proclamation" (Campanella 2014).

3. In developing this analytical frame, I take inspiration from Paul Gilroy's conceptualization of the black Atlantic, which emphasizes its fractal, international, and transcultural formation, testing and transcending more absolutist structures and designations, for example, of geography, nation, race, and ethnicity (Gilroy 1993, 4). Gilroy is interested in "the stereophonic, bilingual, or bifocal cultural forms originated by, but no longer the exclusive property of, blacks dispersed within the structures of feeling,

producing, communication, and remembering" that is the black Atlantic world (3). The Black urban delta operates in a similar sense, illuminating the fluidity and purchase of Black social and cultural practices in a place that has been otherwise defined but that in reality offers no firm footing as physical and symbolic ground productively shifts and as structures and boundaries are crossed, reconfigured, or bypassed.

4. http://www.datacenterresearch.org/data-resources/katrina/facts-for-impact/.

5. Such processes followed a neoliberal model of disaster capitalism with distinctly racist overtones and focused on the repopulation of the city through the destruction of public housing and the criminalization and exclusion of poor Black residents. As Arena argues, "The pronouncements and actions taken by . . . powerful political and economic actors in New Orleans, Baton Rouge, and Washington in the immediate aftermath of Katrina made it clear that public-housing communities were not part of the 'completely different' city they were imagining. . . . Yet Hurricane Katrina and the forced displacement of residents provided an opportunity to fast-track the revanchist agenda—to drown public housing in a fully human-made 'neoliberal deluge'" (Arena 2012, 146–47; see also Klein 2007; Woods 2005; Gunewardena and Schuller 2008; Johnson 2011).

6. Although relations between Europeans and Native Americans were mutually beneficial—for example where navigation, agriculture, trade, and defense were concerned (Hall 1992, 14–20)—they were also the source of deadly conflict. Such complexity, as historian Daniel Usner argues, is best understood through a more balanced analysis of the Native-colonial encounter. Rather than a common characterization of the development of "Indian society" during this period as a "downward spiral," Usner recognizes an unpredictable mix of "intratribal and intertribal relations, intracolonial and intercolonial relations, and shifting interests of both Indian and colonial societies" (Usner 1992, 10).

7. In 1717 the French crown privatized the development of the colony, transferring its management to John Law and his Company of the West, which later expanded and was renamed the Company of the Indies (Hall 1992, 5). Bienville was appointed as *commandant-général*, the highest royal official in the colony (Powell 2012, 42).

8. Bienville pushed for the development of the capital city at this particular site, seeing the strategic advantage it allowed for commerce and defense and recognizing the extent to which he would benefit because of the land holdings he had already established (Powell 2012, 42).

9. The argument that New Orleans was an "exceptional" colonial city because of its geography, population, social structure, economy, or culture is the subject of continued debate. While some scholars characterize the city as more racially and socially fluid, and therefore less orderly (Tannenbaum 1946; Hall 1992; Usner 1992; Hanger 1997; see also Clark 2000), others have argued that New Orleans was no different from any other racially

polarized slave society in North America and characterized not by cultural disorder but rather a struggle for order and power in a tri-racial slave society fueled by geographic position, the lure of wealth, and subsequent economic and urban development (Ingersoll 1999). A useful contribution to this debate is Shannon Dawdy's identification of the characterizations of order and disorder that were housed in place and population alike and their use to justify the short-term failures of imperialism in the New World (Dawdy 2008, 21).

10. For example, the importation of slaves increased after 1771, when royal decree accelerated the trade through special exemptions such as lower import duties to meet the growing labor needs of a revived port and plantation economy (Powell 2012, 228). However, it was halted from 1796 to 1800 for fear of continued slave revolt, particularly following the slave conspiracy in Pointe Coupée, Louisiana, and with the Haitian Revolution then underway on the French colony of Saint-Domingue. The slave trade began again in 1800, demanded by Louisiana planters and town merchants rushing into sugar production and profit.

11. Such practices were also part of a strategic move by the Spanish crown to expand a prosperous society, fill the roles of an established social hierarchy, and encourage freedom by peaceful diligence and merit rather than force (Hanger 1997, 24).

12. For example, in 1778 a new Code Noir (Loi Municipale) was proposed that resurrected many tenets of the French Code Noir, such as disallowing for slaves' gun ownership, horseback travel, assembly, the reporting of abuse, and manumission, among other things (Powell 2012, 235). This new code was never enacted, however, falling by the wayside in a complicated series of political maneuverings involving the colonial governor, Bernardo de Gálvez, the councilors of the municipal government, merchants and planters, and the Spanish crown (Din 1999, 79).

13. One need only consider the many acts of resistance and revolt that enslaved Africans initiated and contributed to in both the French and Spanish periods. These include the Natchez Uprising in 1729, when enslaved Africans joined with members of the Natchez Nation to resist French encroachment, killing over two hundred French colonists. Also significant were the maroon societies that grew along the rivers and bayous surrounding the city. One of the most established was a settlement in Bas du Fleuve led by Juan San Maló, which by 1777 was home to 2,484 people (Hall 1992, 206, 245).

14. As Scott summarizes, by the middle of the nineteenth century there were approximately 1,500 sugar plantations in the Louisiana territory. The enslaved population was concentrated in fourteen leading sugar parishes, which "held 116,000 slaves and produced about 87,000 metric tons of sugar, along with cotton and corn" (Scott 2005, 12).

15. It is important to acknowledge the role of technology here, beginning in the 1830s with the construction of steam-engine-powered pumps that

drained the swamp through an integrated system of canals. State levee districts were created to manage this system, and at the national level, Congress created the Mississippi River Commission in 1879, which worked in partnership with the Army Corps of Engineers (Campanella 2008, 206).

16. In the New Orleans Race Riot, July 1866, a mob of ex-Confederates, white supremacists, and members of the New Orleans police force massacred hundreds of Black citizens, including delegates to the Louisiana Constitutional Convention (Hollandsworth 2001).

17. While federal intervention prevented the White League from overthrowing the Republicans outright, subsequent elections secured their claim to authority. As Scott (2005, 71) notes, "As the curtain came down on Reconstruction, white-line Democratic dominance was reasserted in the legislature, in the town halls, and in the militia. A new state constitution in 1879 expunged the guarantee of equal 'civil, political and public rights' that had figured in the 1868 constitution, though it stopped short of openly mandating racial separation. Much of the power of the state could now be exercised directly against the interests of former slaves and their descendants."

18. As historian C. Vann Woodward (1955, 7) explains, Jim Crow laws were segregation statutes and codes that served collectively as "public symbols and constant reminders of [the Negro's] inferior position." The system was all encompassing, "the most elaborate and formal expression of sovereign white opinion upon the subject" (7). Its reach thus extended "to churches and schools, to housing and jobs, to eating and drinking . . . to virtually all forms of public transportation, to sports and recreations, to hospitals, orphanages, prisons, and asylums, and ultimately to funeral homes, morgues, and cemeteries" (7–8).

19. Religious and community leaders had lobbied the city in the late 1970s to honor King's legacy and work, first by changing the name of a portion of Melpomene Street to Martin Luther King Jr. Boulevard and then by creating a memorial to King at its end, at the intersection with Claiborne Avenue. I give the history of this memorial in greater detail in chapter 3.

20. Living conditions for Blacks across the city were poor. In 1970, 44 percent of African American residents earned incomes below the poverty level, and poverty was concentrated in public housing, where residents had the lowest median family income and the highest rate of unemployment (Spain 1979, 94).

21. In just one example, the Lakeview area at the edge of Lake Pontchartrain was drained and developed in the early 1900s, and large-scale residential development began in the mid-1940s, after World War II. Racist deed contracts prevented African Americans and others from purchasing the land; thus, a middle-class white community essentially "leapfrogged over the black back-of-town" to settle in this new, though still low-lying, area (Campanella 2007, 709).

22. In chapter 2, I discuss the many efforts to improve these conditions in Central City, including protest, social and political movement, and related programs that worked for fairness in housing and employment, the improvement of infrastructure and services, and increased political representation.
23. In census data from the year 2000, just five years before Hurricane Katrina, the population of Orleans parish was estimated at 484,674. Over two-thirds (67.3 percent) was African American. Whites accounted for 28.1 percent, Hispanics or Latinos made up 3.1 percent, Asians accounted for 2.3 percent, and smaller ethnic groups made up the remainder. Overall, 27.9 percent of the total population lived below the poverty level. The poor, mainly poor African Americans, primarily resided in back-of-town neighborhoods such as Central City, in public-housing projects, and in wards and subdivisions farther afield.

CHAPTER TWO

1. http://www.democracycorps.com/wp-content/files/tulane-democracy-corps-survey-analysis.pdf.
2. This information, which remains incomplete and difficult to verify, is culled from several sources, including a crime report from the New Orleans Times-Picayune (Thevenot 2007), obituaries, and a local blog by writer Mark Folse (2017) that lists the names of homicide victims (*Toulouse Street: Odd Bits of Life in New Orleans*, https://toulousestreet.wordpress.com/2008/01/11/silence-is-violence-remembers/).
3. Louisiana does not require background checks before the sale or transfer of a firearm between unlicensed parties and does not require gun owners to register weapons. The state also does not prohibit the transfer or possession of assault weapons nor restrict magazine capacity. It is legal to openly carry a firearm that is ready to use, although certain places such as schools are off limits, and concealed carry is not allowed without permit.
4. https://www.ncjrs.gov/ondcppubs/publications/enforce/hidta2001/gulf-fs.html.
5. As ethnomusicologist Matt Sakakeeny (2013, 163) notes, even Dinerral Shavers, the beloved musician whose death led to the march on city hall, had a prior arrest that made it into media reports, although it was widely known that he had not been the intended target of the shooting. Shavers's life and death were elevated in part "because his killing coincided with that of Helen Hill, a white filmmaker who was murdered in her home by an intruder. The twin victims—one black, one white; both innocent; and both upstanding citizens and beloved members of sprawling social networks—pained a city suffering from a homicide rate ten times the national average" (169).
6. Richard Pennington was the chief of police in New Orleans from 1994 to 2002. After losing the City of New Orleans's mayoral election to Ray Nagin

in 2002, Pennington resigned and relocated to Georgia, where he became the chief of police for the City of Atlanta.

7. The Order of Saint Ursula (OSU) was founded by Angela Merici, later Saint Angela. Born in Italy in 1474, as a young Christian woman Angela was divinely directed through prayer to found a "company of virgins" focused on the education of girls. The order began in Brescia in 1532 and received the approval of the Holy See in 1544 (Heaney 1993).

8. Our Lady and Ezili Danto have a close and intersected relationship that reflects the synergies that exist between Vodou and Catholicism. Some say they "walk the same path"; others describe their identities as "conflated"; still others consider Ezili Danto to be the "counterpart" to Our Lady. As Karen McCarthy Brown asserts, however, "the question is not whether Ezili Danto is the Virgin Mary. The answer to that is both yes and no. The real question is: 'Which name for her should be used in which circumstance?'" This is the question, she argues, "that reveals the social class issues and the power politics" (K. M. Brown [1991] 2001, 180).

9. Within this history, some scholars and practitioners include Catholicism as a key influence, arguing that the foundations of Voodoo are more closely related to Catholicism than to any of the West African traditions. As one local Vodou priest (oungan), asserted, "the base of New Orleans Voodoo is not really African, it's Catholicism, with the saints given the attributes of the African deities." By this account, the pantheon of deities typically found in Haitian Vodou is largely absent in New Orleans, replaced instead by the Catholic saints, many of whom have been Africanized and appear in accordance with the histories, realities, and needs of local practitioners.

10. Questions of authenticity are significant in an increasingly diverse religious landscape. While Africans and African Americans have historically been the practitioners of Vodou and Voodoo, the religions have an increasingly broad appeal. One local practitioner, for example, described a wide range of beliefs and approaches, from the persistence of underground folk practices to their more aboveground commercial display. Some tension thus exists about who is practicing, how they are practicing, and how the African history and legacy of the tradition is represented. Fandrich (2006, 126) gives some indication of this complexity when she argues that Vodou traditions, "at their core . . . have always remained African despite their amazing capacity to incorporate and assimilate elements from other faith traditions."

11. Drug kingpin Richard Pena cornered much of the city's cocaine market in the mid-1990s. In one of the most widely publicized local corruption cases, former New Orleans police officer David Singleton confessed to being a Pena lieutenant, dealing kilos of cocaine and orchestrating the kidnapping of one of Pena's rivals. The investigation confirmed that as many as twenty-nine New Orleans police officers were involved, protecting a cocaine supply warehouse with over two hundred pounds of the drug (Flaherty 2005). A six-year investigation concluded in 1999 with Pena's

conviction for murder and drug trafficking, the arrest of thirty-five other defendants, the closure of sixteen murder investigations, and the seizure of four million dollars in drug-related assets.

12. Here Martine refers to Legba, the Marasa, Loko, and Ayizan. As she described it, "We do Legba first; then the Marasa, the twins who are the first children of God so they are the first ancestors and the first in; then Loko; and then Ayizan. Loko and Ayizan accompany Legba, and they are the original priest and priestess, and they make sure that you can handle the forces that you're bringing through and that you're not bringing through something that's going to destroy you."

13. As Karen McCarthy Brown (1997, 66–67) explains, the Lwa "were once divided into several *nanchon*, 'nations'—Rada, Petro, Kongo, Nago, Ibo, and so on. In most cases, their names clearly indicate their African origins. This pattern is still used in some rural parts of Haiti. However, in and around Port-au-Prince, Haiti's major urban center, two pantheons, the Rada and the Petro, have emerged as dominant, largely by absorbing the other nations into themselves."

CHAPTER THREE

1. These historical periods correspond roughly to Cornel West and Eddie S. Glaude Jr.'s tracing of African American religious life across five periods of historical and scholarly significance. These are (1) African American religion as the problem of slavery (mid-eighteenth century to 1863); (2) African American religion and the problem(s) of emancipation (1864–1903); (3) African American religion, the city, and the challenges to racism (1903–1954); 4) African American religion and the Black freedom struggle (1954–1969); and (5) the golden age of African American religious studies (1969–present) (West and Glaude 2003, xiii–xiv; see also White 2016, 10).

2. Michael E. Crutcher Jr. details the overlapped development and decline of this neighborhood in *Tremé: Race and Place in a New Orleans Neighborhood* (2010).

3. In 1993 the New Orleans Theater of the Performing Arts was renamed as the Mahalia Jackson Theater for the Performing Arts.

4. Armstrong was born and raised not far from this site; his memoir refers to a difficult childhood spent in a rough "Back o' Town" neighborhood "in the very heart of what is called the Battlefield" (L. Armstrong 1954, 7–8).

5. For example, the Silver Bluff Baptist Church, whose cornerstone dated to 1750, was located on the Savannah River and established by a enslaved man named George Liele. The African Baptist "Bluestone" Church was established in 1758 on the William Byrd plantation in Mecklenberg, Virginia (Lincoln and Mamiya [1990] 2003, 23).

6. As Sobel (1979, 101) maintains, "Blacks actually created a new world view that, despite their status as slaves, established order, values, and the possibility

of personal development, and even fulfillment. In so doing, they became Baptist American at the same time as they made a quasi-African Sacred Cosmos at home in the New World".

7. Matthew 28:19 (King James Version), "Go ye therefore, and teach all nations, baptizing them in the name of the Father, and of the Son, and of the Holy Ghost."

8. Dorrien thus provides a comprehensive and long overdue recovery of the black social gospel in two impressive works: *The New Abolition: W. E. B. Du Bois and the Black Social Gospel* (2015) and *Breaking White Supremacy: Martin Luther King Jr. and the Black Social Gospel* (2018).

9. While I maintain that this trajectory directs us to the work of Black churches such as Liberty Street, it leaves out many key moments and figures. In fact, and as Dorrien (2015, 3) writes, "to confine this work to the figures that joined Du Bois in the Niagara Movement and the NAACP, espoused liberal theology, and led to Mays and King would miss nearly half the story." While I remain aware of this pitfall, I nonetheless take my cues from the clergy and parishioners at Armstrong Park who congregated and prepared to "go ye therefore into the world," and I use this trajectory to think through the resonating histories while tracing also their continued influence.

10. The Uptown growth of Black Protestantism also reinforced a growing social and spatial divide within the Black community, one that "separate[d] the shrinking Creole population from the emancipated population, the educated from the less educated, the Catholic from evangelical Protestant" (Frey 2012, 232).

11. The NBCA, the association of which Liberty Street was a member, has experienced tremendous growth since its founding. Headquartered in Shreveport, Louisiana, the organization has an estimated membership of five million people. At the time of my fieldwork, it was the second largest Baptist organization in the world, behind the Southern Baptist Convention.

12. My focus on the religious activism of Black Protestants in Central City should not overshadow the long fight for equality and civil rights that was rooted in other areas in New Orleans, such as the Tremé. What seems more useful, while beyond the scope of this work, is a social and geographic mapping of civil rights work along an expanding back-of-town corridor following the contours of a growing, though far from inclusive, city.

13. https://kinginstitute.stanford.edu/king-papers/documents/statement-south-and-nation-issued-southern-negro-leaders-conference.

14. See also Aldon Morris's (1984) study of the origins and development of the civil rights movement, which focuses in particular on the local roots of the Black struggle and emphasizes activism at specific community-based organizations and institutions.

15. http://okra.stanford.edu/transcription/document_images/Vol03Scans/451_3-Dec-1956_Facing%20the%20Challenge%20of%20a%20New%20Age.pdf.

16. Smith and Zepp ([1974] 1998) outline three major theological presuppositions for the beloved community that shed further light on its conceptualization and influence. The first is based on a liberal version of the doctrine of creation, which for King meant that "all persons are created in the image of God and are therefore inseparably bound together" (143). The second is "the prophetic vision of justice, peace, freedom, equality, and harmony associated with the Messianic era" (143), a vision that King conceived of in this world, achieved within history rather than in the world to come. The third presupposition is Christian love (agape), which King defined as "the love of God operating in the human heart" (144; see also King [1958] 2010, 93–95)—an unselfish love that leads to genuine relations between people and the building of a truly integrated society.

CHAPTER FOUR

1. These processes also fit with a view of "entextualization," an idea developed by Ato Quayson in an analysis of the city street in Accra, Ghana's capital city. Drawing on the work of anthropologist Karin Barber, Quayson envisions the street as a "lively expressive archive" where discourse emerges in inventive ways via writing and other forms of emplacement. The inscription of THOU SHALT NOT KILL, therefore, might also be understood as contributing to a "rich urban [transcript]" that defines "an arc of enchantment," although such a transcript still competes with dominant inscriptions of disenchantment and destruction (Quayson 2014, 129–30; see also Barber 2007, 72).
2. A survey of Central City residents conducted by the Metropolitan Crime Commission (MCC), revealed that before Hurricane Katrina 45 percent of surveyed residents stated that they felt safe from crime. This percentage fell even lower, to 31 percent, after the storm (MCC 2007, 14–15). Residents cited a range of concerns including widespread drug activity; murders; few opportunities for young people to learn, work or advance; poor infrastructure and services; poor housing conditions; and blight (5).
3. As Lincoln and Mamiya ([1990] 2003, 393) confirm, "church mergers are among the most complicated of human endeavors, and the restructuring of ecclesiastical entities seem to founder more often than they succeed. Human interests vested in positions of power and leadership must be resolved once the doctrinal and ritual preferences have been resolved. Traditions are not readily relinquished, even in the face of the obvious, and emotions sometimes speak with more authority than either reason or practicality."
4. John 12:20–22 (King James Version), "And there were certain Greeks among them that came up to worship at the feast: The same came therefore to Philip, which was of Bethsaida of Galilee, and desired him, saying, Sir, we would see Jesus. Philip cometh and telleth Andrew: and again

Andrew and Philip tell Jesus. And Jesus answered them, saying, The hour is come, that the Son of man should be glorified."

5. Romans 12:19 (King James Version), "Dearly beloved, avenge not your-selves, but rather give place unto wrath: for it is written, Vengeance is mine; I will repay, saith the Lord."

6. In fact, the deaths of children had long fueled religious mobilization against violence in New Orleans. It was the killing of two children in the mid-1990s that had brought clergy and parishioners from several Black churches together in a show and march of unity—a response that, for Pastor Samuel, led directly to the THOU SHALT NOT KILL ministry at Liberty Street.

CHAPTER FIVE

1. The influence here of Black feminist theory, through both scholarly work and social and political activism, cannot be overstated. Duchess Harris (2001, 282) traces the work of three key groups from 1961 to 1980: John F. Kennedy's Presidential Commission on the Status of Women (PCSW), the National Black Feminist Organization (NBFO), and the Combahee River Collective (CRC) with its "more radical and polyvocal focus on gender, race, class, and sexual orientation."

2. My intent is not to suggest a dichotomy between research that focuses on social, civic, and political movement and research that attends to belief, experience, and practice. However, testimonies such as Danielle's suggest the need for an integrated approach, for example, by situating religious belief and practice in relation to the conditions of the city and by simultaneously exploring how the realities of daily life relate to and inform religious engagement.

3. Alice Walker ([1979] 2006, 7) first coined the term *womanist*, which appears in her short story "Coming Apart". Key scholars and activists who subsequently developed its corresponding theological framing include Delores S. Williams ([1987] 1993), Katie G. Cannon (1988, 1995), and the other members of a 1989 roundtable discussion on "Christian Ethics and Theology in Womanist Perspective" (Cheryl J. Sanders, Emilie M. Townes, M. Shawn Copeland, bell hooks, and Cheryl Townsend Gilkes) (Kirk-Duggan 2014, 268).

4. The theological and physical recovery of the Black female body is especially crucial here given the systems of oppression and violence that continue to strip away bodily possession (Carter 2014, 182). Katie Cannon (2013, 352) describes the context as a "US post-industrialist political economy of advanced capitalism [which] perpetuates ruthless, volatile, and cruel dehumanization of poor African American women on a continual basis." Keri Day (2012, 3) reminds us, however, of the essential role the Black Church can continue to play as a "community of transcendence" at the intersection of Black women's religious faith, daily struggle, and activism—"a

black religious site that can offer not only hope and cultural flourishing for poor black women but can also participate in a project of economic justice toward their well-being."

5. For example, Higginbotham (1993, 3) finds that Black Baptist women's efforts at organization and contribution were frequently muted by "male-biased traditions and rules of decorum . . . [which] provide[d] men with full manhood rights, while offering women a separate and unequal status."

6. This inquiry aligns with another, which focuses on the extent to which Black women have become the iconic symbols of sorrow within the conditions of vulnerability, violence, and death that extend across the diaspora (Sharpe 2016, 74), testing and sometimes challenging this characterization through "obvious and not-so-obvious," "mundane . . . and spectacular" interventions (C. A. Smith 2016b, 6). Continuing inquiries, which detail but are not necessarily focused on rituals of death and dying themselves, include Zenzele Isoke's (2013) study of political resistance for Black women in Newark, Keisha-Khan Y. Perry's (2014) ethnography of Black women activists in Brazil, Riché Barnes's (2015) study of middle-class Black women's negotiations of family and career, Marcia Chatelain's (2015) ethnohistorical examination of Black girlhood and the Great Migration in early twentieth century Chicago, and Aimee Meredith Cox's (2015) ethnography of Black girls and citizenship set in a homeless shelter in Detroit. Cox (2015, 7) develops in particular a useful notion of "shapeshifting" to examine how Black girls "[shift] the terms through which educational, training, and social service institutions attempt to shape young Black women into manageable and respectable members of society whose social citizenship is always questionable and never guaranteed." However, by following the ways in which Black girls creatively and strategically "engage with, confront, challenge, invert, unsettle, and expose the material impact of systemic oppression" (7), Cox leads us to the "collective strategies" they inspire "for living fuller, self-defined lives without the threats of extinction that . . . generally incur when you are young and Black" (8).

7. Williams has a background in Africana studies and performance studies, and her work both interrogates the archive of Black maternal grief and traces its mobilization toward social, political, and performative ends. This is a powerful intersection in an inquiry simultaneously concerned with the poetics and other liberating aspects of radical Black mothering. Tracing its threads reveals a range of existing work and influences, for example, by Stephanie L. Batiste, scholar of Black studies and English, whose play/solo-show *Stacks of Obits* (2005) draws on her own family's experience of loss and mourning (following the murder of her first cousin). The performance works through a collected archive of obituaries of young Black people killed by gun violence in Los Angeles and uses these artifacts to "[relay] the entangled experiences of love, loss, and family . . . against very real experiences of death, murder, and violence in a place called Home" (123). More

broadly, Batiste connects performance to witnessing and truth-telling, situating these as "community-making practice" in the context of death mediated by a call for a "loving response" (124).

8. Talking to the dead is overall an act of remembrance, Manigault-Bryant maintains, an engagement with one's forbears through practices of two primary types. The first are "customs traditionally interpreted as religious, which include prayer, seekin' (a process of gaining church membership), shouting or experiencing ecstatic spiritual moments, and sacred music traditions" (Manigault-Bryant 2014, 104–5). The second "includes cultural activities that may not be typically understood as religious: storytelling, sweetgrass basketry, dreaming, and the concept of remembering" (105). These activities are fundamental to the religious and spiritual traditions of Gullah/Geechee women. Talking to the dead is thus not a metaphor, it is "as literal to these women as their belief in God. It is an essential aspect of their very existence as human beings, as African Americans, and as Christian women of faith" (104).

CHAPTER SIX

1. Ephesians 6:12 (King James Version), "For we wrestle not against flesh and blood, but against principalities, against powers, against the rulers of the darkness of this world, against spiritual wickedness in high places." Psalm 138:6 (King James Version), "Though the LORD be high, yet hath he respect unto the lowly: but the proud he knoweth afar off."

2. Numbers 23:19 (King James Version), "God is not a man, that he should lie; neither the son of man, that he should repent: hath he said, and shall he not do it? or hath he spoken, and shall he not make it good?"

3. For a comparative perspective, see Robert Orsi's (2016, 162–200) historical examination of "real presence," particularly the relationships between the living and the dying and the dead found among Catholics in the late twentieth and early twenty-first centuries in the United States.

4. 1 Thessalonians 4:13 (King James Version), "But I would not have you to be ignorant, brethren, concerning them which are asleep, that ye sorrow not, even as others which have no hope."

5. As Taussig (1997, 77) argues, the storyteller gains power by "summoning death to the stage of the living human body so as to render, through repeat performance, the authority of death that lies at the source of the story-form." In making this claim, Taussig draws inspiration from Walter Benjamin's essay "The Storyteller," specifically, the idea that knowledge or wisdom becomes first transmissible at the moment of death (Benjamin [1936] 2002, 6). Thus, the authority of "death-work" that Taussig claims through storytelling comes from "the sudden revelation of a sequence of images of the self set in motion . . . *inside* a dying person as life approached its end" (Taussig 1997, 79, emphasis in original).

6. As Gilkes (2001, 137) also confirms, "Testimony does not resolve black problems but does transform them from the private troubles of distressed individuals into the public issue of a covenant community." Identifying Black women as "the best testifiers in the community," Gilkes further understands testimony as an important antecedent to social movement and change.

CONCLUSION

1. Dr. James Puckette Carter Sr., interview by Edward Dees, 2004, transcript, Amistad Research Center, New Orleans, LA.
2. https://www.facebook.com/permalink.php?story_fbid=1090233291064627&id=168304409924191.

References

Abrams, Andrea C. 2014. *God and Blackness: Race, Gender, and Identity in a Middle Class Afrocentric Church*. New York: New York University Press.

Abrums, Mary Elyeen. 2010. *Moving the Rock: Poverty and Faith in a Black Storefront Church*. Walnut Creek, CA: AltaMira.

Alcoff, Linda. 1991. "The Problem of Speaking for Others." *Cultural Critique*, no. 20, 5–32.

Alexander, Michelle. 2010. *The New Jim Crow: Mass Incarceration in the Age of Colorblindness*. New York: New Press.

Anderson, Elijah. 1990. *Streetwise: Race, Class, and Change in an Urban Community*. Chicago: University of Chicago Press.

———. 1999. *Code of the Street: Decency, Violence, and the Moral Life of the Inner City*. New York: W. W. Norton.

———. 2008. *Against the Wall: Poor, Young, Black, and Male; The City in the 21st Century*. Philadelphia: University of Pennsylvania Press.

Angel-Ajani, Asale. 2004. "Expert Witness: Notes toward Revisiting the Politics of Listening." *Anthropology and Humanism* 29 (2): 133–44.

Arena, John D. 2004. "Repression, Racism, and Resistance: The New Orleans Black Urban Regime and a Challenge to Racist Neoliberalism." In *Race and Ethnicity: across Time, Space, and Discipline*, edited by Rodney D. Coates, 365–69. Leiden: Brill.

———. 2012. *Driven from New Orleans*. Minneapolis: University of Minnesota Press.

Armstrong, Louis. 1954. *Satchmo: My Life in New Orleans*. Boston: Da Capo.

Armstrong, Tonya D. 2010. "African and African-American Traditions in America." In *Religion, Death, and Dying*, edited by Lucy Bregman, 3:83–109. Santa Barbara, CA: ABC-CLIO.

Auyero, Javier, and Kristine Kilanski. 2015. "Introduction." In *Violence at the Urban Margins*, edited by Javier Auyero, Philippe Bourgois, and Nancy Scheper-Hughes, 1–20. Oxford: Oxford University Press.

Bailey, Julius, and David J. Leonard. 2015. "Black Lives Matter: Post-Nihilistic Freedom Dreams." *Journal of Contemporary Rhetoric* 5 (3/4): 67–77.

Barber, Karin. 2007. *The Anthropology of Texts, Persons and Publics: Oral and Written Culture in Africa and Beyond*. Cambridge: Cambridge University Press.

Barnes, Riché J. Daniel. 2015. *Raising the Race: Black Career Women Redefine Marriage, Motherhood, and Community*. New Brunswick, NJ: Rutgers University Press.

Barrett, Ronald K., and Karen S. Heller. 2002. "Death and Dying in the Black Experience." *Journal of Palliative Medicine* 5 (5): 793–99.

Basso, Keith H. 1996. *Wisdom Sits in Places: Landscape and Language among the Western Apache*. Albuquerque: University of New Mexico Press.

Batiste, Stephanie L. 2005. "Stacks of Obits: A Performance Piece." *Women & Performance: A Journal of Feminist Theory* 15 (1): 105–125.

Beckett, Katherine, and Theodore Sasson. 2004. *The Politics of Injustice: Crime and Punishment in America*. Thousand Oaks, CA: Sage.

Bell, Sylvana, and E. V. Banks. 1946. "I Am On the Battlefield." Arranged by Thomas A. Dorsey. Chicago: n.p.

Benjamin, Walter. (1936) 2002. "The Storyteller: Reflections on the Works of Nikolai Leskov." In *Walter Benjamin: Selected Writings*, vol. 3, *1935–1938*, edited by Howard Eiland and Michael W. Jennings, 143–66. Cambridge, MA: Belknap Press of Harvard University Press.

Bennett, James B. 2005. *Religion and the Rise of Jim Crow in New Orleans*. Princeton, NJ: Princeton University Press.

Bergmann, Luke. 2009. *Getting Ghost: Two Young Lives and the Struggle for the Soul of an American City*. Ann Arbor: University of Michigan Press.

Berube, Alan, and Natalie Holmes. 2015. "Concentrated Poverty in New Orleans 10 Years after Katrina." In *The Avenue: Rethinking Metropolitan America*. Metropolitan Opportunity Series. Washington, DC: Brookings Institution. https://www.brookings.edu/blog/the-avenue/2015/08/27/concentrated-poverty-in-new-orleans-10-years-after-katrina/.

Biehl, João G., Byron Good, and Arthur Kleinman. 2007. *Subjectivity: Ethnographic Investigations*. Berkeley: University of California Press.

Biondi, Martha. 2003. *To Stand and Fight: The Struggle for Civil Rights in Postwar New York City*. Cambridge, MA: Harvard University Press.

Bolles, A. Lynn. 2001. "Seeking the Ancestors: Forging a Black Feminist Tradition in Anthropology." In *Black Feminist Anthropology: Theory, Politics, Praxis, and Poetics*, edited by Irma McClaurin, 24–48. New Brunswick, NJ: Rutgers University Press.

Bouie, Jamelle. 2016. "Brothers in White Resentment: What Gave Us Donald Trump Is What Gave Us Dylann Roof." *Slate*, December 15, 2016. http://www.slate.com/articles/news_and_politics/politics/2016/12/what_gave_us_donald_trump_is_what_gave_us_dylann_roof.html.

Bourgois, Philippe I. 1995. *In Search of Respect: Selling Crack in El Barrio*. Cambridge: Cambridge University Press.

Bourgois, Philippe I., and Jeff Schonberg. 2009. *Righteous Dopefiend*. Berkeley: University of California Press.

Boylorn, Robin M. 2013. *Sweetwater: Black Women and Narratives of Resilience*. New York: Peter Lang.

Breunlin, Rachel, and Helen A. Regis. 2006. "Putting the Ninth Ward on the Map: Race, Place, and Transformation in Desire, New Orleans." *American Anthropologist* 108 (4): 744–64.

Brown, Karen McCarthy. (1991) 2001. *Mama Lola: A Vodou Priestess in Brooklyn*. Berkeley: University of California Press.

———. 1997. "Systematic Remembering, Systematic Forgetting: Ogou in Haiti." In *Africa's Ogun: Old World and New*, edited by Sandra T. Barnes, 65–89. Bloomington: Indiana University Press.

Brown, Vincent. 2009. "Social Death and Political Life in the Study of Slavery." *American Historical Review* 114 (5): 1231–49.

Butler, Anthea. 2007. *Women in the Church of God in Christ: Making a Sanctified World*. Chapel Hill: University of North Carolina Press.

Cacho, Lisa Marie. 2012. *Social Death: Racialized Rightlessness and the Criminalization of the Unprotected*. New York: New York University Press.

Campanella, Richard. 2006. *Geographies of New Orleans: Urban Fabrics before the Storm*. Lafayette: Center for Louisiana Studies, University of Louisiana at Lafayette.

———. 2007. "An Ethnic Geography of New Orleans." *Journal of American History* 94 (3): 704.

———. 2008. *Bienville's Dilemma: A Historical Geography of New Orleans*. Lafayette: Center for Louisiana Studies, University of Louisiana at Lafayette.

———. 2014. "A Glorious Mess: A Perceptual History of New Orleans Neighborhoods." *New Orleans Magazine*, June 2014. http://www.myneworleans.com/New-Orleans-Magazine/June-2014/A-Glorious-Mess/.

Campt, Tina. 2012. *Image Matters: Archive, Photography, and the African Diaspora in Europe*. Durham, NC: Duke University Press.

Cannon, Katie G. 1988. *Black Womanist Ethics*. Atlanta: Scholars Press.

———. 1995. *Katie's Canon: Womanism and the Soul of the Black Community*. New York: Continuum.

———. 2013. "Unfinished Business: Black Women, the Black Church, and the Struggle to Thrive in America by Keri Day." Review of *Unfinished Business: Black Women, the Black Church, and the Struggle to Thrive in America*, by Keri Day. *Theology Today* 70 (3): 352–54.

Cannon, Katie G., and Anthony B. Pinn, eds. 2014. *The Oxford Handbook of African American Theology*. Oxford: Oxford University Press.

Carsten, Janet. 2000. "Introduction: Cultures of Relatedness." In *Cultures of Relatedness: New Approaches to the Study of Kinship*, edited by Janet Carsten, 1–36. Cambridge: Cambridge University Press.

———. 2007. *Ghosts of Memory: Essays on Remembrance and Relatedness*. Malden, MA: Blackwell.

Carter, J. Kameron. 2014. "Humanity in African American Theology." In *The Oxford Handbook of African American Theology*, edited by Katie G. Cannon and Anthony B. Pinn, 174–84. Oxford: Oxford University Press.

Casey, Edward S. 1996. "How to Get from Space to Place in a Fairly Short Stretch of Time." In *Senses of Place*, edited by Steven Feld and Keith H. Basso, 13–52. Santa Fe, NM: School of American Research Press.

Casselberry, Judith. 2013. "The Politics of Righteousness: Race and Gender in Apostolic Pentecostalism." *Transforming Anthropology* 21 (1): 72–86.

———. 2017. *The Labor of Faith: Gender and Power in Black Apostolic Pentecostalism*. Durham, NC: Duke University Press.

Chaddha, Anmol, and William Julius Wilson. 2008. "Reconsidering the 'Ghetto.'" *City & Community* 7 (4): 384–88.

Chappell, David L. 2004. *A Stone of Hope: Prophetic Religion and the Death of Jim Crow*. Chapel Hill: University of North Carolina Press.

Chase, John Churchill. (1949) 2007. *Frenchmen, Desire, Good Children: And Other Streets of New Orleans*. Gretna, LA: Pelican.

Chatelain, Marcia. 2015. *South Side Girls: Growing Up in the Great Migration*. Durham, NC: Duke University Press.

Chudacoff, Howard P. 1989. *How Old Are You? Age Consciousness in American Culture*. Princeton, NJ: Princeton University Press.

Clark, Emily. 2000. Review of *Mammon and Manon in Early New Orleans: The First Slave Society in the Deep South, 1718–1819*, by Thomas N. Ingersoll. *William and Mary Quarterly* 57 (4): 855–57.

———. 2007. *Masterless Mistresses: The New Orleans Ursulines and the Development of a New World Society, 1727–1834*. Chapel Hill: University of North Carolina Press.

Coates, Ta-Nehisi. 2017. "My President Was Black: A History of the First African American White House—and of what Came Next." *Atlantic*, January/February 2017. https://www.theatlantic.com/magazine/archive/2017/01/my-president-was-black/508793/.

Collier-Thomas, Bettye. 1997. *Daughters of Thunder: Black Women Preachers and Their Sermons, 1850–1979*. San Francisco: Jossey-Bass.

———. 2010. *Jesus, Jobs, and Justice: African American Women and Religion*. New York: Alfred A. Knopf.

Collins, Patricia Hill. 1994. "Shifting the Center: Race, Class, and Feminist Theorizing about Motherhood." In *Mothering: Ideology, Experience, and Agency*, edited by Evelyn Nakano Glenn, Grace Chang, and Linda Rennie Forcey, 45–65. New York: Routledge.

———. 2000a. *Black Feminist Thought: Knowledge, Consciousness, and the Politics of Empowerment*. New York: Routledge.

———. 2000b. *Gender, Black Feminism, and Black Political Economy*. Thousand Oaks, CA: Sage.

Cone, James H. 1999. *Risks of Faith: The Emergence of a Black Theology of Liberation, 1968–1998*. Boston: Beacon.

Contreras, Randol. 2012. *The Stickup Kids: Race, Drugs, Violence, and the American Dream*. Berkeley: University of California Press.

Copeland, M. Shawn. 2013. "Blackness Past, Blackness Future—and Theology." *South Atlantic Quarterly* 112 (4): 625–40.

———. 2010. *Enfleshing Freedom: Body, Race, and Being*. Minneapolis, MN: Fortress.

Cox, Aimee Meredith. 2015. *Shapeshifters: Black Girls and the Choreography of Citizenship*. Durham, NC: Duke University Press.

Crumbley, Deidre Helen. 2012. *Saved and Sanctified: The Rise of a Storefront Church in Great Migration Philadelphia*. Gainesville: University Press of Florida.

Crutcher, Michael E., Jr. 2010. *Tremé: Race and Place in a New Orleans Neighborhood; Geographies of Justice and Social Transformation*. Athens: University of Georgia Press.

Currie, Elliott. 1998. *Crime and Punishment in America*. New York: Metropolitan Books.

Daniel, E. Valentine. 1996. *Charred Lullabies: Chapters in an Anthropography of Violence*. Princeton, NJ: Princeton University Press.

Das, Veena, and Clara Han. 2015. *Living and Dying in the Contemporary World: A Compendium*. Berkeley: University of California Press.

David, Bruno, and Meredith Wilson, eds. 2002. *Inscribed Landscapes: Marking and Making Place*. Honolulu: University of Hawai'i Press.

Davis, Angela, and Fania Davis. 2016. "The Radical Work of Healing: Fania and Angela Davis on a New Kind of Civil Rights Activism." Interview by Sarah van Gelder. *Yes!*, February 18, 2016. http://www.yesmagazine.org/issues/life -after-oil/the-radical-work-of-healing-fania-and-angela-davis-on-a-new-kind -of-civil-rights-activism-20160218.

Davis, Dana-Ain. 2006. *Battered Black Women and Welfare Reform: Between a Rock and a Hard Place*. Albany: State University of New York Press.

Dawdy, Shannon Lee. 2008. *Building the Devil's Empire: French Colonial New Orleans*. Chicago: University of Chicago Press.

Day, Keri. 2012. *Unfinished Business: Black Women, the Black Church, and the Struggle to Thrive in America*. Maryknoll, NY: Orbis Books.

Desjarlais, Robert R. 2015. "A Good Death, Recorded." In *Living and Dying in the Contemporary World: A Compendium*, edited by Veena Das and Clara Han, 648–61. Berkeley: University of California Press.

———. 2016. *Subject to Death: Life and Loss in a Buddhist World*. Chicago: University of Chicago Press.

Devalcourt, Joel A. 2011. "Streets of Justice? Civil Rights Commemorative Boulevards and the Struggle for Revitalization in African American Communities: A Case Study of Central City, New Orleans." Master's thesis, University of New Orleans.

DeVega, Chauncey. 2017. "Trump's Election Has Created 'Safe Spaces' for Racists: Southern Poverty Law Center's Heidi Beirich on the Wave of Hate Crimes."

Salon, March 8, 2017. https://www.salon.com/2017/03/08/trumps-election -has-created-safe-spaces-for-racists-southern-poverty-law-centers-heidi-beirich -on-the-wave-of-hate-crimes/.

DeVore, Donald E. 2015. *Defying Jim Crow: African American Community Development and the Struggle for Racial Equality in New Orleans, 1900–1960.* Baton Rouge: Louisiana State University Press.

Dickerson, Dennis C. 2005. "African American Religious Intellectuals and the Theological Foundations of the Civil Rights Movement, 1930–55." *American Society of Church History* 74 (2): 217–35.

Din, Gilbert C. 1999. *Spaniards, Planters, and Slaves: The Spanish Regulation of Slavery in Louisiana, 1763–1803.* College Station: Texas A&M University Press.

Dorrien, Gary. 2015. *The New Abolition: W. E. B. Du Bois and the Black Social Gospel.* New Haven, CT: Yale University Press.

———. 2017. "King and His Mentors." *Commonweal Magazine* 144 (16): 17–21.

———. 2018. *Breaking White Supremacy: Martin Luther King Jr. and the Black Social Gospel.* New Haven, CT: Yale University Press.

Dotson, Kristie. 2013. "Radical Love: Black Philosophy as Deliberate Acts of Inheritance." *Black Scholar* 43 (4): 38–45.

Drake, St. Clair, and Horace R. Cayton. 1945. *Black Metropolis: A Study of Negro Life in a Northern City.* Chicago: University of Chicago Press.

Du Bois, W. E. B. (1901) 1969. *The Black North in 1901: A Social Study.* New York: Arno Press.

Duneier, Mitchell. 2016. *Ghetto: The Invention of a Place, the History of an Idea.* New York: Farrar, Straus and Giroux.

Fabian, Johannes. 1972. "How Others Die: Reflections on the Anthropology of Death." *Social Research* 39 (3): 543–67.

———. 1979. "The Anthropology of Religious Movements: From Explanation to Interpretation." *Social Research* 46 (1): 4–35.

Fairclough, Adam. (1995) 2008. *Race and Democracy: The Civil Rights Struggle in Louisiana, 1915–1972.* Athens: University of Georgia Press.

Fandrich, Ina J. 2006. "Vodou in the United States: The Case of New Orleans." In *African Diaspora Traditions and Other Americans Innovations*, edited by Eugene V. Gallagher and W. Michael Ashcraft, 125–48. Vol. 5 of *Introduction to New and Alternative Religions in America.* Santa Barbara, CA: Greenwood.

———. 2007. "Yoruba Influences on Haitian Vodou and New Orleans Voodoo." *Journal of Black Studies* 37: 775–91.

Fitts, Leroy. 1985. *A History of Black Baptists.* Nashville: Broadman.

Flaherty, Jordan. 2005. "Crime and Corruption in New Orleans." *AlterNet*, October 16. https://www.alternet.org/story/26871/crime_and_corruption _in_new_orleans.

Fleegler, Eric W., Lois K. Lee, Michael C. Monuteaux, David Hemenway, and Rebekah Mannix. 2013. "Firearm Legislation and Firearm-Related Fatalities in the United States." *JAMA Internal Medicine* 173 (9): 732–40.

Folse, Mark. 2017. "Silence Is Violence." *Toulouse Street: Odd Bits of Life in New Orleans*, last modified January 11. https://toulousestreet.wordpress.com/?s=silence+is+violence.

Franklin, Sarah, and Susan McKinnon. 2001. "Introduction: Relative Values: Reconfiguring Kinship Studies." In *Relative Values: Reconfiguring Kinship Studies*, edited by Sarah Franklin and Susan McKinnon, 1–28. Durham, NC: Duke University Press.

Fraser, Gertrude Jacinta. 1998. *African American Midwifery in the South*. Cambridge, MA: Harvard University Press.

Frazer, Sir James George. (1890) 1940. *The Golden Bough: A Study in Magic and Religion*. London: Macmillan.

Frazier, David. 2003. "I Need You to Survive." Macon, GA: God's Music Inc.; L'il Dave's Music Inc.

Frederick, Marla Faye. 2003. *Between Sundays: Black Women and Everyday Struggles of Faith*. Berkeley: University of California Press.

Freud, Sigmund. (1917) 1953. "Mourning and Melancholia." In *Sigmund Freud Collected Papers*, translated by Joan Riviere, edited by Sigmund Freud, 4:152–70. London: Hogarth Press.

Frey, Sylvia. 2012. "Acculturation and Gendered Conversion: Afro-American Catholic Women in New Orleans, 1726–1884." In *Beyond Conversion and Syncretism: Indigenous Encounters with Missionary Christianity, 1800–2000*, edited by David Lindenfeld and Miles Richardson, 213–42. New York: Berghahn Books.

Fussell, Elizabeth. 2007. "Constructing New Orleans, Constructing Race: A Population History of New Orleans." In "Through the Eye of Katrina: The Past as Prologue?," special issue, *Journal of American History* 94, no. 3 (December): 846–55.

Garbin, David. 2012. "Introduction: Believing in the City." In *Believing in the City: Urban Cultures, Religion and (Im)Materiality*. Special issue, *Culture and Religion* 13 (4): 401–4.

Garza, Alicia. 2014. "A Herstory of the #BlackLivesMatter Movement." *Feminist Wire*, October 7, 2014. http://www.thefeministwire.com/2014/10/blacklivesmatter-2/.

Gilkes, Cheryl. 2001. *"If It Wasn't for the Women . . .": Black Women's Experience and Womanist Culture in Church and Community*. Maryknoll, NY: Orbis Books.

Gill, Hannah. 2004. "Finding a Middle Ground between Extremes: Notes on Researching Transnational Crime and Violence." *Anthropology Matters* 6 (2): 2–9.

Gilroy, Paul. 1993. *The Black Atlantic: Modernity and Double Consciousness*. Cambridge, MA: Harvard University Press.

Giroux, Henry A. 2006. *Stormy Weather: Katrina and the Politics of Disposability*. Boulder, CO: Paradigm.

———. 2017. "White Nationalism, Armed Culture and State Violence in the Age of Donald Trump." *Philosophy and Social Criticism* 43 (9): 887–910.

Glazier, Stephen D., ed. 2001. *The Encyclopedia of African and African-American Religions*. New York: Routledge.

Goffman, Alice. 2014. *On the Run: Fugitive Life in an American City.* Chicago: University of Chicago Press.

Goldberg, Jeffrey. 2015. "A Matter of Black Lives." *Atlantic,* September 2015. https://www.theatlantic.com/magazine/archive/2015/09/a-matter-of-black-lives/399386/.

Gregory, Steven. 1998. *Black Corona: Race and the Politics of Place in an Urban Community.* Princeton, NJ: Princeton University Press.

Griffiths, J. Gwyn. 1966. "Hecataeus and Herodotus on 'A Gift of the River.'" *Journal of Near Eastern Studies* 25 (1): 57–61.

Grogger, Jeff, and Michael Willis. 2000. "The Emergence of Crack Cocaine and the Rise in Urban Crime Rates." *Review of Economics and Statistics* 82 (4): 519–29.

Gunewardena, Nandini, and Mark Schuller, eds. 2008. *Capitalizing on Catastrophe: Neoliberal Strategies in Disaster Reconstruction.* Lanham, MD: AltaMira.

Hall, Gwendolyn Midlo. 1992. *Africans in Colonial Louisiana: The Development of Afro-Creole Culture in the Eighteenth Century.* Baton Rouge: Louisiana State University Press.

Hallam, Elizabeth, and Tim Ingold. 2007. *Creativity and Cultural Improvisation.* Oxford: Berg.

Hanger, Kimberly S. 1997. *Bounded Lives, Bounded Places: Free Black Society in Colonial New Orleans, 1769–1803.* Durham, NC: Duke University Press.

Hannerz, Ulf. 1969. *Soulside: Inquiries into Ghetto Culture and Community.* Chicago: University of Chicago Press.

Harding, Rosemarie Freeney, and Rachel Elizabeth Harding. 2015. *Remnants: A Memoir of Spirit, Activism, and Mothering.* Durham, NC: Duke University Press.

Harding, Vincent. [1967] 2010. Introduction to *Where Do We Go from Here: Chaos or Community?,* edited by Martin Luther King Jr., xi–xxi. Boston: Beacon Press.

Harjo, Joy. (1983) 2008. *She Had Some Horses.* New York: W. W. Norton.

Harkin, Michael E., ed. 2004. *Reassessing Revitalization Movements: Perspectives from North America and the Pacific Islands.* Lincoln: University of Nebraska Press.

Harris, Duchess. 2001. "From the Kennedy Commission to the Combahee Collective: Black Feminist Organizing, 1960–1980." In *Sisters in the Struggle: African-American Women in the Civil Rights–Black Power Movement,* edited by Bettye Collier-Thomas and V. P. Franklin, 280–305. New York: New York University Press.

Harris, Fredrick C. 1999. *Something Within: Religion in African-American Political Activism.* Oxford: Oxford University Press.

Harrison, Faye Venetia, ed. 1997. *Decolonizing Anthropology: Moving Further Toward an Anthropology for Liberation.* Arlington, VA: Association of Black Anthropologists, American Anthropological Association.

Hartman, Saidiya. 2007. *Lose Your Mother: A Journey along the Atlantic Slave Route.* New York: Farrar, Straus and Giroux.

Haynes, Bruce, and Ray Hutchison. 2008. "The Ghetto: Origins, History, Discourse." *City and Community* 7 (4): 347–52.

Haynes, George Edmund. 1913. "Conditions among Negroes in the Cities." *Annals of the American Academy of Political and Social Science* 49 (1): 105–19.

Heaney, Jane Frances. 1993. *A Century of Pioneering: A History of the Ursuline Nuns in New Orleans, 1727–1827.* New Orleans: Ursuline Sisters of New Orleans, Louisiana.

Hearn, Lafcadio. (1907) 2007. *Letters from the Raven: Being the Correspondence of Lafcadio Hearn with Henry Watkin.* Rockville, MD: Wildside Press.

Hennesey, James J. 1981. *American Catholics: A History of the Roman Catholic Community in the United States.* Oxford: Oxford University Press.

Hertz, Robert. (1907) 1960. *Death and the Right Hand.* New York: Routledge.

Hicks, William. (1914) 1998. *History of Louisiana Negro Baptists and Early American Beginnings from 1804 to 1914,* edited by Sue L. Eakin. Lafayette: Center for Louisiana Studies, University of Southwestern Louisiana.

Higginbotham, Evelyn Brooks. 1993. *Righteous Discontent: The Women's Movement in the Black Baptist Church, 1880–1920.* Cambridge, MA: Harvard University Press.

Holland, Sharon Patricia. 2000. *Raising the Dead: Readings of Death and (Black) Subjectivity.* Durham, NC: Duke University Press.

Hollandsworth, James G. 2001. *An Absolute Massacre: The New Orleans Race Riot of July 30, 1866.* Baton Rouge: Louisiana State University Press.

Holloway, Karla F. C. 2002. *Passed On: African American Mourning Stories; A Memorial.* Durham NC: Duke University Press.

hooks, bell. 1994. *Outlaw Culture: Resisting Representations.* New York: Routledge.

———. 2004. *The Will to Change: Men, Masculinity, and Love.* New York: Simon and Schuster.

Howarth, Glennys. 2000. "Dismantling the Boundaries between Life and Death." *Mortality* 5 (2): 127–38.

Howell, Nancy. 1990. *Surviving Fieldwork: A Report of the Advisory Panel on Health and Safety in Fieldwork.* Washington, DC: American Anthropological Association.

Hurston, Zora Neale. 1937. *Their Eyes Were Watching God.* Philadelphia: J. B. Lippincott.

Ingersoll, Thomas N. 1999. *Mammon and Manon in Early New Orleans: The First Slave Society in the Deep South, 1718–1819.* Knoxville: University of Tennessee Press.

Ingold, Tim. (2009) 2011. "Against Space: Place, Movement, Knowledge." In *Being Alive: Essays on Movement, Knowledge, and Description,* edited by Tim Ingold, 144–55. New York: Routledge.

Isoke, Zenzele. 2013. *Urban Black Women and the Politics of Resistance.* New York: Palgrave Macmillan.

Jackson, John L. 2001. *Harlemworld: Doing Race and Class in Contemporary Black America.* Chicago: University of Chicago Press.

Jacobs, Claude F., and Andrew J. Kaslow. 1991. *The Spiritual Churches of New Orleans: Origins, Beliefs, and Rituals of an African-American Religion.* Knoxville: University of Tennessee Press.

Jargowsky, Paul, and Mary Jo Bane. 1991. "Ghetto Poverty in the United States, 1970–1980." In *The Urban Underclass*, edited by Christopher Jencks and Paul E. Peterson, 253–73. Washington, DC: Brookings Institution Press.

Johnson, Cedric. 2011. *The Neoliberal Deluge: Hurricane Katrina, Late Capitalism, and the Remaking of New Orleans*, edited by Cedric Johnson. Minneapolis: University of Minnesota Press.

Kelman, Ari. 2007. "Boundary Issues: Clarifying New Orleans's Murky Edges." *Journal of American History* 94 (3): 695–703.

Kennedy, Randall. 2004/2005. "Finding a Proper Name to Call Black Americans." *Journal of Blacks in Higher Education*, no. 46 (Winter): 72–83.

Kilanski, Kristine, and Javier Auyero. 2015. "Introduction." In *Violence at the Urban Margins*, edited by Javier Auyero, Philippe I. Bourgois, and Nancy Scheper-Hughes, 1–20. Oxford: Oxford University Press.

King, Martin Luther, Jr. (1956). "Facing the Challenge of a New Age." Stanford University. The Martin Luther King, Jr. Papers Project. http://okra.stanford.edu/transcription/document_images/Vol03Scans/451_3-Dec-1956_Facing%20the%20Challenge%20of%20a%20New%20Age.pdf.

———. (1958) 2010. *Stride toward Freedom: The Montgomery Story*. Boston: Beacon Press.

———. (1967) 2010. *Where Do We Go from Here: Chaos or Community?* Boston: Beacon Press.

Kirk-Duggan, Cheryl A. 2014. "Womanist Theology as a Corrective to African American Theology." In *Oxford Handbook of African American Theology*, edited by Katie G. Cannon, 267–79. Oxford: Oxford University Press.

Klass, Dennis. 1997. "The Deceased Child in the Psychic and Social Worlds of Bereaved Parents during the Resolution of Grief." *Death Studies* 21 (2): 147–76.

Klass, Dennis, Phyllis R. Silverman, and Steven Nickman, eds. 1996. *Continuing Bonds: New Understandings of Grief*. Philadelphia: Taylor and Francis.

Klein, Naomi. 2007. *The Shock Doctrine: The Rise of Disaster Capitalism*. New York: Picador.

Laborde, Peggy Scott, and John Magill. 2006. *Canal Street: New Orleans' Great Wide Way*. Gretna: Pelican.

Landrieu, Mitch. 2012. "2012 State of the City Address." May 22, 2012. https://www.nola.gov/nola/media/Mayor-s-Office/Files/2012%20SOTC/2012-State-of-the-City-Address-Mayor-Mitch-Landrieu.pdf.

———. 2017. "Truth: Remarks on the Removal of Confederate Monuments in New Orleans." May 19, 2017. https://assets.documentcloud.org/documents/3730572/Truth-Remarks-on-the-Removal-of-Confederate.pdf.

Levin, Jeffrey S. 1984. "The Role of the Black Church in Community Medicine." *Journal of the National Medical Association* 76 (5): 477–83.

Lewin, Ellen. 2018. *Filled with the Spirit: Sexuality, Gender, and Radical Inclusivity in a Black Pentecostal Church Coalition*. Chicago: University of Chicago Press.

Liebow, Elliot. 1967. *Tally's Corner: A Study of Negro Streetcorner Men*. New York: Little, Brown.

Lincoln, C. Eric, and Lawrence H. Mamiya. (1990) 2003. *The Black Church in the African American Experience*. Durham, NC: Duke University Press.

Lipsitz, George. 2011. *How Racism Takes Place*. Philadelphia: Temple University Press.

Low, Setha M. 1996. "The Anthropology of Cities: Imagining and Theorizing the City." *Annual Review of Anthropology* 25 (1): 383–409.

Manigault-Bryant, LeRhonda S. 2014. *Talking to the Dead: Religion, Music, and Lived Memory among Gullah/Geechee Women*. Durham, NC: Duke University Press.

Marcus, George E. 2006. "Where Have All the Tales of Fieldwork Gone?" *Ethnos: Journal of Anthropology* 71 (1): 113–22.

Martin, Civilla D., and Charles H. Gabriel, "His Eye Is On the Sparrow." In *Revival Hymns: A Collection of New and Standard Hymns for Gospel and Social Meetings, Sunday Schools and Young People's Societies*, edited by Daniel B. Tower and Chas M. Alexander, 108. Chicago: Bible Institute Colportage Association, 1905.

Mattingly, Cheryl. 2014. *Moral Laboratories: Family Perils and the Struggle for a Good Life*. Berkeley: University of California Press.

McClaurin, Irma. 2001. *Black Feminist Anthropology: Theory, Politics, Praxis, and Poetics*. New Brunswick, NJ: Rutgers University Press.

McKittrick, Katherine, and Clyde Woods. 2007. *Black Geographies and the Politics of Place*. Toronto: Between the Lines Books.

McLoughlin, William G. 1978. *Revivals, Awakenings, and Reform: An Essay on Religion and Social Change in America, 1607–1977*. Chicago: University of Chicago Press.

Medley, Keith Weldon. 2001. "Dryades Street/Oretha Castle Haley Boulevard: Remembrance and Reclamation." *New Orleans Tribune*, April 2001.

———. 2014. *Black Life in Old New Orleans*. Gretna: Pelican.

Merry, Sally Engle. 1981. *Urban Danger: Life in a Neighborhood of Strangers*. Philadelphia: Temple University Press.

Metropolitan Crime Commission (MCC). 2007. *Crime and Safety in Central City: A Community's Perspective Summer/Fall 2006*. New Orleans: Metropolitan Crime Commission. http://metrocrime.org/wp-content/uploads/2013/05/Central -City-Safety-Assessment-Jan-2007-full-report.pdf.

Morris, Aldon D. 1984. *The Origins of the Civil Rights Movement: Black Communities Organizing for Change*. New York: The Free Press.

Mosher, Anne E., Barry D. Keim, and Susan A. Franques. 1995. "Downtown Dynamics." *Geographical Review* 85 (4): 497.

Muhammad, Khalil Gibran. 2010. *The Condemnation of Blackness: Race, Crime, and the Making of Modern Urban America*. Cambridge, MA: Harvard University Press.

Mullings, Leith. 1997. *On Our Own Terms: Race, Class, and Gender in the Lives of African American Women*. New York: Routledge.

Mullings, Leith, and Alaka Wali. 2001. *Stress and Resilience: The Social Context of Reproduction in Central Harlem*. New York: Kluwer Academic/Plenum.

Ochs, Elinor, and Lisa Capps. 1996. "Narrating the Self." *Annual Review of Anthropology* 25 (1): 19–43.

Osbey, Brenda Marie. 1996. "One More Last Chance: Ritual and the Jazz Funeral." *Georgia Review* 50 (1): 97–107.

———. 2015. *All Souls: Essential Poems*. Baton Rouge: Louisiana State University Press.

Orsi, Robert A. 2016. *History and Presence*. Cambridge, MA: Belknap Press of Harvard University Press.

Palgi, Phyllis, and Henry Abramovitch. 1984. "Death: A Cross-Cultural Perspective." *Annual Review of Anthropology* 13 (1): 385–417.

Parnell, Philip, and Stephanie Kane. 2003. *Crime's Power: Anthropologists and the Ethnography of Crime*. New York: Palgrave Macmillan.

Parsons, Chelsea, and Eugenio Vargas Weigend. 2016. *America under Fire: An Analysis of Gun Violence in the United States and the Link to Weak Gun Laws*. Washington, DC: Center for American Progress.

Patterson, Orlando. 1982. *Slavery and Social Death: A Comparative Study*. Cambridge, MA: Harvard University Press.

Pattillo, Mary. 2003. "Negotiating Blackness, for Richer or for Poorer." *Ethnography* 4 (1): 61–93.

Perry, Hosea L. 1993. "Mourning and Funeral Customs of African Americans." In *Ethnic Variations in Dying, Death, and Grief: Diversity in Universality*, edited by Donald P. Irish, Kathleen F. Lundquist, and Vivian J. Nelsen, 51–66. Philadelphia: Taylor and Francis.

Perry, Keisha-Khan Y. 2014. *Black Women against the Land Grab: The Fight for Racial Justice in Brazil*. Minneapolis: University of Minnesota Press.

Pius, N. H. 1911. *An Outline of Baptist History: A Splendid Reference Work for Busy Workers; A Record of the Struggles and Triumphs of Baptist Pioneers and Builders*. Nashville, TN: National Baptist Publishing Board.

Powell, Lawrence N. 2012. *The Accidental City: Improvising New Orleans*. Cambridge, MA: Harvard University Press.

Quayson, Ato. 2014. *Oxford Street, Accra: City Life and the Itineraries of Transnationalism*. Durham, NC: Duke University Press.

Quillen, Kimberly. 2009. "New Orleans Area Lost 3,000 Jobs between April 2008 and April 2009." *Times-Picayune*, May 26, 2009. http://blog.nola.com/tpmoney/2009/05/new_orleans_area_lost_3000_job.html.

Ralph, Laurence. 2014. *Renegade Dreams: Living through Injury in Gangland Chicago*. Chicago: University of Chicago Press.

———. 2015. "The Limitations of a 'Dirty' World." *Du Bois Review* 12 (2): 441–51.

Ralph, Michael, Aisha M. Beliso-De Jesús, Laurence Ralph, and Maggie Gates. 2016. "Editor's Note." *Transforming Anthropology* 24 (1): 3–4.

Reagon, Bernice Johnson. 1983. "Coalition Politics: Turning the Century." In *Home Girls: A Black Feminist Anthology*, edited by Barbara Smith, 343–56. New York: Kitchen Table—Women of Color Press.

Regis, Helen A. 2001. "Blackness and the Politics of Memory in the New Orleans Second Line." *American Ethnologist* 28 (4): 752–77.

Reinders, Robert C. (1964) 1989. *End of an Era: New Orleans, 1850–1860*. Gretna: Pelican.

Reyes, Victoria. 2018. "Three Models of Transparency in Ethnographic Research: Naming Places, Naming People, and Sharing Data. *Ethnography* 19 (2): 204–26.

Rios, Victor M. 2011. *Punished: Policing the Lives of Black and Latino Boys*. New York: New York University Press.

———. 2015. "Decolonizing the White Space in Urban Ethnography." *City & Community* 14 (3): 258–61.

Robben, Antonius C. G. M. 2004. "Death and Anthropology: An Introduction." In *Death, Mourning, and Burial: A Cross-Cultural Reader*, edited by Antonius C. G. M Robben, 1–16. Malden, MA: Blackwell.

Rogers, Kim Lacy. 1993. *Righteous Lives: Narratives of the New Orleans Civil Rights Movement*. New York: New York University Press.

Rosaldo, Renato. (1989) 2001. *Culture and Truth: The Remaking of Social Analysis*. Boston: Beacon Press.

Rosenblatt, Paul C., and Beverly R. Wallace. 2005. *African American Grief*. New York: Routledge.

Sakakeeny, Matt. 2013. *Roll with It: Brass Bands in the Streets of New Orleans*. Durham, NC: Duke University Press.

Scheper-Hughes, Nancy. 1993. *Death without Weeping: The Violence of Everyday Life in Brazil*. Berkeley: University of California Press.

Scheper-Hughes, Nancy, and Philippe I. Bourgois. 2004. *Violence in War and Peace: An Anthology*. Malden, MA: Blackwell.

Scott, Rebecca J. 2005. *Degrees of Freedom: Louisiana and Cuba after Slavery*. Cambridge, MA: Belknap Press of Harvard University Press.

Sexton, Rocky L., Robert G. Carlson, Harvey A. Siegal, Carl G. Leukefeld, and Brenda M. Booth. 2006. "The Role of African-American Clergy in Providing Informal Services to Drug Users in the Rural South: Preliminary Ethnographic Findings." *Journal of Ethnicity in Substance Abuse* 5 (1): 1–21.

Sharpe, Christina. 2016. *In the Wake: On Blackness and Being*. Durham, NC: Duke University Press.

Smith, Christen A. 2015. "Blackness, Citizenship, and the Transnational Vertigo of Violence in the Americas." *American Anthropologist* 117 (2): 384–87.

———. 2016a. "Facing the Dragon: Black Mothering, Sequelae, and Gendered Necropolitics in the Americas." *Transforming Anthropology* 24 (1): 31–48.

———. 2016b. "Sorrow as Artifact: Radical Black Mothering in Times of Terror—A Prologue." *Transforming Anthropology* 24 (1): 5–7.

Smith, Drew R. 2014. "The Church in African American Theology." In *The Oxford Handbook of African American Theology*, edited by Katie G. Cannon and Anthony B. Pinn, 228–41. Oxford: Oxford University Press.

Smith, Kenneth L., and Ira G. Zepp Jr. (1974) 1998. *Search for the Beloved Community: The Thinking of Martin Luther King, Jr.* Valley Forge, PA: Judson Press.

Sobel, Mechal. 1979. *Trabelin' On: The Slave Journey to an Afro-Baptist Faith*. Westport, CT: Greenwood Press.

Spain, Daphne. 1979. "Race Relations and Residential Segregation in New Orleans: Two Centuries of Paradox." *Annals of the American Academy of Political and Social Science* 441 (1): 82–96.

Stack, Carol B. 1974. *All Our Kin: Strategies for Survival in A Black Community*. New York: Harper and Row.

Stark, Rodney. 1996. "Why Religious Movements Succeed or Fail: A Revised General Model." *Journal of Contemporary Religion* 11 (2): 133–46.

Sublette, Ned. 2008. *The World That Made New Orleans: From Spanish Silver to Congo Square*. Chicago: Lawrence Hill Books.

Susser, Ida. 1982. *Norman Street: Poverty and Politics in an Urban Neighborhood*. Oxford: Oxford University Press.

Tannenbaum, Frank. 1946. *Slave and Citizen: The Negro in the Americas*. New York: Alfred A. Knopf.

Tapia, Ruby C. 2011. *American Pietàs: Visions of Race, Death, and the Maternal*. Critical American Studies Series. Minneapolis: University of Minnesota Press.

Taussig, Michael T. 1984. "Culture of Terror—Space of Death: Roger Casement's Putumayo Report and the Explanation of Torture." *Comparative Studies in Society and History* 26 (3): 467–97.

———. 1987. *Shamanism, Colonialism, and the Wild Man: A Study in Terror and Healing*. Chicago: University of Chicago Press.

———. 1997. *The Magic of the State*. New York: Routledge.

Taylor, Robert Joseph, and Linda M. Chatters. 1988. "Church Members as a Source of Informal Social Support." *Review of Religious Research* 30: 193–202.

Tempalski, Barbara, and Hilary McQuie. 2009. "Drugscapes and the Role of Place and Space in Injection Drug Use-Related HIV Risk Environments." *International Journal of Drug Policy* 20 (1): 4–13.

Thevenot, Brian. 2007. "Killings Bring the City to Its Knees." *Times-Picayune*, January 26, 2007.

Thurman, Howard. 1961. *Mysticism and the Experience of Love*. Wallingford, PA: Pendle Hill.

Trethewey, Natasha D. 2010. *Beyond Katrina: A Meditation on the Mississippi Gulf Coast*. Athens: University of Georgia Press.

Usner, Daniel H. 1992. *Indians, Settlers, and Slaves in a Frontier Exchange Economy: The Lower Mississippi Valley before 1783*. Chapel Hill: Published for the Institute of Early American History and Culture, Williamsburg, Virginia, by the University of North Carolina Press.

Van Gennep, Arnold. (1909) 1960. *The Rites of Passage*. Translated by Monika B. Vizedom and Gabrielle L. Caffee. Chicago: University of Chicago Press.

Venkatesh, Sudhir Alladi. 2008. *Gang Leader for a Day: A Rogue Sociologist Takes to the Streets*. London: Penguin.

Vigil, James Diego. 1988. *Barrio Gangs: Street Life and Identity in Southern California*. Austin: University of Texas Press.

Wacquant, Loïc J. D. 1997. "Three Pernicious Premises in the Study of the American Ghetto." *International Journal of Urban and Regional Research* 21 (2): 341–53.

———. 2014. "Marginality, Ethnicity and Penality in the Neo-Liberal City: An Analytic Cartography." *Ethnic and Racial Studies* 37 (10): 1687–1711.

Walker, Alice. (1979) 2006. "Coming Apart." In *The Womanist Reader*, edited by Layli Phillips, 3–11. New York: Routledge.

Walker, Corey D. B. 2013. "Love, Blackness, Imagination: Howard Thurman's Vision of *Communitas.*" *South Atlantic Quarterly* 112 (4): 641–55.

Wallace, Anthony F. C., and Sheila C. Steen. 1970. *The Death and Rebirth of the Seneca*. New York: Knopf.

Walsh, Patrick. 2010. "Changes in the Illegal Drug Market in New Orleans after Hurricane Katrina." In *Crime and Criminal Justice in Disaster*, edited by Dee Wood Harper and Kelly Frailing, 161–85. Durham, NC: Carolina Academic Press.

Warner, Coleman. 2001. "Freret's Century: Growth, Identity, and Loss in a New Orleans Neighborhood." *Louisiana History: The Journal of the Louisiana Historical Association* 42 (3): 323–58.

Waterston, Alisse. 1999. *Love, Sorrow, and Rage: Destitute Women in a Manhattan Residence*. Philadelphia: Temple University Press.

Weisenfeld, Judith. 1997. *African American Women and Christian Activism: New York's Black YWCA, 1905–1945*. Cambridge, MA: Harvard University Press.

Wellford, Charles, Brenda J. Bond, and Sean Goodison. 2011. "Crime in New Orleans: Analyzing Crime Trends and New Orleans' Responses to Crime." March 15, 2011. https://www.nola.gov/getattachment/NOPD/Reform-and-Publications/BJA-Crime-in-New-Orleans-Report-March-2011.pdf/.

West, Cornel. (1993) 2017. *Race Matters*. Boston: Beacon Press.

West, Cornel, and Eddie S. Glaude. 2003. *African American Religious Thought: An Anthology*. Louisville, KY: Westminster John Knox Press.

White, Carol Wayne. 2016. *Black Lives and Sacred Humanity: Toward an African American Religious Naturalism*. Oxford: Oxford University Press.

Williams, Delores S. (1987) 1993. "Womanist Theology: Black Women's Voices." In *Black Theology: A Documentary History*, vol. 2, *1980–1992*, edited by James H. Cone and Gayraud S. Wilmore, 265–72. New York: Orbis Books.

Williams, Rhaisa Kameela. 2016. "Toward a Theorization of Black Maternal Grief as Analytic." *Transforming Anthropology* 24 (1): 17–30.

Wilson, William J. 1987. *The Truly Disadvantaged: The Underclass, the Ghetto and Public Policy*. Chicago: Chicago University Press.

Wimberly, Anne Streaty. 1994. *Soul Stories: African American Christian Education*. Nashville, TN: Abingdon Press.

Witte, John. 2006. "Facts and Fictions about the History of Separation of Church and State." *Journal of Church and State* 48 (1): 15–45.

Woods, Clyde Adrian. 2005. "Do You Know What It Means to Miss New Orleans? Katrina, Trap Economics, and the Rebirth of the Blues." *American Quarterly* 57 (4): 1005–18.

Woodward, C. Vann. 1955. *The Strange Career of Jim Crow*. New York: Oxford University Press.

Index

Abramovitch, Henry, 173–74
African American (as term and identity), 232n2. *See also* research process
African Baptist "Bluestone" Church, 241n5
Afro-Baptist cosmos, 101, 105–6, 111, 147, 210. *See also* Black Baptist Church
Alexander, Michelle, 7, 217–18
American Baptist Missionary Convention, 110
American National Baptist Convention, 110
American Pietás: Visions of Race, Death, and the Maternal (Tapia), 179
Anabaptists, 103
Anderson, Elijah, 55
anthropology of death, 173–79
antiviolence ministries, 63–64, 68–89, 216–21; Catholic prayer group, 64, 68–75, 81; Episcopal Victims of Violence ministry, 64, 81–87, 88; interdenominational coalition-building in, 134–37, 243n3; Vodou anticrime ceremonies, 64, 75–81. *See also* Liberty Street Baptist Church
Arena, John D., 236n5
Armstrong, Louis, 97, 103, 241n4
Armstrong, Tonya, 175
Atchafalaya River, 42

Baldwin, James, 120
Banks, E. V., 97

Baptist Church. *See* Black Baptist Church; Black social Christianity
Baptist Foreign Mission Convention, 110
Barber, Karin, 243n1
Barnes, Riché, 245n6
Barrett, Ronald, 193
Batiste, Stephanie L., 245n7
Beckett, Katherine, 66
Bell, Sylvana, 97
Bennett, James B., 110
Biehl, João G., 191
Biondi, Martha, 232n2
birthdays, 3–4, 155–58, 169, 180–86, 190–91, 210
Black (as term and identity), 232n2. *See also* research process
black Atlantic, 235n3
Black Baptist Church: activism and outreach of, 96, 107, 112; history of, 103–6, 109–10, 112–13, 241n6; new abolitionist movement in, 101; religious responses to death in, 187; women's roles in, 161–62, 166–67, 245n5. *See also* Black social Christianity
Black Church. *See* Black Baptist Church; Black social Christianity
Black death, 4, 173–79, 181–82, 205, 211–12. *See also* death; space of death and transformation
Black feminist theory, 217–18, 234n17, 234–35n20, 244n1

Black humanity, 4–8, 98–120; Black social
Christianity's assertion of, 4–5, 7–8, 19,
63, 100–102, 202, 234nn15–16; black
social gospel and, 101–2, 107–8, 111–14,
122–23, 147, 210; embodied practices,
relatedness, and care in, 98–102, 115–
20, 123, 130–31, 144–47, 158, 243n16,
244n6; King's evocations of, 89, 116–19,
243n16; post-Katrina focus on, 123,
131–34; racist assessments of, 145–46,
182, 193; as sacred, 64, 88, 100, 107–8,
119–20, 209; womanist theology and,
162–63, 234n18
Black knowledge, 217–18
*Black Lives and Humanity: Toward an African
American Religious Naturalism* (White),
119–20
Black Lives Matter movement, 6–8, 212,
217, 220
Black social Christianity, 16–24, 59–60, 97–
120, 216–18; African American religious
ideal in, 4–5, 100–101, 122, 130; assertion of Black humanity in, 4–5, 7–8,
19, 63, 88, 100–102, 107–8, 111–20,
202, 234nn15–16; black social gospel
of, 101–2, 107–8, 111–14, 122–23, 147,
210, 242nn8–9; civil rights activism of,
102, 108, 111–15; as dynamic mediating
institution, 18–19, 218–21; embodied
claiming of space in, 102, 114–15,
130–31, 243n1; ethnography and
field work on, 21–24, 208–10; formal
organization of, 109–11, 242nn10–11;
guiding covenant of, 94, 100, 105–6,
187; historical periods of, 101–6, 210,
241n1, 241–42nn5–6; male elites of,
101–2, 113–14, 163, 166–67; restorative
kinship in, 20–21, 24, 163, 167–79, 184,
188–206, 210, 234–35nn19–20; role in
community of, 159–60; spiritual consciousness in, 89, 96; spiritual journey
and rebirth in, 105–8, 242n7; women's
religious labor of, 19–21, 96, 161–63,
166–68, 234nn17–18, 244–45nn2–5. *See
also* Black Baptist Church; Black humanity; Liberty Street Baptist Church; Mothers Group at Liberty Street
black social gospel, 101–2, 107–8, 111–14,
122–23, 147, 210, 242nn8–9
Black urban delta, 8, 24, 33–60, 209–10,
235n3; classification of homicide as

inherent to, 65–68; criminalization of
race in, 16, 57, 63, 66–67, 175, 236n5;
evolution of precarity in, 38; freeing
geographies of agency in, 12–13, 37–38;
ghettoized understandings of, 10–12, 55,
233nn8–9; historical context of, 41–59,
235nn1–3; population decreases in, 8–9,
40, 233n5; poverty rate in, 112, 124,
211, 239n23; public housing policies in,
53–59, 238–39nn20–23; public responses
to violence in, 9–10, 17, 33–35, 38, 54,
61–63. *See also* Hurricane Katrina; New
Orleans; violence and crime
Black women, 24, 155–79, 210; motherwork
of, 189–90; radical black mothering of, 177, 234–35n20, 245nn6–7;
research and scholarship on, 161–63,
244nn1–2; restorative kinship of, 20–21,
24, 163, 167–79, 184, 188–206, 210,
234–35nn19–20; sorrow of, 175–79,
245nn6–7; systematic suppression of,
19, 56–59, 160–61, 168, 234n17, 244n4;
traditional religious labor of, 19–21,
96, 161–63, 234n18, 244–45mn2–5;
womanist theology of, 162–63, 234n18,
244nn3–4. *See also* Mothers Group at
Liberty Street
Bourgois, Philippe, 11, 25
Boyd, Roland H., 110
Boyz II Men, 2
Brown, Karen McCarthy, 240n8, 241n13
Brown, Vincent, 15–16, 233n13
Brown v. Board of Education, 112
Burroughs, Nannie H., 108
Bush, George W., 213

Cacho, Lisa Marie, 16
Campbell, Andrew, 223
Campbell, Hilary, Jr., 63
Cannon, Katie G., 244nn3–4
capitalization of "black," 232n2
Capps, Lisa, 197
Carsten, Janet, 21, 234n19
Carter, Jimmy, 55–56
Carter, J. Kameron, 163, 234n16
Casselberry, Judith, 20, 162, 167
Catholic prayer groups, 64, 68–75, 81,
240nn8–9; focus on sin and conversion
in, 74–75; Our Lady of Prompt Succor of,
68–70, 75, 87, 240n8; prayers of, 70–73
Cavelier, René-Robert, 42

Made in the USA
Monee, IL
01 September 2022